THE PIGGY WIGGY BLUES

by Fergus Henderson

Why are we so good to eat, why? *oink oink oink oink*

You can brine us then smoke us for bacon,
that's the Gloucester Old Spot's lot

Cure our limbs and you've got ham *oink oink oink oink*

Looking for fat, how about that, middle white, lard on legs

Get on up like a lardon machine *oink oink oink oink*

This is what you do to me charcuterie

Put your horse's bone in my thigh *oink oink*

The onomatopoeic lop, flavour is loppishish,
needs an Alice band for those ears

The giant orange sofa Tamworth, ladies and gents *oink oink oink oink*

Trotters bring unctuous sticky, tails that go crispy

The little things like chitterlings, poo pipe, woohoo!

Roast chop sandwich, raised pork pie

Ears cheeks and nose I tell no lie, pigs head is the tops woohoo woohoo!

The table is laid, your number is up, it's dinner time pig *oink oink squeal squeal!*

Sizzle, woohoo woohoo!

I'd like to dedicate this book to my mother, who ignited my lifelong interest in food and whom I miss very much indeed.

An Hachette UK Company
www.hachette.co.uk

First published in Great Britain in 2015
by Mitchell Beazley, a division of Octopus Publishing Group Ltd,
Endeavour House, 189 Shaftesbury Avenue, London WC2H 8JY
www.octopusbooks.co.uk

ISBN 978 1 84533 923 4
A CIP catalogue record for this book is available
from the British Library.

Printed and bound in China
10 9 8 7 6 5 4 3 2 1

Publishing Director Stephanie Jackson
Senior Editor Sybella Stephens
Art Direction & Design Juliette Norsworthy
Photographer Paul Winch-Furness
Illustrator Abigail Read
Home Economist & Food Stylist Richard H. Turner
Recipe Tester & Home Economist Kat Mead
Prop Stylists Polly Webb-Wilson & Linda Berlin
Senior Production Manager Peter Hunt

RICHARD H. TURNER

HOG

PROPER PORK RECIPES FROM THE SNOUT TO THE SQUEAK

MITCHELL BEAZLEY

"The difference between involvement and commitment is like ham and eggs. The chicken is involved; the pig is committed. "

MARTINA NAVRATILOVA

CONTENTS

FOREWORD BY JOSH OZERSKY

The pig, the most perfect of all animals, never stops giving. From its snout to its tail, its chops and its cheeks all the way down the jellied feet that float in brine atop seedy American bars, the pig epitomizes the commitment of carnivores not to waste one bit of living flesh. What you can't use goes into sausages, and what can't go into sausages goes into scrapple. Eventually nothing is left but fat (one's own) and happy memories.

Which isn't to say that just anyone knows how to cook pork.

Like any animal, a pig is made up of many muscles, each one adapted to a different task -- the shoulder for propulsion, say, or the tail for expression, and they can't all be cooked the same way. Each is made up itself of multiple disparate elements: muscle tissue, collagen, sinew, nerve, bone, fat and tendon. Each one cooks at a slightly different rate, and of course, no two animals are ever exactly alike. The real pork masters, from Hong Kong to the Carolinas, don't so much cook pork as draw it out, as one might a shy girl on a first date, or a glass of Scotch that needs just a few drops of tap water to be its own best self.

A great pork cook uses hot fires, slow fires, salt, a few spices here and there, and that's it: the rest happens more or less by itself. And the rest, at its best, can easily be astounding. The Tamworth and Berkshire hogs sourced by Richard Turner for his restaurants have creamy, firm and fragrant fat, the kind that you could spread on toast if you needed to, the kind that secretly powers half the good things that come out of the world's kitchens. The meat is red and strong, and tastes like the animal it's from: a hardy, independent-minded forager, fearless and inexhaustible. Those massive, all-consuming jaws are powered by some of the densest and most delicious muscles in the animal kingdom; the hams come from legs that jump and strut, big powerful muscles that are in almost constant motion, at least in the wild. The best pork, of the sort Turner sells at his craft butcher shop, comes from pigs that feed in the sun, copulate freely and live a good life. Sadly, though, I have to admit a melancholy fact few conscientious meat eaters will admit openly: even the worst pork is still pretty good. The murder mills of the United States are an atrocity, but the bacon they produce affects even sober men like marijuana, and their cheapest blade chops seethe with sweet juices and soft, pillowy pockets of fat.

As I write this, in the next room, leftover spare ribs, stiff from the refrigerator, are slowly softening and sizzling in a toaster oven. They come from commodity animals, and are being cooked in a cheap appliance weighing less than the book you are holding. I just ate one, and it was better than any tournado; two others are still warming and crisping as the time clicks away, and all I need to do is continue ignoring them. Pork is the most forgiving of meats, and for that reason the best for beginning cooks. It takes a lot to ruin it.

It is possible, of course. I never get over how many recipes assume otherwise. Modernist cookbooks are especially wrongheaded, assuming pork to be the raw material for the chef's creative genius, or the virtuosity of his technique. But the pig doesn't need geniuses or virtuosi. It doesn't need to be in tuiles or cocktails. It doesn't require its image on the forearms of oversexed line cooks. No, all it needs is love, and patience, and a deep but invisible skill on the part of the person cooking it. Such a person is Richard Turner. Listen to what he says, follow his instruction faithfully, and you won't go far wrong. The pig will see to that.

Josh Ozersky
Restaurant Editor, *Esquire*

TRIBUTE BY DIANA HENRY

I know when Richard Turner is in my house. The photography for his books is done here and I have to hide upstairs in my study as the smell of pork, in all its wonderful guises, drifts up through floorboards and open windows and makes me weep with hunger. Occasionally I venture downstairs and embarrass myself. The kitchen is so full of luscious things I know neither where to start nor where to stop. His terrines: the most perfect I have ever tasted (French men! Hang your heads in shame!). His pork burgers: I ate one with so much enthusiasm that the juices dripped down my chin and had to be mopped up by Richard before I left the house. His ham in cola: my children loved this so much they begged me to marry him. His deep-fried pickled mushrooms: how the hell did he even think these up (and why didn't I get there first)? Rillettes, Scotch eggs, quiche, you may think you've tasted good versions of these, but Richard's cooking makes you think again about such classics (as well as bringing new dishes to your life). And this big bourbon-drinking, porcine-loving hunk is also great at salads (I've paid him the ultimate compliment by stealing many of them).

I'm pretty fussy, hard to please. Nobody ever seasons well enough for me, or they get the flavour balance slightly wrong. But Richard Turner's food *sends* me. He simply has an amazing palate. He's touchingly (and unexpectedly) modest too. When I go 'Oh my God Richard, that is *so* good!' he says (blushing) 'Really? Do you think so?' and he means it.

Of course he does have his drawbacks. He leaves, in his wake, a trail of empty bourbon bottles. He makes everyone he knows eat too much. And my freezer is always full of his bloody pork fat (#notaeuphemism). But he is a love, great craic and a bloody fantastic cook. May he always return to my kitchen.

Diana Henry

Diana Henry
Food writer, London

INTRODUCTION

I have been fascinated by pork all my life. Like many people, I grew up on pork sausages, bacon and ham, with big old joints of roast pork at the weekend, memories of my mother cooking the Sunday roast, the smell enveloping the whole house, and the crackling, ohhh the crackling...

Fast forward 15 years and I'm working long hours, with only Sundays off, in top Michelin-starred-to-the-hilt restaurants and am deluded enough at this point to fancy myself as a bit of a chef. When I cook a Sunday roast, friends and family find ways of turning up -- I'm a chef, right? So my Sunday roast must be something to behold, and it is. The meat is perfectly cooked, my vegetables are *al dente* (the trend at the time), the roast potatoes crispy *and* fluffy. The gravy is a bit overworked but, hey, I don't

yet have the confidence to cook with total simplicity. There is one niggling problem though. It never quite attains the smell and flavour of my mother's roast, especially when I cook pork. It smells different, it tastes different, the texture is wrong and where is the bloody crackling?

Ten years later and I have joined Hawksmoor, the London steakhouse where the cooking is simple, relying on the quality of the produce. As Alain Ducasse so eloquently said, 'No geniuses have ever come from the kitchen. We are simply the bridge between nature and our clients.' Nowhere is this illustrated so well as at Hawksmoor. They have strong links with their butcher/farmer, Tim Wilson of The Ginger Pig, and during countless trips to his farm I finally taste the roast of my memories – Tamworth pork roasted in Tim's farmhouse kitchen, with a deep meaty porkiness, crispy crunchy crackling and translucent wobbly fat. It is an epiphany.

Later I meet Tom Adams, a young lad cooking up a storm in a van on the south bank of the Thames in London, and we plot to open Pitt Cue Co. in Soho together. On one of our research trips to the United States, Tom overdoes it a tad and upon our return he takes time off to recuperate. During this time we walk through the woods at the bottom of his parents' garden where we scheme great piggery. Four beautiful Middle Whites duly arrive and run free in Pitt Woods, hand-fed and cared for by Tom during his convalescence. It's here that I fall in love with pigs, and when the day comes for those Middle Whites to make their final journey, they must be the most loved and cared-for pigs in England. The resulting pork is as

good, or maybe even better, than what I tasted in that Yorkshire farmhouse years before, and I begin to understand what went so wrong with my attempts at roasts ten years previously.

This book is about that epiphany, and how the rearing of pigs directly informs the taste of the pork at the end of their journey. My hope is that by understanding that journey we can make informed decisions on what and where we buy. The chapters, together with the features between them, set out a rudimentary map of what it takes to make great pork.

Although the features on piggery are a fundamental part of that map, I am not expecting you to go out and buy two pigs tomorrow. I just want to engender a better understanding of what it takes to make good-quality meat. I'm lucky enough to be involved with amazing companies – from Turner & George to Meatopia, Tavern, Hawksmoor, Foxlow, Pitt Cue Co. and The Ginger Pig – all of which labour to promote the appreciation and understanding of proper, jaw-droppingly good meat. It is through working for and with these companies that I've realized we have all been the victims of a terrible crime against our stomachs. But it is not too late – read the features on piggery and take up the mantle with zeal, vote with your wallets and buy only the best. You will thank me when you taste the results.

The meat of this marvellous beast can be some of the best-tasting, most popular and versatile in the world, and we have developed a bewildering number of ways to preserve, keep and cook nearly every part of the pig, more so than any other animal. Almost every region has unique and interesting ways of preparing pork – you could spend a lifetime researching pigs and pork and still not know it all.

It's important to respect an animal that has been raised for meat, firstly by giving it a good life and a humane death, and secondly by using every part of the animal. You'd be amazed at what can be done with a pig's feet, ears or snout, and if this book conveys that nose-to-tail ethos, then my job is mostly done. It is by no means comprehensive – pork is entirely too versatile for one book to manage – but I have tried to cover every part of a pig in recipes.

I am indebted to the amazing chefs and cooks that took time out of their busy schedules to contribute a recipe. I hope I did you justice. Meredith Erickson, Aaron Franklin, Fergus Henderson, Judy Joo, Neil Rankin, Mitch Tonks and Valentine Warner, I salute you.

Hog is a celebration of all things porcine. My hope is that by understanding the whole picture, we can all make informed decisions about what we consume. And if we consume the best pork, we will enjoy it all the more.

Now it's over to you: read, digest, lick your lips, source some great pork and cook to your heart's content.

Richard
x

Richard H. Turner
London

PIGS, HOGS AND SWINE – SOME USEFUL TERMINOLOGY

Barrow A castrated male pig

Boar A male pig that has not been castrated

Dam A mother pig

Gilt A young female pig at least six months of age that has had no more than one litter of piglets

Herd A group of pigs

Hog An adult castrated male pig usually over 54kg

Hybrid A cross of two or more breeds of one species

Litter A group of piglets born together

Maiden A young female before being mated

Pig Any of the animals in the genus Sus, within the Suidae family of even-toed ungulates

Piglet A baby pig, aged eight weeks or less

Porker A pig reared to a weight of around 60kg, slaughtered at around six months

Runt The smallest piglet in a litter, often requiring extra care

Shoat A weaned, adolescent pig

Sire A father pig

Sow An adult female pig that has had at least one litter of piglets

Suckling pig A piglet, slaughtered at 6–8 weeks

Suid Any member of the family Suidae, including pigs and wild boar

Swine Pigs

Weaner A young piglet that has been weaned

Working boar An adult male pig used for breeding

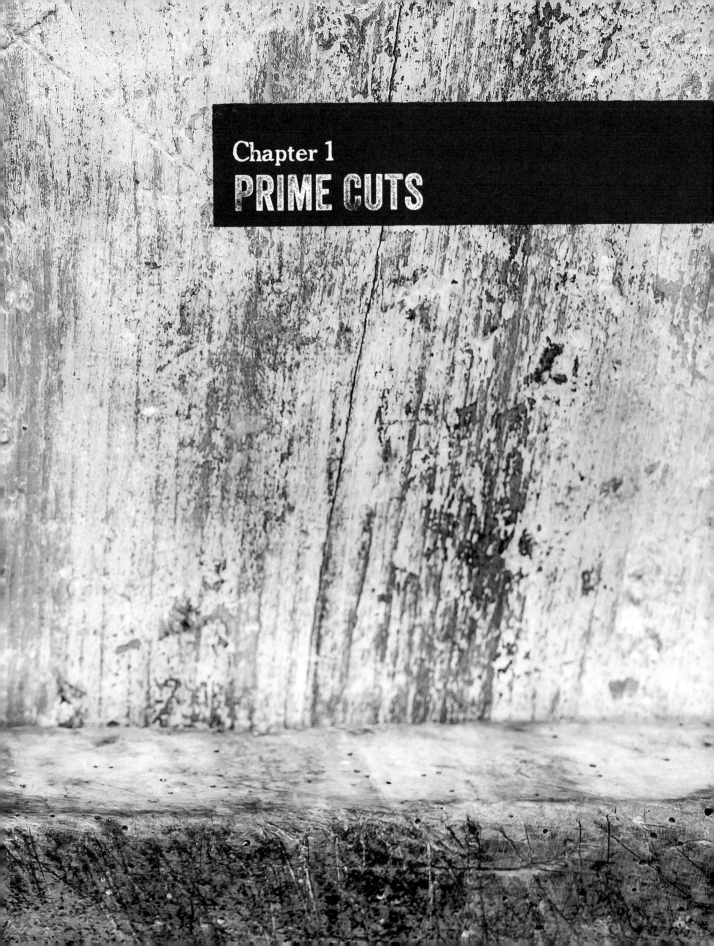

Chapter 1
PRIME CUTS

100g pork lard

2 onions, chopped

1 head of garlic, peeled and chopped

offal from the suckling pig, chopped

1 apple, peeled and grated

1kg sausagemeat of choice (see Basic Pork Sausages, page 146)

1 small loaf of bread, cut into chunks

fine sea salt and freshly ground black pepper

1 whole (10kg) suckling pig, gutted, cleaned, singed and shaved

To serve

bread rolls

butter

mustard

You will also need a big enough oven and a roasting tray to hold your pig, a butcher's needle and thread, and a meat thermometer

I've been serving whole suckling pigs for nigh on a decade now and they are just as impressive today as when I started. They never fail to elicit appreciative noises from all around the table upon arrival.

WHOLE ROAST SUCKLING PIG Serves 10

Melt the pork lard and sauté the onions and garlic over a medium heat until soft. Add the chopped offal and grated apple and toss to combine and seal the offal. Allow to cool.

Put the sausagemeat into a large bowl, add the cooled offal mixture and the bread chunks and combine well. Season the cavity of the suckling pig with salt and pepper, then stuff with the mixture and sew the belly together, using a large needle and butcher's thread.

Preheat the oven to 160°C/gas mark 3. Score the skin of the pig and rub with fine salt, then place it belly down with the legs tucked underneath in a large roasting tray. A 10kg pig will take about 6 hours to roast, and should reach an internal temperature at the shoulder of about 85°C when cooked.

Transfer the pig to a large wooden serving board and leave to rest for 30 minutes before carving. Serve with bread rolls, butter and mustard.

1 bottle of red wine

1 large haunch of wild boar

3 carrots, peeled and cut into chunks

1 leek, washed and cut into chunks

1 onion, cut into quarters

1 faggot of herbs, made with bay leaf, thyme and rosemary

1 spice bag, made with cloves, juniper and orange peel

100g pork dripping

Maldon sea salt flakes and freshly ground black pepper

500ml Master Pork Broth (see page 335)

100g butter

1 recipe Cranberry Ketchup (see page 339)

There is something slightly medieval about a haunch of wild boar as the hunting of boars in medieval Europe was a popular martial pastime. Dogs would hound the animal over miles of countryside until it was cornered, whereupon the noble would dismount his horse and finish it with a dagger. Attendants to the noble would carry the carcass back to his place of noble abode, where it would be butchered and roasted over an open fire.

ROAST HAUNCH OF WILD BOAR WITH CRANBERRY KETCHUP Serves 4

Pour the red wine into a large non-reactive dish, deep enough to hold the haunch. Add the carrots, leek, onion, faggot of herbs and spice bag.

Prick the haunch in several places and place it in the marinade, then cover with clingfilm and put the dish into the refrigerator for 24 hours, turning the meat over after 12 hours.

The next day, remove the meat from the marinade and pat dry. Reserve the marinade.

Preheat the oven to 200°C/gas mark 6.

Score the skin of the haunch with a sharp knife, making small incisions, then rub the meat with the pork dripping and season with salt and pepper. Roast for 15 minutes, then lower the oven temperature to 160°C/gas mark 3 and cook for about 1 hour, turning the meat regularly and basting with the juice.

The cooking time will depend on the size of the haunch – to check it's done, pierce the meat with a skewer. When the juice that flows is clear and free of blood, it's ready.

Remove the haunch from the oven and put it into a clean dish to rest for 30 minutes.

Deglaze the roasting tray with the reserved marinade and simmer over a low heat until reduced by half, then add the pork broth and continue to reduce to a sauce consistency. Whisk in the butter, adjust the seasoning if necessary, then pass through a fine sieve.

Serve the sauce alongside the wild boar, with Cranberry Ketchup on the side.

2 fennel bulbs, trimmed
and roughly chopped

2 carrots, roughly chopped

2 onions, roughly chopped

1 bunch of fresh thyme

1 head of garlic, split in half

2 teaspoons black peppercorns

2 teaspoons fennel seeds

20g Maldon sea salt flakes

1 large leg of pork

pork dripping or lard

500ml cider

500ml Master Pork Broth
(*see* page 335)

100g unsalted butter

1 recipe Rhubarb Ketchup
(*see* page 338)

The medieval English favoured fruit with meat, and served fruit sauces with pork, lamb and even beef. Over the centuries apples have become synonymous with pork, but rhubarb works equally well.

SLOW-ROAST LEG OF PORK WITH RHUBARB KETCHUP   Serves 4

Preheat the oven to 200°C/gas mark 6. Put the roughly chopped vegetables into a large roasting tray with the thyme and garlic.

Crush the black peppercorns and fennel seeds with the sea salt in a pestle and mortar until fine. Score the pork all over about 2mm deep at 1cm intervals with a sharp knife, rub the skin with pork dripping, then rub with the crushed seasoning mix.

Place the pork on the vegetables and roast for 20–30 minutes, or until it's beginning to colour, then turn the temperature down to 120°C/gas mark ½ and continue to cook for 9–12 hours until the meat is soft and you can pull it apart easily with a fork.

Pour the cider and pork broth into the roasting tray and let it cook for another hour, then remove from the oven, transfer the pork to a clean dish and let it rest for 30 minutes.

Bring the liquid in the roasting tray to a gentle simmer and whisk in the butter to thicken it. Pass it through a fine sieve and serve with the pork, alongside Rhubarb Ketchup.

100g small shallots, peeled

25g butter

100g cooking apple,
cut into 2cm chunks

100g Blood Pudding (see
page 174), cut into 2cm
chunks

100g white sourdough
bread, torn into chunks

200g Basic Pork Sausage
mix (see page 146)

Maldon sea salt flakes and
freshly ground black pepper

16-rib pork loin crown roast
(to prepare, see below)

To serve

roast potatoes

steamed broccoli

steamed carrots

pork gravy

rocket leaves

Apparently 7 March is National Crown Roast of Pork Day, but this dish is good enough to make an appearance more often than once a year. I promise much gasping, ooh-ing and smacking of lips should you bring this to your Sunday table.

CROWN ROAST OF PORK Serves 12

To make the stuffing, sauté the shallots in a little butter, allowing them to brown. Add the chunks of apple and continue cooking for a few minutes, then put into a bowl and allow to cool. Mix in the chunks of Blood Pudding, white sourdough and pork sausagemeat and season with salt and pepper.

Preheat the oven to 200°C/gas mark 6. Loosely scrunch up some foil and place in the middle of the crown roast. Cover the exposed bones with more foil to prevent them from burning, but leave the meat uncovered. Roast for 30 minutes.

Remove the foil from the centre of the roast and fill with the stuffing mix. Roast for 30 minutes more. Leave the crown roast to rest at 60°C for a further 30 minutes, loosely covered with a sheet of foil. When ready to serve, carve the pork chops by cutting between the bones, and serve with the stuffing, roast potatoes, steamed broccoli and carrots, pork gravy and a rocket leaf garnish.

HOW TO PREPARE A CROWN ROAST

Lay 2 strips of pork loin horizontally on a cutting board in front of you. With a sharp knife, carefully make a cut from one end of the 2 loins to the other, perpendicular to the bones, about 3cm from the top of the bone. Carefully remove the meat from between the cut you just made and the top of the bone using a small knife; you can save it for another use. Cut away enough meat to expose the bones. Do this for both strips of loin. Using a boning knife, cut away the meat between each bone so that 3cm of bone is exposed. Cut away any fat and meat from the top 3cm of each bone until they're as close to bare bone as you can manage. Lay the strips of loin on the cutting board horizontally in front of you, bone side up and with the bones facing away from you. With a small knife, make a shallow incision through the meat halfway between each bone. Your cuts should extend from the bottom of the meat up between each bone to the top of the meat.

Stand the strips up with the bones facing upwards and the meatiest part of the meat facing inwards. Shape the 2 strips into a circle. With a long length of butcher's string, tie the meat together in a circle. One string should tie the roast across midway up the outward-facing bones, and another string should tie it below the bones in the meaty portion of the strips. All of this, of course, is entirely redundant should you know a good butcher!

1 large bunch of fresh flat-leaf parsley, chopped

1 bunch of fresh sage, chopped

2 garlic cloves, crushed

200g fresh white breadcrumbs

100g butter, cubed and softened

Maldon sea salt flakes and freshly ground black pepper

1 French trimmed loin of pork, about 2.4kg

You will also need a meat thermometer

I've eaten this crust stuffed under the skin of a chicken and again on top of a slab of turbot. Paired with pork, the crust adds texture and soaks up precious juices to make a delicious contrast to the flesh.

ROAST RACK OF PORK WITH A GARLIC & HERB CRUST
Serves 8

Preheat the oven to 160°C/gas mark 3.

In a food processor, blend the parsley, sage, crushed garlic and breadcrumbs to very fine green crumbs. Mix in the butter and season with salt and pepper.

Wash and thoroughly dry the pork rack, then score the skin at least 1mm deep with a very sharp knife. Rub the pork all over with salt and roast in the oven for 1 hour.

Remove the pork from the oven, take off the cooked skin and return this to the oven separately to crisp up.

Coat the exposed meat in the green breadcrumbs, pressing it on to the part-cooked flesh, return it to the oven and cook for a further 20 minutes. When an internal temperature of 60°C is reached, remove the pork from the oven and let it rest for 20 minutes. If necessary, turn the oven up to 200°C/gas mark 6 to finish crisping the crackling.

Slice the pork into chops, taking care to keep the crust intact, and serve with strips of the crackling and pork gravy.

1 rack of pork from an 8kg suckling pig

milk, to cover

vegetable oil, for deep-frying

plain flour, seasoned with Maldon sea salt flakes and freshly ground black pepper

I first ate these in a very busy tapas bar during a trip to Madrid, where piles of them were being ferried from kitchen to table. It's unlikely you will find chops as small as I ate so I've specified a rack from an 8kg piglet cut into thin chops.

FRIED SUCKLING PIG CHOPS Serves 4

Cut the suckling pig chops 1cm thick, getting 2 thin chops per bone so that alternate chops will be bone in. Put them into a bowl, pour over milk to cover, and leave to soak for at least 2 hours, or overnight if possible.

Heat the oil to 180°C in a deep-fat fryer or large saucepan. Remove the chops from the milk and dust them generously with the seasoned flour.

Deep-fry them in small batches until crispy and crunchy and cooked through – about 6 minutes.

Drain on kitchen paper, then season with salt and pepper and serve with Barbecue or Red Barbecue Sauce (*see* page 337–8).

4 double pork rib chops,
around 4cm thick

400g Basic Pork Sausage mix
(*see* page 146)

50g shallots, finely chopped

50g Parmesan cheese, grated

50g pork dripping

10g Pork Rub (*see* page 334)

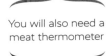
You will also need a
meat thermometer

It's a big ask to improve pork chops, but one thing that could
do it might be a liberal stuffing of sausagemeat, as sausage
and bacon improve everything.

SAUSAGE-STUFFED PORK CHOPS Serves 4-6

Preheat the oven to 180°C/
gas mark 4.

Using a sharp knife, cut a pocket
between the rib bones in each
chop, hollowing out the double
chops to form a pork 'bag'.

Mix the sausagemeat with the
shallots and Parmesan and stuff
the pork chops until bursting.

Rub the chops with the pork
dripping and dust liberally with
the Pork Rub, then place them
upright on an ovenproof baking
tray. Bake the chops for
30 minutes, or until golden brown
and an internal temperature of
60°C has been reached.

Allow to rest for up to 20 minutes
before serving with an interesting
mixed salad.

500ml milk

200ml honey

1 faggot of fresh herbs, made with rosemary, thyme and bay

1 small spice bag, made with 1 star anise, ½ cinnamon stick, 2 cm piece of fresh root ginger, 3 cloves and a few peppercorns

100g Maldon sea salt flakes

4 pork chops, untrimmed

any neutral oil, for brushing

To serve

mustard of choice

watercress salad

Parsnip, Potato & Apple Cake (*see* page 343), optional

You will also need a charcoal barbecue

The ancient Persians had a delightfully fascinating, if brutal, method of torture and execution involving milk and honey, that I'm afraid my lovely, sensitive publisher has censored [because we don't want to discourage anyone from making this lovely dish! *Ed.*]. Here is a far more civilized use for milk and honey.

MILK & HONEY BRINED PORK CHOPS Serves 4

Bring the milk, honey, faggot of herbs, spice bag and sea salt to the boil, then remove from the heat and allow to cool completely.

Pour the cooled milk mixture into a shallow dish. Submerge the pork chops in the milk mixture and refrigerate overnight.

Preheat a barbecue, preferably charcoal. Remove the chops from the milk and honey brine and dry them, then brush with oil and cook on the barbecue until charred all over and cooked through. There is a fine line between beautifully charred and burnt, so be careful – better to take the chops off when a perfect colour is achieved and finish them in a low oven than risk burning them.

Allow the chops to rest for 10 minutes in a warm place, then serve with your mustard of choice and a watercress salad, or a Parsnip, Potato & Apple Cake.

1 litre sweet cider

50g Maldon sea salt flakes

4 bone-in, thick-cut pork chops

100g interesting mustard
(Maille do many variations)

50g light muscovado sugar

100ml cider vinegar

100ml Master Pork Broth
(*see* page 335)

10ml Worcestershire sauce

1 garlic clove, crushed

8 cornichons, split or chopped

25g unsalted butter

extra Maldon sea salt
flakes and freshly ground
black pepper

You will also need a
meat thermometer

GRILLED CIDER-BRINED PORK CHOPS WITH MUSTARD SAUCE Serves 4

Brining not only seasons meat, but due to some scientific wizardry makes for a juicier end result. Moisture loss of up to 30 per cent of the raw weight occurs normally during the cooking of meat, because heat causes raw, individual coiled proteins in the fibres to unwind, then join together with one another. But brining can reduce that by half, enhancing juiciness in several ways. First, raw meat absorbs liquid during the brining period, increasing weight by 6-8 per cent. Second, brining causes some proteins in the muscle fibres to dissolve, turning them from solid to liquid. Lastly, the salt in the brine causes some of the proteins in muscle fibres to unwind and swell. As they unwind, the bonds that hold the proteins together break. Water from the brine then binds directly to and between these proteins when the meat cooks. Some of this would happen anyway during cooking, but the brine unwinds more proteins and exposes more bonding sites. Are you with me? As I said, scientific wizardry.

In a medium bowl, whisk the cider with the sea salt until the salt has dissolved. Pour this brine into a large plastic tub, add the pork chops, then seal and refrigerate for a few hours or overnight.

In a small saucepan, combine the mustard with the sugar, cider vinegar, pork broth, Worcestershire sauce and garlic. Simmer, stirring occasionally, until thickened – about 10 minutes. Stir in the butter and season with salt and pepper. Keep warm.

Remove the pork chops from the brine and pat dry with kitchen paper. Season the chops with salt and pepper. Grill over a high heat until the pork is nicely browned – about 5 minutes on each side. Reduce the heat to moderate or, if using a charcoal grill, move the coals to one side and transfer the pork chops so they're opposite the coals. Continue cooking the chops until a meat thermometer inserted in the thickest part of the chops registers 60°C – about 10 minutes. Let the chops rest for 10 more minutes.

Strain the warm mustard sauce over the cornichons and serve with the chops.

4 thin-cut pork chops

Maldon sea salt flakes and freshly ground black pepper

2 garlic cloves, chopped

50g fresh breadcrumbs

50g Parmesan cheese, grated

2 free-range eggs, seasoned and beaten

50g plain flour seasoned with Maldon sea salt flakes and freshly ground black pepper

100ml olive oil, for frying

Parmesan cheese makes a great crust for frying pork. Don't be tempted to use pre-grated Parmesan just because it's for frying; you never know how long that stuff has been sitting in its cardboard tube.

FRIED PORK CHOPS IN A PARMESAN & GARLIC CRUST Serves 4

Lightly season the pork chops with salt and pepper and set aside.

In a food processor, blend the garlic, breadcrumbs and Parmesan to a sandy texture, then place in a shallow bowl. Place the eggs in another bowl and the seasoned flour in a third bowl.

Douse the pork chops in the seasoned flour, then dip them in the beaten egg and finally coat them with the Parmesan and garlic breadcrumbs.

Heat the olive oil in a shallow skillet over a medium heat and fry the crumbed chops 2 at a time until cooked through.

Drain the chops on kitchen paper and serve with pasta or a risotto.

20g pork dripping or lard

2 large white onions,
thinly sliced

Maldon sea salt flakes and
freshly ground black pepper

4 pork blade chops, 2cm
thick, with any bone removed

4 burger buns (potato or half
brioche for preference)

mustard, to serve

Maxwell Street is a street in Chicago, in one of the city's oldest residential districts. It is notable as the location of the famous Maxwell Street Market, the birthplace of Chicago blues and the Maxwell Street Polish sausage sandwich. You can also buy pork chop sandwiches prepared in a similar way, and they are quite delicious.

MAXWELL STREET PORK CHOP SANDWICHES Serves 4

Heat half the dripping in a cast iron skillet, then add the sliced onions and fry until golden, seasoning with salt and pepper and tossing from time to time – they will take about 10 minutes to cook down. Remove the onions and keep warm.

Add the remaining dripping to the skillet, season the pork chops and fry until brown all over – about 3 minutes on each side. Add the chops to the onions, then cover and leave to rest in a warm place, about 60°C, for up to 20 minutes – the residual heat will finish the cooking.

Split each bun and toast until golden. Spread one half with onions, top with a chop and close the sandwiches. Serve with mustard, of course.

100ml soy sauce

100ml orange juice

1 teaspoon cornflour

50g pork dripping or lard

4 free-range eggs

1 tablespoon fresh root ginger, chopped

1 tablespoon garlic, peeled and chopped

500g pork blade chop, cut into thin strips

800g mixed vegetables, to include onions, celery, carrots, peppers, tenderstem broccoli, bok choi, pak choi and any other vegetables to hand, cut into slices

Maldon sea salt flakes and freshly ground black pepper

4 spring onions, finely sliced diagonally

Chop suey is an American dish based on *tsap seui* (mixed leftovers) from Toisan, Canton, the original home of many early Chinese immigrants to the West.

PORK CHOP SUEY Serves 4

Mix the soy sauce, orange juice and cornflour in a bowl and set aside.

Heat half the dripping in a wok until sizzling, then crack in the eggs and mix with chopsticks until just set. Tip out of the wok and reserve on a plate.

Heat the remaining dripping in the wok and add the ginger and garlic, followed by the pork strips, giving the wok a good toss as you go. Now start to add the vegetables – first the onions, then the celery and carrots, followed by the peppers.

Keep tossing the wok and add the rest of the vegetables – the whole process should take about 5 minutes. Finally add the soy sauce/orange juice mix and give a final toss to coat. The cornflour should thicken immediately, but if it doesn't, continue tossing until it does.

Remove from the heat, adjust the seasoning and turn out on to 4 plates. Tear the omelette into 4 and garnish each plate with a piece of omelette and some sliced spring onions.

800g wild boar loin

250g mushrooms

50g butter

1 large sprig of fresh thyme

100ml dry white wine

20 slices of dry-cured
streaky bacon

800g Rough Puff Pastry
(*see* page 149)

flour, for dusting

2 eggs, beaten

The lovely Stephanie Jackson of Octopus Publishing had this one Christmas in Germany and suggested I give it a go. I'm very glad she did -- it's just as good as a classic Beef Wellington.

WILD BOAR WELLINGTON Serves 4

Preheat the oven to 200°C/gas mark 6.

Season the meat and seal it all over in a hot pan, then roast in the oven for 10 minutes. Remove from the oven and allow to cool, then chill in the refrigerator for about 10 minutes.

While the wild boar is cooling, chop the mushrooms very finely. Heat the butter in a large pan and fry the mushrooms over a medium heat, with the thyme sprig, for about 10 minutes, stirring often, until you have a softened mixture. Season with salt and pepper, pour in the wine and cook for about 10 minutes, until all the wine has been absorbed. The mixture should hold its shape when stirred. Remove the mushroom mixture from the pan to cool and discard the thyme.

Overlap 2 pieces of clingfilm on a large chopping board. Lay the bacon on the clingfilm, slightly overlapping, in rows. Spread half the mushroom mixture over the bacon, then sit the sealed meat on top and spread the remaining mushroom mix over. Use the edges of the clingfilm to draw the bacon around the loin, then roll it into a sausage shape, twisting the ends of the clingfilm to tighten it as you go. Chill the loin while you roll out the pastry.

Dust your work surface with flour and roll out a third of the pastry to an 18 x 30cm strip. Place on a nonstick baking sheet. Roll out the remaining pastry to about 28 x 36cm. Unravel the rolled loin from the clingfilm and sit it in the centre of the smaller strip of pastry. Brush the edges of the pastry, and the top and sides of the wrapped loin, with beaten egg. Using a rolling pin, carefully lift and drape the larger piece of pastry over the loin, pressing well into the sides. Trim the edges to about a 4cm rim and seal by pinching or with a fork. Slash the top with a knife, then glaze all over with the beaten egg and chill for at least 20 minutes.

Preheat the oven to 200°C/gas mark 6 again, then brush the Wellington with a little more egg and cook until golden and crisp – about 30 minutes. Allow to stand for 15 minutes, then cut into thick slices to serve.

60ml olive oil

2 pork tenderloins

½ onion, sliced into 4 (like half-moons)

1 teaspoon Maldon sea salt flakes

1 teaspoon freshly ground black pepper

½ tomato, cut into 4

240ml hot water

240ml soured cream

PORK SAURKRAUSEN Serves 4–6

BY MEREDITH ERICKSON

I met my husband at Joe Beef, a restaurant in Montreal. Back then it was more of a neighbourhood spot, not the fabled destination restaurant it is now. Oliver was a local and I was his waitress*. In the years that followed, I co-authored the *Joe Beef* cookbook, got married and spent a whole lot of time with my fiery mother-in-law, Sybille Sasse. Born and raised near Hamburg, Sybille has a contagious love for life and specifically a love for Kirsch, red wine, white wine, caviar, vodka and more Kirsch. She's quite fabulous, or 'faboo-lus' as she says it (and she says it often!). I'm not sure if she was always a good cook, but being married to a hotel general manager (Oliver's dad Frank) and a constant entertainer she certainly became one. Of all the cookbooks we have in our house -- and there are hundreds -- the book we turn to most often is the one she created for Oliver, a collection of his favourites. It's full of simple and quick recipes that remind us of home. Comfort food that is still quite, well, faboo-lus.

* To the men out there who think this union in some way legitimizes your pervy advances with waitresses: it doesn't.

In a flameproof casserole, heat the olive oil over a medium heat. Once the pan gets nice and hot, add the tenderloins and brown them on both sides – about 2 minutes on each side. Add the onion, salt and pepper. Reduce the heat to low and stir to combine.

Add the tomato and stir for another minute. Add the hot water so it fills the pan 3–4cm from the bottom. Cover and allow it to simmer for 20 minutes.

Preheat the oven to 110°C/gas mark ¼. Using a slotted spoon or your trusty tongs, transfer the meat to a baking tray or an ovenproof dish and place in the oven to keep warm while you make the sauce.

Back on the hob, increase the heat to medium and add the soured cream. Reduce for about 5–7 minutes, or until you get that signature rosé colour.

Remove the tenderloins from the oven and put them on a chopping board. Slice them into medallions and divide them between plates. Pour the sauce on top of each medallion, making sure to distribute the onions equally.

For the pickled pork

500ml water

250ml cider vinegar

50g Maldon sea salt flakes

6 garlic cloves, crushed

20g sugar

20ml Sriracha or other
hot sauce

1 teaspoon yellow
mustard seeds

½ teaspoon fennel seeds

½ teaspoon black
peppercorns

250g ice cubes

1kg pork loin,
cut into 5cm dice

To serve

200g jar of pickled jalapeños

8 garlic cloves, peeled

8 soft white buns, split

100g Vinegar Slaw
(see page 341)
or any other slaw

8 lettuce leaves

Before the days of refrigeration and commercial curing plants, pork from a very recently butchered hog would be cured in large batches and kept in barrels. Pickled pork was a staple in the Creole kitchen and is still fairly easy to find in New Orleans. Pork is usually pickled in sufficient quantity to last for some time, as it should keep (particularly now we have refrigeration), but it can also be pickled in small quantities, as here.

PICKLED PORK LOIN SANDWICHES Makes 8

Combine all the pickled pork ingredients except the ice and the pork in a stainless steel saucepan, then set over a high heat and bring to the boil. Reduce the heat and maintain a simmer for 3 minutes, then remove from the heat, add the ice and stir.

Place the diced pork loin in a large sealed plastic container or sterilized glass jar and add the cooled pickling liquid, then place in the refrigerator for at least 3 days, turning occasionally.

When pickled, preheat the oven to 120°C/gas mark ½.

Drain the meat and place in a lidded casserole with the jar of jalapeños (juice as well) and the garlic cloves. Place the casserole in the oven and cook for 6–8 hours, or until the pork is tender.

Drain the pork, shred the meat and serve piled high in soft white buns, with Vinegar Slaw and lettuce.

100g plain flour

100g fresh breadcrumbs

100ml milk

6 eggs

4 pork cutlets, about 200g each 1cm thick

Maldon sea salt flakes and freshly ground black pepper

60g unsalted butter

8 Cantabrian anchovy fillets

1 teaspoon chopped fresh parsley

2 teaspoons Lilliput capers

juice of 1 lemon

To serve

sliced tomatoes

chopped spring onions

The Arabs brought back breaded and fried meat from one of their forays into the provinces of the Byzantine Empire, and Spain is said to have acquired the dish when the Arabs invaded Andalucía in the 8th century. Later, the Spanish soldiers of Emperor Charles V breaded and fried their meat in the same way during their occupation of Rome in the 16th century, and from Italy the schnitzel made its way to Austria, where it acquired the name Wiener schnitzel and was made with veal. Variations can now be found all over the world, but I think this version is perhaps the best, Holstein referring to the garnish of fried egg, anchovies, capers, lemon and parsley.

PORK SCHNITZEL HOLSTEIN Serves 4

Place the flour and breadcrumbs on separate plates. Whisk together the milk and 2 of the eggs in a bowl.

Season the cutlets with salt and pepper, then coat them in the flour, dip them in the egg mixture and finally dredge them in the crumbs.

Heat a quarter of the butter in a skillet over a medium-high heat. Add 2 of the cutlets and cook, turning, for about 4 or 5 minutes, or until browned and cooked through. Transfer to a plate and repeat with the other 2 cutlets. Return the skillet to the heat,

add another quarter of the butter and crack in the remaining eggs; cook until the whites are firm – about 3 minutes. Place an egg on each cutlet and top each one with 2 anchovy fillets.

Return the skillet to the heat, add the rest of the butter and cook until brown and nutty – about 30 seconds. Stir in the parsley, capers and lemon juice and pour over the cutlets.

Serve with a simple tomato and spring onion salad on the side.

100g Maldon sea salt flakes

50g light muscovado sugar

50g garlic, minced

½ bunch of fresh sage, chopped

2 pork fillet barrels (the middle of the fillet)

40g cracked black pepper

For the charcuterie cream sauce

25g unsalted butter

6 banana shallots, finely diced

100ml cider

250ml Master Pork Broth (*see* page 335)

250ml double cream

30g gherkins, finely diced

30g superfine capers

¼ bunch of fresh parsley, chopped

You will also need a piece of muslin large enough to wrap the pork and some butcher's string

Pork takes well to all kinds of curing, and in this case a few hours are enough to change the character of a less exciting pork cut. It is very important to undercook slightly and rest long, to keep the meat as moist as possible.

SEMI-CURED PORK FILLET WITH CHARCUTERIE CREAM SAUCE Serves 4

Mix the sea salt, sugar, garlic and sage to make a cure and leave overnight to dry on a tray. Alternatively, this can be done in 2 hours in a very low oven.

Trim the fillet barrels and rub with the cure mix, then layer in a tray with 1cm of cure mix above and below.

Turn every hour for 4 hours until ready and firm to touch, then wash thoroughly. Roll the pork in cracked black pepper, then wrap in muslin and tie up. Hang free in the refrigerator to air-dry and continue curing and drying for 24 hours.

When ready to serve, make the sauce. In a heavy-based saucepan add the butter and gently sweat the shallots until they turn a golden honey colour – about 10 minutes or so.

Increase the heat, add the cider and boil rapidly to reduce by half. Add the pork broth and reduce by half again, before adding the double cream and reducing once more to around half. This should result in about 250ml of sauce. To finish, stir in the gherkins, capers and parsley and keep warm.

Unwrap the cured pork and cut into tournedos. Fry them in a little butter until just cooked, then allow to rest for at least 10 minutes before serving with sautéed or charcutière potatoes and the charcuterie cream sauce.

160g butter, softened

3 garlic cloves, crushed

a small handful of chopped fresh parsley

Maldon sea salt flakes and freshly ground black pepper

600g pork fillet, cut into 4 equal pieces

100g plain flour

a pinch of paprika

2 large free-range eggs, beaten

100g dried breadcrumbs

50ml vegetable oil

To serve

finely grated cabbage

finely grated carrot

parsley leaves

In the 18th century, the Russian Empress Elizabeth sent her chefs in St Petersburg to study in Paris, and one of them returned with a recipe for *côtelettes de volaille*. A revolution and two World Wars later, the cutlets were served to honour a Ukrainian delegation returning from Berlin to Kiev, and since then they have been known as chicken Kiev. Pork makes a great variation -- perhaps even an improvement.

PORK FILLET KIEV Serves 4

Preheat the oven to 180°C/gas mark 4.

Mix the softened butter with the garlic and parsley, and season with salt and pepper.

Using a small, sharp knife, make a slit in the flesh of each piece of pork fillet from top to bottom, creating a pocket. Spoon the butter mixture into a piping bag and pipe it into the pocket.

Mix the flour and paprika in a shallow bowl and season with salt and pepper. Pour the beaten eggs into another shallow bowl and place the breadcrumbs in a third. First toss the stuffed fillet portions in the flour to coat, shaking off any excess, then slide them one at a time into the egg and turn until covered. Finally, dip each one into the breadcrumbs, again shaking off any excess. Lay the fillets, slit sides down, on a plate and chill to help firm up the crumb coating.

Heat the oil in an ovenproof frying pan over a medium heat, then add the pork fillet Kievs and cook for 1–2 minutes on each side, or until lightly golden. Transfer the pan to the oven and cook for about 10 minutes, or until golden brown and the pork is just cooked through.

Allow to rest for 10 minutes, then serve with a finely grated cabbage, carrot and parsley salad.

For the marinade

400g pork fillet, cut into 3cm dice

25ml soy sauce

10ml rice wine

For the batter

100g rice flour

100ml rice wine

25ml rice wine vinegar

2g baking powder

pinch of Maldon sea salt flakes

cooking oil, for frying

For the sauce

20g fresh root ginger, finely diced

20g garlic cloves, finely diced

20ml oyster sauce

20ml rice wine vinegar

20ml tomato ketchup

20ml clear honey

20ml pineapple juice

To garnish

50g red pepper (about half a pepper), cut into 2cm squares

50g green pepper (about half a pepper), cut into 2cm squares

75g spring onions, cut into 2cm lengths

75g fresh pineapple, cut into 2cm dice

Ah, sweet and sour pork, the linchpin of any Chinese takeaway menu. There are authentic Chinese sweet and sour pork recipes, but this is not one of them -- it's unashamedly Western and is the dish we are all familiar with. These ingredients were settled upon by Chinese immigrants struggling to source exotic preserved plums or hawthorn candy upon their arrival in the West.

SWEET & SOUR PORK Serves 4

Marinate the pork fillet in 25ml soy sauce and 10ml rice wine for 15–20 minutes.

Meanwhile, make the batter by mixing together the rice flour, rice wine, rice wine vinegar, baking powder and salt until smooth, then set aside.

Blend the ginger, garlic, oyster sauce, rice wine vinegar, tomato ketchup, honey and pineapple juice until smooth, then set aside.

In a deep-fat fryer or deep heavy-based saucepan, heat up enough cooking oil to cover the pork.

Transfer the pork pieces to the batter and toss to ensure they are well coated. Deep-fry the pork pieces in batches until they turn golden brown, then remove and drain on a plate lined with kitchen paper.

Heat a wok over a high heat and add a little cooking oil. Add the bell peppers and pineapple pieces. Stir-fry until you smell the peppery aroma from the peppers, then add the sweet and sour sauce. As soon as the sauce is hot, add the crispy fried pork to the wok and stir well with the sauce. Add in the spring onions, toss to combine, then serve with steamed white rice.

400g pork fillet, cut into medallions 3cm thick

Maldon sea salt flakes and freshly ground black pepper

100g Air-cured Ham (*see* page 206) or prosciutto, sliced

8 large fresh sage leaves

100ml Marsala wine

50g unsalted butter

2 tablespoons capers

Saltimbocca means 'jumps in the mouth', and though usually made with veal it is equally tasty when made with pork. Here it's paired with Marsala, an Italian fortified wine, but if you struggle to find it Madeira makes a fine alternative.

SALTIMBOCCA Serves 4

Pound the slices of meat between 2 pieces of clingfilm to make them thinner – they should be about 1cm thick. Lightly season the meat with salt and pepper and lay the sliced prosciutto on top. Place a sage leaf in the centre of each piece and secure it with a cocktail stick.

Put the Marsala into a small saucepan and place it over a gentle heat to warm through. Heat the butter in a frying pan and fry the slices of pork, sage side down, for 2 minutes, then turn the pieces over and fry them for another minute until just cooked through.

Pour in the hot Marsala and let it bubble and reduce for a minute or so until sauce-like. Remove from the heat and allow to rest for a few minutes, then transfer the pork to warm serving plates. Remove the cocktail sticks and spoon the sauce over. Garnish with a few capers and serve with a mixed salad.

700g pork loin, cut into thick slices

Maldon sea salt flakes and freshly ground black pepper

2 eggs

1 tablespoon vegetable oil

plain flour

panko breadcrumbs

vegetable oil, for deep-frying

For the tonkatsu sauce

equal parts ketchup, brown sauce, Japanese soy sauce and Worcestershire sauce

To serve

white cabbage

cooked Japanese rice

You will also need a food thermometer

Pork tonkatsu originated in Japan in the 19th century – here it's served with finely shredded cabbage, but it's often also used as a sandwich filling or in combination with curry sauce.

PORK TONKATSU   Serves 4

Shred the white cabbage very finely indeed, and set aside.

Pound the slices of meat between 2 pieces of clingfilm to 1cm thick and season well with salt and pepper.

In a large bowl or plate, whisk the eggs with the oil. Dredge the pork in flour, then dip in the egg mixture, and finally coat with the panko breadcrumbs.

Heat the oil to 180°C in a wok over a medium-high heat. Gently lower the pork into the oil. Keep watching the temperature of the oil and make sure it doesn't go above 180°C. Deep-fry the pork for 2 minutes on each side, or until golden and cooked through, then drain on kitchen paper.

Serve with Japanese rice, finely shredded white cabbage and the tonkatsu sauce.

FROM WILD BOARS TO BERKSHIRES

It is unclear exactly when early man pulled off the clever trick of making fire, but this discovery allowed us to consume and digest protein in substantially larger amounts than at any time in history, giving our evolution the boost that ultimately launched civilization as we know it. One of those protein sources was the wild boar, which was widespread in Eurasia and northwest Africa. It had been around a whole lot longer, but was unlikely to have been of much interest until we could cook it. Nowadays, more than two hundred breeds have been developed, the most relevant of which are detailed on these pages.

Pre-domestication, some wild boar that were less shy than their herd mates would tolerate human proximity and exploit settlements as a food source, eventually becoming semi-tame and almost certainly breeding. They were mostly used for food, but their hides were also useful for shields and shoes, their bones for tools and weapons, and their bristles for brushes. Later they had other roles: their feeding behaviour in searching for roots churned up the ground and made it easier to plough, and their omnivorous nature enabled them to eat human rubbish, keeping settlements cleaner. Human presence offered protection from large carnivores, except us, of course – we took advantage of our newfound village mates by eating a few of them.

THE RISE OF THE DOMESTICATED PIG

This inquisitive, opportunistic beast may, in part, have domesticated itself by choosing to come freely into association with humans. Human control would have been easily accomplished, and the next step – unconscious selection – began the long process of evolving regional distinctions in the animal's conformation. Gradually the wild boar began to change: its head became smaller, its nose and legs shorter, its body longer and wider, its hair finer and smoother and its tail curled. In the Neolithic period, early pigs from central Europe were bred with those of southern Europe to increase their size, and the Romans further improved the pig by better feeding and breeding.

For most of their domesticated history, swine were kept in one of two ways: free-ranging in forests or contained in settlements. In neither situation did they compete with humans for food, although pigs have the capacity to eat and thrive on the same nutrients. For the free-range pig, both plant and animal matter – on and beneath the forest floor – was sought. While pigs contained in settlements were fed scraps and leftovers, they were also given sporadic access to forage. In western Europe, where domesticated swine have been known since before 4000BC, they ate acorns, chestnuts, beechnuts, hazelnuts and wild fruit such as berries, apples, pears and hawthorns. Their powerful mobile snouts and sharp teeth were able to dig mushrooms, tubers, roots, worms and grubs from the ground. In fact, the use of pasturing in a forest to feed pigs was recorded from antiquity, and pigs were once so common in the wooded parts of England that woods were measured in the Domesday Book by how many pigs they could support. In the early Middle Ages, there was better income to be had from grazing livestock in woods than there was from the sale of timber. Indeed, this practice still exists in some British forests.

HAVE PIGS, WILL TRAVEL

At the end of the Middle Ages in 1493, Christopher Columbus sailed to the New World for the second time taking live pigs as a food supply, eight lucky pigs survived this voyage and were released on the island of Hispaniola in the Caribbean where they multiplied and became feral. Semi wild descendants of those animals were then later rounded up as needed and put on board ships bound for central and south America and all the islands en route. Later, in 1531, the Spanish conquistador Francisco Pizarro took live pigs on to the Andean highlands where they were well suited to move along with the expedition parties as a mobile fresh meat supply. Tropical America afforded few nuts, but instead an abundance of foraged wild fruit and seed-pods provided nourishment.

The first pigs in North America arrived from Cuba with Hernando de Soto's expedition of 1539, the explorer gave gifts of live pigs to the Native Americans, and when he died in 1542 near what is now Fort Smith, Arkansas, seven hundred pigs were counted among his property. These 'razorbacks' still survive in the southern United States, and Ossabow Island, off the coast of Georgia, harbours a breed of swine considered to be direct descendants of those brought by the Spaniards.

Further introductions came from Britain, most notably in 1607 to John Smith's settlement at Jamestown, and by 1615 they had multiplied to several hundred. Pigs fitted well into the forested countryside of North America as foragers, abundant oak and chestnut mast in the Appalachians offered a good return for little investment in feed or care. In late autumn, the semi-feral animals were rounded up and slaughtered, and their fatty flesh was made into salt pork, which along with Indian corn was a staple of the early American diet, and in the early 19th century, these Appalachian pigs were commercialized, their flesh salted and their fat rendered.

Developing breeds involves fixing and enhancing desirable characteristics while eliminating or reducing undesirable traits, and when the trade routes opened up and other pigs from Asia and southern Europe arrived in northern Europe, new breeds were refined. Piglets with desirable traits were grown on for breeding while those with undesirable traits were eaten. This, aided by the prolificacy of pigs, meant the process of evolution went into hyper-drive with the emergence of distinctive breeds as we know them today.

During the agricultural revolution, Britain became the centre of pig-breed development, with classic breeds such as the Berkshire, the Hampshire and the Yorkshire developing in different parts of the country. With the import of pigs from Asia and Italy, the features of these native pigs dramatically changed. Native pigs were crossed with imported pigs to produce bulkier animals with more meat. This pig breeding was not very scientific and the results owed as much to natural selection as human intervention, but it was incredibly influential because the new breeds were shipped worldwide and became the genetic basis for the development of local breeds elsewhere.

Wild Boar

MODERN METHODS

Before the re-engineering of pork in the 20th century, pork in Europe and North America was traditionally an autumn dish – pigs and other livestock came to the slaughter in the autumn after growing in the spring and fattening during the summer. Pork, being particularly suited to preservation methods such as pickling, curing and smoking, could be kept throughout the winter and eaten as needed. But with the advent of refrigeration in the late 19th century, it became possible to keep pork all year round, and seasonal pig rearing slowly became redundant.

Refrigeration also paved the way for pork farming to become more efficient – which ultimately led to the intensive post-war farming practices that are responsible for the poor quality of much of today's pork. Pork producers began to shift to the current, more profitable system that treats pigs as production units, with thousands of pigs being crowded into dimly lit warehouses with mesh floors for excrement to fall through. After artificial insemination, pregnant sows are kept in gestation crates just large enough to hold their bodies. Once they have given birth, they are moved to farrowing crates with a grate between them and their litters, so the piglets have access to milk but none of the mother nurture – the partitions' purpose being to prevent any loss of 'product' as a result of the sows rolling on to the piglets.

The piglets are taken from their mothers at three to four weeks (ten weeks earlier than they would separate in the wild) and fed a drug-fortified feed that makes them grow faster than with mothers' milk. They are slaughtered around the six-month mark, when through intensive processes these young pigs may have reached a weight of over 80kg (176lb), something that can take up to a year when pigs are raised naturally.

The slaughtered pigs are the lucky ones. The mothers return to be artificially inseminated again, then go back into the gestation crate followed by the farrowing crate. This cycle of torture is repeated for ten or more years until the sow is finally worn out and is slaughtered.

All of this makes for tasteless, unappealing pork, but fortunately we are starting to wake up to how barbaric this way of rearing animals for meat is, and small numbers of farmers are returning to old, less greedy, more ethical ways of rearing pigs – and guess what? It tastes better!

BREEDS OF INTEREST

Part of a renewed interest in extensive farming methods is a return to the slow-growing rare breeds that taste so good. Today's pig breeds are the result of decades of selective breeding combined with local environmental factors that have led to regional traits. They can be categorized into traditional, modern or hybrid breeds, and then further divided into bacon

Old English

Neapolitan

Siamese

pigs, lard pigs or meat pigs. Modern-day pigs come in a surprising multitude of shapes, colours and sizes, and the variety is really quite astounding. Valerie Porter's *Pigs: A Handbook to the Breeds of the World* describes two hundred or so of these, although up until the mid-1800s there were far fewer. The breeds that follow are, in my opinion, the most relevant either historically or for eating nowadays.

Wild boar

The Eurasian wild boar originated in Southeast Asia, and from this animal came all the many breeds of domestic pig. It is grey-brown in colour, and medium-sized with a narrow head and thick shoulders that run into a hump at the top. It has strong, sturdy forequarters that are protected by small tusks. Wild boar is farmed in Europe (though still hunted in some areas, such as Germany), and its meat, which has little fat and is low in cholesterol, often sells at a premium. In the United States, where it is not a native, it is hunted and considered a pest. Wild boar is remarkable – deeply meaty and with a porkiness matched only by Mangalitsa or the Iron Age Pig, but it should be cooked carefully so that it does not dry out.

Old English

The Old English was a woodland pig common throughout England in the 18th and 19th centuries.

There were several colour combinations, depending on where in the country it came from: red and black, red and mustard, black, or patches of red, black or mustard. It was a large, hairy pig with thick, sturdy legs and a narrow, short body. There was a slight hollow in its back and its long, narrow head had lop ears. It had little or no jowl, narrow shoulders and a ridge of hair along its back. These pigs often lived semi-feral and were slow to grow, surviving on scraps and waste supplemented by foraging in woodlands. The Old English disappeared as it bred with foreign stock.

Neapolitan

The Neapolitan pig hailed from Italy and can be traced back to Roman times. In the 15th century it was used for Parma ham and was considered one of Italy's finest pigs. In the 18th century it was exported to improve European stock. Almost uniformly black in colour, it was medium-sized with wrinkled jowls at its jaw, a slightly dished face, forward-pointing ears and almost hairless skin. The Neapolitan was an important bloodline used to improve modern pig breeds but ultimately died out when superseded by today's pigs.

Siamese

The Siamese arrived in Britain in the 18th century and bore a resemblance to the Neapolitan, to which it was probably related. Either black or slate-coloured and

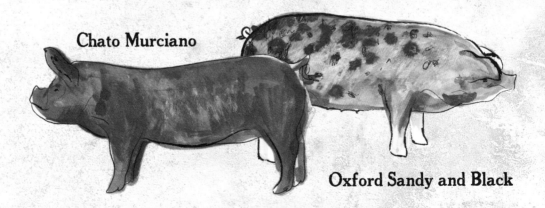

Chato Murciano

Oxford Sandy and Black

medium-sized, it matured early and was hardy and docile in temperament. It had short legs and a medium-sized head with a straight nose and upright ears. This quiet and tractable pig made for tender and tasty pork with white flesh and was important in improving British pigs, but with the gradual improvement of pigs in the agricultural revolution it became another casualty.

Chato Murciano

The Chato Murciano is a traditional Spanish breed. Black fur is the most common colour but some have white patches on the tail and legs, which are believed to have been inherited from the Berkshire, with which the Spanish improved the primitive Murcian breed. Hair is found all over the pig's body except on the sow's teats, and – as the Spanish word chato ('flat') indicates – it has a short nose. Although once endangered, Murcia's only surviving breed now flourishes because the Spanish have worked hard to promote the excellence of its hams and sausages.

Oxford Sandy and Black

The Oxford Sandy and Black Pig, sometimes referred to as the Plum Pudding or Oxford Forest Pig, is one of the oldest British pig breeds. It has existed for more than two hundred years. A large and beautiful pig, it is ginger in colour, with white feet and tail and black patches, strong, medium-length legs, lop ears and a medium-length nose. Tractable and easily managed,

it is an exceptional forager and prolific breeder that carries less fat than other breeds, and it makes great bacon. I have used Plum Pudding bacon for years as it is delicious, with the added bonus of a great name!

Large Black

The Large Black, Britain's only totally black pig, is a cross between black pigs hailing from the West Country and the east of England. It has a long back with broad shoulders and large hams, and a wide head with lop ears and a long snout. It is a docile pig that makes a good mother and is a great forager suitable for extensive farming practices. Unfortunately, with the rise of intensive farming this breed has suffered and is today considered rare. It is mostly used for bacon and ham.

Middle White

The Middle White is a rare but distinctive breed – there are more giant pandas in the world than Middle Whites. Originating in Yorkshire, England, it was given its name because it was roughly between the Large White and the now extinct Small White in size. It was fully recognized as a breed in 1884. The Middle White is an all-white pig of medium size with a short, snub-nosed, dished face, large, downward-facing ears and a broad, strong neck. In the 1930s it was exported to Japan, where the Emperor would only eat pork from Middle Whites. He even erected a statue to this outstanding rare breed. This 'beautifully ugly' pig more than deserves

Middle White

Large Black

British Saddleback

its fame as the pork pig of England, boasting a much-appreciated taste, almost forgotten in these days of modern commercial production. Middle Whites make great pork and are justly favoured by restaurants.

British Saddleback

The British Saddleback, a combination of the Essex Saddleback and the Wessex Saddleback, is a striking animal of black with a continuous belt of white hair encircling the shoulders and forelegs. The body is both deep and long, reflecting its advantages as an excellent breeding animal and producer of high-quality meat. It has a medium-length head with a very slightly dished face and a jaw free from jowl. Its ears are medium-sized and carried forward, but do not obscure vision. These hardy pigs are well known for their grazing ability, which makes them really popular in outdoor and organic production. The breed is used almost exclusively for bacon.

Gloucestershire Old Spot

This old breed, originally known as the Orchard Pig, originated around the Berkeley Vale in southwest England. It traditionally foraged windfall fruit from local orchards, and according to folklore the spots on its back are bruises from the falling fruit. It is large, is white in colour with a minimum of one distinct black spot, and has lop ears that almost cover the face of a mature pig, a medium-length head and a nose that is

very slightly dished. Its ears are well set apart and drop forward, and its back is long and level. Good husbandry produces top-quality meat all round, used for pork chops, roasting joints and sausages. Due to popular demand, it is now a butcher's speciality.

Berkshire

The Berkshire came from the Old Berkshire and was a rust-coloured pig with dark spots until the 19th century, when Asian blood was used to improve the breed. Nowadays, it is black in colour, with white on the face, feet and tip of the tail – as standardized in 1884, when the breed society was formed. Medium-sized, it weighs a few kilograms (around 6 pounds) less than the Old Berkshire. It has a dished snout of medium length, is wide between the eyes and has fairly large ears carried erect or inclined slightly forward and fringed with hair. It gets to pork weight early and is well known for its quality and flavour. Queen Victoria and the author Beatrix Potter both kept this breed.

American Berkshire

The Old Berkshire was exported to the USA from England in 1823, with the breed society being formed there in 1875, but following World War II it suffered a drop in quality, until new stock was imported from England in 2005 to improve the lines. It is black with white feet, nose and tail, medium-sized, with a short, dished face, alert prick ears, a long body, large hams

Gloucestershire Old Spot

Old Berkshire

Berkshire

and a fine shoulder on short legs. The American Berkshire is a little larger than its English ancestors and is noted for good intramuscular fat distribution, which makes for particularly succulent and delicious pork.

Tamworth

Originating from Tamworth in Staffordshire, England, the Tamworth is one of the most distinctive British breeds, with its richly coloured coat that can range from pale ginger to the deepest auburn. Its head is of medium length, with a slightly dished face, it is wide between the ears, the jowl is light, and the ears, which have a fine fringe, are rather large, carried rigid and slightly inclined. It is among the oldest of pig breeds and, as with many older breeds of livestock, is not well suited to modern production methods. The Tamworth is one of the stunners of the pig world and certainly produces some of the best pork – and it is the pig that the legendary Ginger Pig farm and butcher are named after. At the Ginger Pig farm in Yorkshire I have seen two beauties called Harwell Yorkshire Lad and Dai Bando – the size of small sofas, they were over 700kg (1,500lb) each!

Iron Age pig

A hybrid between a wild boar and a Tamworth, the Iron Age pig recreates the type of pig represented in European Iron Age artworks. It was developed in the 1970s for a BBC television series by rare-breeds conservationist Joe Henson, who crossed a male wild boar from London Zoo with Tamworth sows to produce an animal that looked like the pig from long ago. It shares traits with both the Tamworth and the wild boar, being lighter in colour than the wild boar but with the long snout seen in both, and a similar general conformation. The piglets are usually striped from nose to tail like those of a wild boar but they lose their stripes as they grow. The infamous 'Tamworth Two' that caused headlines in British newspapers in the 1990s were actually Iron Age pigs, which explains their lengthy liberty, as the wild-boar blood helped to keep them alive and healthy through forage alone. The pork is rich and flavoursome, with enough fat to avoid the dryness seen in wild boar meat.

Hampshire

The Hampshire pig probably started its history in the New Forest in Hampshire and is characterized by a black body with a whitish band around the middle, covering the front legs. Its head is medium-sized, with small, erect ears and a clean jowl, and it has a wide chest, strong, medium-length legs and a well-muscled back. It is noted for being a rapid grower and for exhibiting good carcass quality when used as a meat animal. It developed later into the Wessex Saddleback, a similarly coloured pig, but with flop ears, which was

American Berkshire   **Tamworth**   **Iron Age**

kept largely for foraging in forests. Residents of Hampshire, in the south of England, are often colloquially referred to as 'Hampshire Hogs', a name that goes back at least to the 1790s.

American Hampshire

The American National Swine Registry notes that this is the fourth 'most recorded breed' of pigs in the United States, and probably the oldest American breed of hogs. Hampshire in England is thought to have exported to America between 1827 and 1839. The American Hampshire is black with a white band taking in the forelegs and has large, muscled shoulders and a longish, narrow head with upright ears and no jowl. It produces good lean meat used for both pork and bacon.

British Lop

A large, long, pure-white modern pig from the West Country of England, the British Lop is a good forager and grazer, docile and self-sufficient outside. The long lop ears for which it was named incline forward over the face and touch the end of the nose and tapered muzzle. It has straight, silky hair with no wrinkles. Being a white pig, it doesn't suffer from the commercial bias against multi-coloured pigs. (Unfortunately, this also works the other way, with many rare-breed keepers considering it too plain a pig to keep.) The pork and bacon from a well-finished Lop are high-quality products.

Yorkshire

One of the most popular modern pigs in the world, the Yorkshire is also known as the Large White. True to its names, it is a big, white-skinned pig from Yorkshire, with erect ears and a dished face. It was originally developed as an outdoor breed, but today it is one of those favoured by commercial pig breeders, lending uniformity to pigs produced for meat on a large scale. The head is fairly long, with large, pointy ears, a light jowl, a clean neck and full shoulders. It is a well-muscled pig with a slightly arched back and broad hams. The Yorkshire has proved itself as a rugged and hardy breed that can withstand variations in climate and other environmental factors. Its ability to cross with and improve other breeds has given the Yorkshire a leading role in commercial pork production and it has influenced pig breeding worldwide. Unlike many breeds, the Yorkshire was not developed by the famous stock improvers of the Agricultural Revolution but by one Joseph Tuley of Keighley in Yorkshire with pig showing in mind!

American Yorkshire

In the 1870s in New York State a Yorkshire Boar from England was crossed with a Cheshire, also from England. From New York State, the American Yorkshire spread to Indiana, Ohio, Iowa and Illinois and is now found all over the USA. It is a large, square-bodied white pig with a dished face and a long nose, a broad,

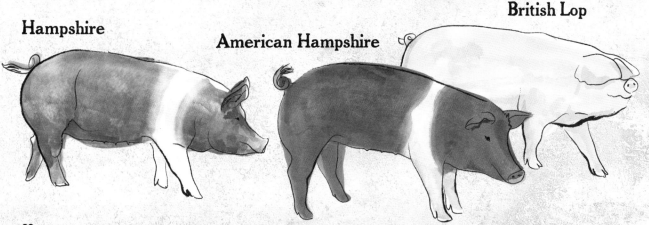

Hampshire

American Hampshire

British Lop

arched back and large shoulders. Its hair is fine and silky with pink skin beneath. It is predominantly used as a bacon pig.

Chester White

The Chester White was developed in Chester County, Pennsylvania, around 1815, when Captain James Jeffries imported from England one white boar that was referred to as a Bedfordshire or Cumberland. This boar was used extensively to mate with white pigs in Chester County, and from these couplings the Chester White breed started. It has a broad head with a short nose and dished face, full shoulders, a long straight back and broad loins. The legs are short and strong, and the skin is pale and thin with white hair. By 1884 a breed association was officially formed, but competing organizations, sometimes for individual strains, continued to appear into the early 20th century. In 1930 all breed organizations were consolidated under the Chester White Swine Record Association, which aided the spread of the breed into the rest of the country. Today the Chester White is a versatile breed suited to both intensive and extensive husbandry. It is used for both pork and bacon.

Piétrain

The Piétrain is a large but lean pig that became popular after World War II, when tastes for lean pork became fashionable. It takes its name from a small village of the Walloon municipality of Jodoigne, Belgium, and is the result of crossing English and French breeds. It is of medium size with a short neck, large shoulders and massive double-muscled hams, and has a medium-sized head with upright ears. The breed became popular in the early 1950s and was exported in the early 1960s to Germany, where it is now bred mostly in Schleswig-Holstein, Nordrhein-Westfalen and Baden-Württemberg. Commonly used in crossbreeding in Germany to improve the quality of pork, the Piétrain produces lean pork of the kind favoured by today's supermarkets.

Blonde Mangalitsa

The Blonde Mangalitsa is the most widespread type of Mangalitsa pig and comes from ancient Hungarian Mangalitsa pigs, which were refined with Serbian Sumadija pigs. Used as a lard pig in its native Hungary, it is late-maturing at around 15 months, has small litters of between three and seven, and is extremely hardy. The coat of the Blonde Mangalitsa ranges from grey to yellow and yellowish red in all variations,

American Yorkshire

Large White

Piétrain

Chester White

depending on the direction from which it is viewed. It is dense and long, curled in winter, and softer, shorter and straighter in summer. The curly hair is a breed trait, and excessive fine woolly fur is not considered desirable. The seasonal change of coat of the Mangalitsa is very typical and noteworthy, being lighter in summer and thicker in winter.

Red Mangalitsa

This comes from a cross of the old Hungarian Blonde with the Transylvanian Szalontai Mangalitsa. Its coat is reddish brown (with the seasonal change that is common to all Mangalitsa breeds), and its height and weight surpass the other Mangalitsas. Consequently, it has a higher growth rate and fertility. The skin is pigmented blackish grey and is visible beneath the coat, which is why the colour seems darker in summer when the coat is naturally sparse. The Red Mangalitsa is a late developer, with a good meaty carcass producing great bacon and salami that are prized throughout Europe.

Swallow Bellied Mangalitsa

The Swallow Bellied Mangalitsa was developed in southern Hungary by crossing the Blonde Mangalitsa with the Croatian Syrmia Mangalitsa. Its mouth, lower neck area and lower half of the body are yellowish white to silver grey. The skin is soft, thin and always grey, and the mouth, snout and teats are dark. It is the smallest Mangalitsa and is slightly less susceptible to running to fat. Like the other Mangalitsas, it is best suited to charcuterie.

Mangalitsa Red

Mangalitsa Blonde

American Duroc

Duroc

Mangalitsa Swallow Bellied

American Duroc

Said to have been named after a famous thoroughbred stallion of the day, the Duroc is an older breed of American pig, which forms the basis for many mixed-breed commercial hogs. It is red-brown, large-framed, medium-length and muscular, with partially drooping ears, and tends to be one of the least aggressive of all the breeds. Its excellent growth rate and conversion of feed to meat makes it particularly prized. The modern breed originated around 1830 from crosses of the Jersey Red and New York's older Duroc. Medium in length, it has strong, straight legs and a slight dish of the face, drooping ears that are not held erect, a wide head and a clean jowl.

British Duroc

Because of its phenomenal weight-gaining ability the Duroc was imported into the UK from America during the 1950s and 1960s by large, commercial pig-breeding companies. By the 1990s it had become accepted as a pure, separate breed. It is best suited to pork production.

Welsh

Known for its hardiness in outdoor farming and its long, pear-shaped body, the Welsh is a smaller white breed with lop ears. Native to Wales, the breed was first mentioned in the 1870s, and is the third most common sire in the UK after the Large White and the British Landrace. The modern Welsh has quite a wide head and a straight nose. The shoulders are flat at the top, supporting a strong back. The white coat covers a thick torso supported by strong, short legs. Its hams are full and firm, its ribs are well spread across the stomach, and its tail is thick. The loin of the Welsh is very muscly and in general the pig is lean and strong. This pig became popular in the mid-20th century as a crucial breed for the British pig industry, but the Welsh is not exported to many countries around the world despite the fact that it can produce good bacon.

British Landrace

The British Landrace is one of the most popular modern breeds in the UK. It originated in the 1949 importation of a dozen Landrace pigs from Denmark – four boars and eight gilts (young females). It is white with medium-sized flop ears that cover most of the face, a medium-length, a light head with a straight nose, and a fine jowl and shoulders. The back is long and slightly arched, leading to wide loins. In 1950 the British Landrace Pig Society was formed and it opened a herd book for the first offspring born from the imported 12. In 1955 a report by the Advisory Committee on the Development of Pig Production advised farmers to increase profitability by focusing on just three breeds of pig – the British Landrace, the

Welsh

Landrace

Large White and the Welsh. Many farmers acted on the report and as a result many rare pig breeds declined. Seven pig breeds were lost in Britain in the 20th century, and the industry became dominated by the British Landrace and the Large White. In the 1980s the breed was developed and its genetic base was expanded by the importation of new bloodlines from Norway and Finland. These developments have made the British Landrace unique among other Landrace breeds. The British Landrace is now also used to improve other breeds.

American Landrace

The Landrace arrived in the USA from Denmark in 1934 and was crossed with the American Yorkshire to produce the bulk of American bacon. A long-bodied, all-white pig with lean hams and loins, a long nose and large flop ears, this pig is often used as a sire to hybridize, as its weight gain and food conversion are better than most other breeds. It is ideally suited to bacon production.

Poland China

The Poland China was first bred in 1816 when a Polish-born farmer took the Big China pig from Philadelphia to Warren County, Ohio, and bred it with the Irish Grazier Pig. Deriving from several breeds including the American Berkshire and Hampshire, it is the oldest American breed. Typically black with white patches, it is known for its large size. Big Bill, the largest hog ever recorded, was a Poland China. He weighed in excess of 1,000kg (2,200lb)! It is said that this breed's pork and bacon are unsurpassed for taste.

Spotted Swine

This large, rugged, black and white pig derived from the Poland China, Berkshire and Gloucestershire Old Spot in the late 19th century and is now found mostly in Indiana, where it is suited to small-scale farming. A rugged, big-boned pig with lop ears, a large head and coarse hair, it has strong, thick legs, powerful shoulders and a cylindrical body. It produces lean meat for pork or bacon and is tough enough to subsist without too much care.

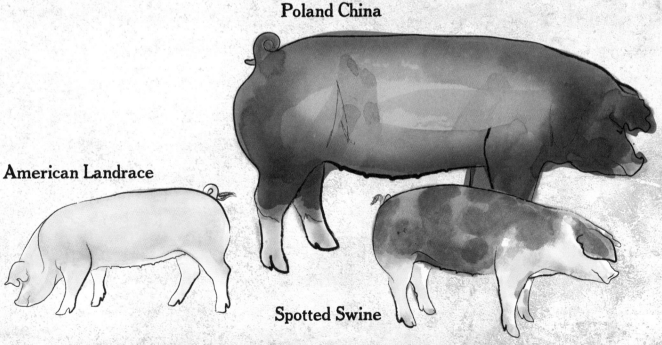

Poland China

American Landrace

Spotted Swine

Chapter 2
NOT-SO-PRIME CUTS

1kg boneless pork shoulder

10g Maldon sea salt flakes

freshly ground black pepper

20g unsalted butter

10ml vegetable oil

500ml full-fat organic milk

1 teaspoon freshly grated nutmeg

juice of 1 lemon

Italian in origin, milk-braised pork is deliciously moist and tender, with a surprisingly complex flavour. As with all simple dishes, the quality of the ingredients is paramount, and while I'm not particularly pro-organic I've specified organic milk, as I believe it will make a difference here.

PORK SHOULDER BRAISED IN MILK Serves 4

Season the pork well with salt and pepper.

In a small heavy-based flameproof casserole, heat the butter and oil over a medium-high heat until the butter has melted. Add the pork and cook, turning occasionally, until browned on all sides. Transfer the pork to a plate. Pour off the fat, then wipe out the casserole and let it cool slightly. Add the milk and nutmeg and return the pork to the casserole.

Bring the milk mixture just to the boil, then reduce the heat to medium-low. Cover the casserole and simmer gently, turning the meat every 30 minutes, until it is tender but not falling apart – about 2 hours. Transfer the meat to a chopping board and let it rest for 10 minutes.

Add the lemon juice and simmer, uncovered, until reduced by two-thirds and small golden curds have formed throughout – about 10 minutes. Season to taste with salt and pepper.

Cut the pork into 1cm slices and arrange on a serving platter. Spoon the curds over and around the pork and serve.

2kg shoulder of pork, bone in, skin on

Maldon sea salt flakes

freshly ground black pepper

2 red onions, halved

2 small fennel bulbs

2 carrots, peeled and halved lengthways

2 celery sticks, halved

1 head of garlic, skin on, smashed

500ml Master Pork Broth (see page 335)

For the anchoïade

30g anchovy fillets

100ml extra virgin olive oil

½ garlic clove

10 fresh thyme leaves

5 fresh basil leaves

1 teaspoon Dijon mustard

1 teaspoon red wine vinegar

freshly ground black pepper

Anchovies are a rich source of umami and salt, and have been used since Roman times as a kind of condiment for seasoning meat. In 1466, the French King Louis XI exempted the *anchoîeurs* from paying the *gabelle* (salt tax), and anchovies grew in popularity as a means of seasoning food. When used in this way, good anchovies have almost no fishy flavour and simply enhance the meatiness of pork, lamb and beef.

SLOW-ROAST PORK WITH ANCHOÏADE Serves 5–6

Preheat the oven to 200°C/gas mark 6. Place the pork on a clean work surface, skin side up, and score it all over with lines about 1cm apart, cutting through the skin into the fat, but not into the meat. Rub salt into all the scores you've just made, pulling the skin apart a little if you need to. Brush any excess salt off the surface, then turn the meat over and season the underside with a few pinches of salt and pepper.

Place the pork, skin side up, in a roasting tray and roast for 30 minutes, or until the skin has started to puff up and you can see it turning into crackling. At this point, lower the heat to 160°C/gas mark 3. Cover the meat with foil and roast for a further 4 hours.

Take the pork out of the oven and remove the foil, then baste the meat with the dripping in the bottom of the tray. Carefully lift up the pork and transfer it to a chopping board. Put all the vegetables, including the garlic, into the roasting tray and stir them into

the dripping. Drain away any excess dripping (keep it for other recipes), then place the pork back on top of everything and return it to the oven, without the foil, to roast for another hour.

Meanwhile, make the anchoïade by blending all the ingredients to a smooth paste.

When the pork is ready, remove it to a serving dish and leave to rest while you make the gravy. Spoon away any fat from the roasting tray, then pour in the pork broth and place on the hob. Bring to a boil, then lower the heat and simmer for a few minutes, stirring constantly with a wooden spoon to scrape up all the stuff on the bottom. When you've got a light viscous gravy, pour it through a sieve into a gravy boat, using your spoon to really push all the juices of the veg through the sieve. Carve the meat and serve with the roasted vegetables, buttered cabbage, potatoes, gravy and the warm anchoïade on the side.

1.5kg boned and rolled pork shoulder

Maldon sea salt flakes

50ml olive oil

2 onions, halved through the root

2 fennel bulbs, halved through the root

4 garlic cloves, sliced

200ml dry white wine

1 litre pork broth or stock

200ml fresh orange juice

400g can chopped tomatoes

100g pitted green olives

2 large oranges, segmented

2 tablespoons fresh oregano leaves

hot smoked paprika, for dusting (optional)

Although not particularly authentic, this braise was inspired by stews I've eaten in Ibiza and is redolent of a hot Iberian summer. Fiona Beckett, a long time oenophile and dispenser of sage advice, recommends a glass or two of Santa Maria del Camí Binissalem from neighbouring Mallorca.

POT ROAST PORK WITH FENNEL, OLIVES, ORANGES & OREGANO Serves 4

Preheat the oven to 200°C/gas mark 6.
Score the skin of the pork with a sharp knife, making small incisions 2cm apart, then rub the skin with salt.

Heat 1 tablespoon of the oil in a large flameproof casserole over a medium heat. Add the onions and fennel and cook for 10 minutes until just softened and golden. Add the garlic and cook for a further 2 minutes.

Add the white wine and reduce by half. Pour in the stock, bring to the boil and reduce by half, then add the orange juice and tomatoes.

Sit the pork in the vegetables and place in the oven, uncovered, for 40 minutes. Add the olives, then cook for a further 20 minutes until the pork is cooked through.

Turn the oven off, add the orange segments and oregano and allow to rest in the oven for 30 minutes before transferring to a chopping board to carve. Serve the pork along with the vegetables, olives and orange segments, drizzled with a spoonful of the pan juice. The lightest dusting of hot smoked paprika at the end adds a lovely warming character.

250g shredded cooked pork shoulder or Pulled Pork (*see* page 312)

50ml hoisin sauce

1 banana shallot, finely chopped

50ml Master Pork Broth (*see* page 335)

2 teaspoons soy sauce

2 teaspoons sesame oil

For the buns

2 teaspoons caster sugar

230ml lukewarm water

7g sachet of dried yeast

20ml vegetable oil

7g (about 1 heaped teaspoon) baking powder

400g plain flour

You will also need a steamer

Steamed pork buns, or *char siu bao*, are a popular dim sum in Chinese restaurants, and these light and fluffy buns are also grab-and-go street food in China. They are sometimes baked and glazed for a crispy result.

STEAMED PORK BUNS Serves 4

Mix together the pork, hoisin sauce, shallot, pork broth, soy sauce and sesame oil. Chill in the refrigerator for several hours.

To make the dough, place the sugar and water in a mixing bowl and stir until the sugar dissolves. Add the yeast and leave to rest for 10 minutes, or until frothy.

Add the vegetable oil and baking powder and sift in the flour. Stir the mixture with your hands until it comes together as a smooth, slightly wet dough. Cover the bowl with a damp cloth and allow the dough to rise – about 1 hour.

When the dough has doubled in size, knock it back and scrape it out of the bowl. Cover with clingfilm and refrigerate until needed.

Shape the dough into balls and roll each one out into a flat circle about the size of a saucer. Put 1 tablespoon of the pork mixture in the centre of each circle, then wrap the dough around the filling. Place seamside down on greaseproof paper squares and let them stand in a warm place until risen – about 20 minutes.

Bring water to the boil in a steamer, then reduce the heat to a medium simmer. Put the buns, still on greaseproof paper, in the steamer basket, cover with a lid and steam for 10 minutes, making sure that water does not come into contact with the buns.

1kg pork shoulder, cut into 3cm dice

50ml ghee or clarified butter

10 fresh curry leaves

1 teaspoon brown mustard seeds

2 onions, finely chopped

1 head of garlic, cloves cut into slivers

2 fresh green chillies, chopped

2 tomatoes, finely chopped

Maldon sea salt flakes, to taste

boiled potatoes or rice, to serve

For the marinade

3 teaspoons cumin seeds

3 teaspoons coriander seeds

½ teaspoon black cardamom seeds

½ teaspoon fenugreek seeds

5 cloves

½ cinnamon stick

10 black peppercorns

½ teaspoon turmeric

3 dried red Kashmiri chillies

75ml cider vinegar

15g tamarind paste

30g light brown muscovado sugar

8 garlic cloves, crushed

3cm piece of fresh root ginger, peeled and sliced against the grain, then chopped

Vindaloo is derived from the Portuguese *carne de vinha d'alhos*, a pork dish made with wine and garlic. It has been modified by the substitution of vinegar for the wine and the addition of red Kashmiri chillies with additional spices, to evolve into the vindaloo we know today. This authentic Anglo-Indian version is marinated in vinegar, chillies, fresh ginger and spices overnight, then cooked with the addition of more spices. The end result has a medium-spiced, 'sweet-sour' flavour and is quite different from what you might find in an Indian restaurant.

GOAN PORK VINDALOO Serves 4

Place all the spices for the marinade except the turmeric and chillies on a baking tray and roast in the oven at 180°C/gas mark 4 until lightly golden and fragrant, but not burnt. Place the warm spices in a food processor with the turmeric and blend to a fine powder, then add the chillies, vinegar, tamarind paste, sugar, garlic and ginger and blend until smooth.

Toss the pork with the marinade and place in a plastic container in the refrigerator for 24 hours.

Heat half the ghee in a frying pan and fry the marinated pork shoulder, then transfer to a large saucepan. Pour the rest of the ghee into the frying

pan and add the curry leaves and mustard seeds. When the seeds begin to pop, add the onions, garlic and green chillies and fry for a few minutes, or until soft.

Add the chopped tomatoes to the pork, add the onion and spice mixture and pour in just enough water to cover. Bring to the boil and skim any impurities from the top. Simmer very gently for 1½ hours, or until tender, then adjust the seasoning and serve with potatoes or rice.

All stews benefit from being made the day before, but a curry in particular is a better dish the following day – and even better three days later...

400g pork shoulder,
cut into 3cm dice

20g curry powder
or 50g curry paste

25g unsalted butter

Maldon sea salt flakes

½ small onion,
finely chopped

3 garlic cloves, crushed

1 Scotch bonnet chilli, pierced
with a knife several times

4 potatoes, peeled and cut
into 3cm dice

400ml Master Pork Broth
(*see* page 335)

40g apricot conserve

100g mixed salad or coleslaw

For the rotis (makes 4)

225g plain flour,
plus extra for dusting

a pinch of Maldon sea
salt flakes

100ml water

75ml vegetable oil, for frying

Originally from India and made using an unleavened flatbread,
roti is also a fast-food item in the Caribbean. The wrap roti was
first created in the mid-1940s in Trinidad to make it easier and
quicker to eat curry. Works for me.

PORK ROTI, WEST INDIAN STYLEE Serves 4

Toss the meat in the curry powder or paste and
refrigerate for a few hours or overnight if possible.

Preheat oven at 140°C/gas mark 1.

Heat the butter in a large casserole, season with salt
and fry the pork, onion, garlic and Scotch bonnet
chilli until lightly coloured. Add the potatoes and the
pork broth, then cover and place in the oven for
2 hours.

Meanwhile, make the dough for your rotis. Mix the
flour, salt, water and half the oil together to form a
dough and allow to rest for 30 minutes.

When the pork is cooked, remove from the oven,
discard the Scotch bonnet and allow to sit while
you cook your rotis.

Heat a large skillet. Divide the dough into 4 and roll
out each piece as thinly as possible to make 4 flat
round rotis. Brush the skillet with the remaining oil
and fry your rotis one at a time, until the dough
starts to bubble and they turn golden brown, with
darker spots here and there. Then turn over and
repeat on the other side.

To assemble, place each cooked roti on a sheet of
greaseproof paper and spread with apricot preserve.
Top with a few spoonfuls of curried pork and a salad
of your choice, then wrap into a fat cigar shape and
twist the ends to hold the roti in place.

800g pork shoulder,
cut into 3cm dice

2 tablespoons curry powder

25ml vegetable oil

Maldon sea salt flakes and
freshly ground black pepper

1 red pepper,
cut into 3cm dice

100g onions, finely chopped

3 garlic cloves, crushed

2cm piece of fresh root
ginger, peeled and finely
chopped

100g canned tomatoes

100g peanut butter

400ml Master Pork Broth
(*see* page 335)

4 sweet potatoes, peeled and
cut into 3cm dice

100g roasted peanuts

½ bunch of fresh coriander,
leaves picked

When writing a cookbook you get to eat a lot of food -- in this case pork. Having consumed my own body weight in pork while writing this book, this is perhaps my favourite dish -- one I think I'll return to again and again. It's not part of the recipe, but a splash of hot sauce or Sriracha could only improve this still further.

WEST AFRICAN PORK & PEANUT STEW Serves 4

Place the meat in a nonreactive bowl and toss in the curry powder. Cover with clingfilm and refrigerate for a few hours, or overnight if possible.

Preheat the oven to 150°C/gas mark 2.

Heat the oil in a large flameproof casserole, season with salt and fry the pork, red pepper, onions, garlic and ginger until lightly coloured. Add the tomatoes, peanut butter and pork broth, then cover and place in the oven for 2 hours.

Remove from the oven, stir in the sweet potatoes, then bake in the oven for a further 20 minutes until the sweet potatoes are tender.

When cooked, adjust the seasoning and serve garnished with the peanuts and coriander leaves.

20g Maldon sea salt flakes

1kg pork belly, bone in

2 litres Master Pork Broth
(*see* page 335)

½ teaspoon Chinese
five-spice powder

2 fresh chillies, chopped

heaped ¼ teaspoon
yellow mustard seeds

½ teaspoon fennel seeds

½ teaspoon black
peppercorns

100ml blackstrap molasses

100ml light soy sauce

100g dates, stoned and
chopped

100g light brown
muscovado sugar

100g dark brown
muscovado sugar

To serve

bok choy

steamed rice

I enjoyed a dish called sticky toffee pork in Hong Kong,
but unfortunately I couldn't discern the ingredients and my
Cantonese is non-existent. Having played around with a similar
preparation and using some classic sticky toffee ingredients,
I came up with this -- it's not identical to what I had but very
much alike and tasty nonetheless.

STICKY TOFFEE PORK Serves 4

Generously salt the pork belly, leave uncovered for 1 hour, then rinse. Place in a large saucepan and cover with the pork broth. Add the rest of the ingredients.

Bring to the boil, then turn down to a simmer. Place a plate or small saucepan lid directly on the pork belly to keep it submerged. Cook at the barest simmer for about 2 hours. When you can pass a skewer through the belly with ease, it is ready.

Meanwhile, preheat the oven to 220°C/gas mark 7.

Take care when removing the pork belly from the stock. Place it on a chopping board and remove the bones and sinews (they should pop out of the tender meat).

Score the skin slightly in a chequered pattern. Place on greaseproof paper on a baking tray and roast for about 20 minutes.

Meanwhile, strain the reserved stock into a saucepan and reduce it until a nice coating consistency is achieved, like a light syrup.

Serve the pork with wilted bok choy and steamed rice, with the sauce drizzled over.

1 tablespoon chopped
fresh oregano

1 tablespoon chopped
fresh sage

1 tablespoon chopped
fresh basil

1 tablespoon chopped
fresh marjoram

2 teaspoons chilli powder

2 teaspoons fennel seeds

2 teaspoons freshly ground
black pepper

2 teaspoons smoked paprika

1 teaspoon chopped onion

1 large garlic clove, chopped

1 heaped tablespoon Maldon
sea salt

1kg pork belly, with ribs

250ml buttermilk

1 free-range egg, beaten

120g plain flour

vegetable oil, for deep-frying

You will also need a
meat thermometer

**For the English, country fried is another name for Southern fried,
and we all love Southern fried stuff -- in moderation, of course.**

COUNTRY FRIED RIBS Serves 4

Preheat the oven to 110°C/gas mark ¼.

In a blender or food processor, blend the herbs,
spices, onion, garlic and salt to a fine powder.
Remove the skin from the ribs and massage with
half the blended mix, then place in a shallow roasting
tray, cover with foil and bake for 4 hours.

When the internal temperature of the centre of the
ribs is 90°C, remove them and sandwich between
2 clean trays. Place a heavy weight on top and
press and chill in the refrigerator. Cut the ribs into
portions, 1 rib thick, and French trim the bones
to form 'lollipops'.

Mix the buttermilk with the egg and submerge the
cold ribs in this mixture. Mix the other half of the
blended spice mix with the flour.

Heat the oil to 180°C in a deep-fat fryer or deep,
heavy-based saucepan. Remove the ribs from the
buttermilk mixture and dredge in the seasoned flour,
then fry until crispy and golden. Serve hot.

1kg pork belly, with ribs

slaw of choice, to serve
(see page 341)

For the spices

45g fennel seeds

1 teaspoon cumin seeds

1 teaspoon coriander seeds

45g black peppercorns

For the marinade

1 onion, grated

1 head of garlic, grated

1 green pepper, finely diced

1 green chilli, finely diced

100ml smoked chipotle
Tabasco

100g English mustard

100g smoked sea salt

100g maple syrup

100ml blackstrap molasses

200g apricot preserve

200ml ketchup

200g grated Granny Smith
apple

In the world of ribs, they don't come any meatier than these, which are essentially pork belly with the bones left in. I'm ridiculously pleased with them and they have appeared on almost every menu I've written over the past decade.

GRILLED MEATY BELLY RIBS Serves 2–3

Preheat the oven to 180°C/gas mark 4. Roast the spices until golden, then blend to a powder in a blender or food processor.

Reduce the oven temperature to 120°C/gas mark ½.

Cook the onion and garlic gently with the spices for 5 minutes, then blend with the remaining marinade ingredients. Remove the skin from the ribs and massage with the marinade, then place in a shallow roasting tray, cover with foil and bake in the oven for 4 hours.

When the internal temperature of the centre of the ribs reaches 90°C, remove them from the oven. Discard the fat from the cooking liquid. Heat the cooking liquor to reduce by half, then leave to cool.

Sandwich the ribs between 2 clean trays, place a heavy weight on top and press and chill in the refrigerator. Cut the ribs into portions, baste liberally with the cool cooking liquor and reserve.

When ready to eat, grill the ribs until hot and caramelized and serve lightly brushed with more of the reduced cooking liquor. Serve with a good slaw (see page 341).

4kg pork belly and loin, from a one-year-old pig, boned

50ml white wine

50g pork lard

50g Maldon sea salt flakes

50g garlic, crushed

2 teaspoons freshly ground black pepper

1 teaspoon wild fennel pollen (available online from www.souschef.co.uk or Amazon)

1 teaspoon chopped fresh thyme leaves

2 teaspoons fine salt

1 litre Master Pork Broth (*see* page 335)

To serve

soft white rolls

mustard of choice

You will also need some butcher's string

Porchetta is the ultimate Italian roast pork and dates back to the days of the Roman Empire. Heavily seasoned, often with wild herbs, and roasted in a wood oven, it is held in such high esteem in Italy that they hold porchetta festivals, where people get together to celebrate by gorging on tender porchetta sandwiches with mounds of crunchy crackling.

PORCHETTA TREVIGIANA Serves 8

Score the skin of the pork belly in a diamond pattern. Turn it over and stab the flesh all over with a knife tip without going right through. Remove the skin from the loin and stab the flesh all over. Mix all the remaining ingredients except the fine salt and the broth to a paste and rub into the pork flesh.

Wrap the belly around the pork loin, tying it at 5cm intervals with butcher's string. Rub the skin with the fine salt and leave to rest for 1 hour.

Preheat the oven to 200°C/gas mark 6. Place the porchetta on a wire rack set over a roasting tin and roast for 1 hour, then lower the heat to 160°C/ gas mark 3 and pour half the pork broth into the roasting tray. Cook for another hour, then add the rest of the pork broth to the tray and turn the oven off.

Allow the porchetta to rest in the cooling oven while you prepare the accompaniments. Braised fennel, garlic potatoes and broccoli raab all go well, and soft rolls are essential.

Remove the pork from the oven, slice and serve with the juices from the roasting tray and mustard of your choice. Any leftovers should be wrapped whole and eaten thinly sliced with salad the next day, when they will possibly be even better than when hot.

2 tablespoons cooking oil

400g pork belly, cut into 4

1 teaspoon minced ginger

1 onion, finely sliced

1 garlic clove, crushed

10cm piece of daikon, finely sliced

2 baby taro, finely sliced

1 carrot, peeled and finely sliced

200g white button mushrooms, sliced

1 litre Master Pork Broth (*see* page 335)

50g miso

200g tofu, cut into 1cm cubes

1 spring onion, thinly sliced

Called *tonjiru* in Eastern Japan (literally 'pig soup'), this is usually made with dashi instead of pork broth, but both work well. More substantial than miso soup, it makes a great light lunch or supper. If daikon or taro prove hard to find, you could substitute turnip or mooli.

PORK & MISO SOUP Serves 4

In a frying pan, heat half the oil over a medium-high heat and add the pork and ginger. Cook until nicely browned, then set aside.

In a large saucepan, heat the remaining oil over a medium-high heat and sauté the onion and garlic until soft.

Add the daikon, taro, carrot and mushrooms and stir until everything is well mixed. Pour in the pork broth. Add the pork and bring the soup to a gentle simmer. Cook until the vegetables are soft and the meat is cooked through, skimming as you go – about 30 minutes.

Remove 100ml of stock to a bowl and whisk in the miso, then return it to the pan. Add the tofu and stir gently without breaking it up, and without letting the soup boil. Place the ingredients separately into bowls, pour the soup over and garnish with spring onions.

I enjoyed a hybrid Portuguese-Chinese dish on a trip to Chicago with the Hawksmoor team and thought I'd try it -- it's a big, complicated and busy dish that is unlike my usual cooking, but give it a go if you can round up the myriad ingredients. It's worth it.

FAT & DIRTY RICE   Serves 4

For the pork

2 garlic cloves, finely chopped

10ml fresh lemon juice

1 teaspoon hot smoked paprika

1kg boneless pork belly,
cut into 10 pieces

For the base

20ml olive oil

2 red peppers, thinly sliced

1 large onion, thinly sliced

Maldon sea salt and freshly ground black pepper

4 garlic cloves, finely chopped

10g tomato purée

1 teaspoon sherry vinegar

1 teaspoon hot smoked paprika

For the rice

Maldon sea salt and freshly ground black pepper

40ml olive oil

250g mini Spanish cooking chorizo sausages, halved

750ml Master Pork Broth
(*see* page 335)

400g paella rice, rinsed

100g Andouille sausage, chopped

100g golden raisins,
soaked in sherry vinegar

For the lobsters and clams

2 garlic cloves, finely chopped

1 teaspoon finely chopped fresh parsley

10g finely chopped pickled Jalapeño chillies

2 small live native lobsters

500g Palourde clams, scrubbed

100ml white wine

Maldon sea salt flakes

For the garnish

10g hot smoked paprika

2 pinches of Maldon sea salt

2 lemons, quartered, seeds removed

2 hard-boiled eggs, halved

a few black olives

a few green olives

a few pickled green chillies

a few pickled sweet cherry peppers

a few thinly sliced spring onions

Continued...

First marinate the pork. Whisk the garlic, lemon juice and paprika in a non-reactive bowl, then add the pork and toss to coat. Cover and chill for at least 6 hours.

To make the base, heat the oil in a large skillet over a medium heat. Add the peppers and onion and season with salt. Cook, stirring often, until softened – about 8–10 minutes. Reduce the heat to low and cook, stirring occasionally, for about 30 minutes, or until the vegetables are caramelized. Add the garlic and tomato purée and continue to cook, stirring occasionally, for a further 10 minutes, or until the tomato purée begins to darken. Mix in the vinegar and paprika, then season with salt and pepper.

Now for the rice. Remove the pork from the marinade and season with salt and pepper. Heat 20ml of the oil in a large lidded flameproof pot over a medium heat and fry the pork until coloured all over, then remove the pork and set aside. Add the chorizo and cook, stirring often, for about 2 minutes, or until crisp, then remove and set aside.

Add the vegetable base and cook, stirring constantly, until sizzling – about 1 minute. Add the broth, scraping up any browned bits, and season with salt. Add the rice, Andouille sausage, chorizo and raisins. Stir and bring to the boil. Reduce the heat, arrange the pork on top, cover the pot and simmer gently, stirring occasionally, for 20–25 minutes, or until the rice is tender. Uncover and increase the heat to medium-high. Drizzle the remaining oil around the edges of the pot and cook, undisturbed, for about 5 minutes more, until the underside of the rice is crunchy.

Meanwhile, cook the lobsters and clams. Mix the garlic, chopped parsley and chillies in a small bowl. Split the lobsters in half through the head to kill them first, then devein. Stuff the cut side with the garlic and parsley mixture, then crack the claws and reserve. If you are at all squeamish you can freeze the lobsters first for an hour to render them unconscious.

Combine the clams and wine in a large skillet. Cover, then cook over a high heat, stirring often, for about 2 minutes, or until the clams open (discard any that remain closed). Using a slotted spoon, transfer the clams to a large bowl.

Reduce the heat to medium-low. Lightly season the lobster with salt and cook in the same skillet until opaque – about 2 minutes on each side. Transfer the lobster to the bowl of clams, and pour the pan juices into a small bowl.

Mix the hot smoked paprika and sea salt in a small bowl. Dip the pointed edges of the lemon wedges into this seasoning mix. Top the rice with the lobster and clams and drizzle with the reserved pan juices. Garnish with the lemon wedges, eggs, olives, pickled chillies, peppers and spring onions.

1 recipe Pork Rub
(*see* page 334)

1 tablespoon fresh thyme
leaves, picked

¼ bunch of fresh sage,
chopped

4 garlic cloves, minced

1 bone-in pork belly, about
2kg, cut into 4 portions

2 litres pork fat

Confit means 'prepared' in French, and is an ancient method of meat preservation before refrigeration. The seasoning semi-cures the meat before it is slow-cooked in a deep reservoir of fat to break down the muscle structure and preserve the meat. The seasoning also matures as the meat sits in the fat, allowing the confit to improve over time.

PORK CONFIT Serves 4

Mix together the pork rub, thyme leaves, sage and garlic and rub all over the pork belly portions. Put the meat into a non-reactive container and leave to cure for 24 hours in the refrigerator.

Preheat the oven to 100°C/gas mark ¼. Rinse the belly and pat dry, then leave to dry completely in the refrigerator for an hour or so.

Warm the pork fat in a saucepan until clear and add the pork belly. Bring to a gentle simmer, then transfer to a roasting tray and roast in the oven, uncovered, until tender – about 3 hours.

Remove from the oven and leave to cool to room temperature. Transfer to a sterilized container and refrigerate for at least 5 days, to allow the flavour to develop. It will keep for 3 months submerged in fat, in the refrigerator.

When needed, scrape off the fat and use as required, or roast in a hot oven at 200°C/gas mark 6 for about 15 minutes, or until the skin is crispy.

440g thinly sliced pork belly (available at Korean stores), or partially freeze skinless pork belly and slice thinly, 3mm

a cup of short-grain (sushi) rice

vegetable oil

6–8 lollo rosso lettuce leaves

3 bunches of spring onions, thinly sliced

For the marinade

2 tablespoons dark sesame oil

3 tablespoons soy sauce

1 tablespoon dark brown sugar

1 tablespoon toasted sesame seeds

1 teaspoon freshly ground black pepper

2 garlic cloves, grated

1 tablespoon peeled and grated fresh root ginger

2 generous pinches of Maldon sea salt flakes

For the *ssam jang* hot sauce

30–40g Korean chilli paste (depending on how spicy you like it)

60g Korean fermented soy bean paste (dwenjang – if you can't find this, use red miso)

25g finely chopped spring onions

30g mirin

1 teaspoon sesame seeds

1 teaspoon dark sesame oil

KOREAN-STYLE PORK BELLY WITH LETTUCE WRAPS ...& THE BEST HOT SAUCE EVER Serves 4–6

BY JUDY JOO

Korean barbecue is one of the most loved and well-known parts of Korean cuisine. And there is little doubt why. The sweet smoke gets your mouth watering just from the first smell. Then you taste the addictive flavours -- and you can't seem to get enough -- a mouthful of umami. Warm succulent sweet meat, nuzzled in steaming rice, cradled with a cool crisp lettuce leaf and topped with an insanely tasty sauce. This *ssam jang* hot sauce is the best thing you have never tried. You'll want to throw it on everything. Best of all, it is all so easy to prepare.

Mix all of the ingredients for the marinade together in a non-reactive bowl. Add the pork belly slices. Massage the marinade well into the meat with your hands, then cover with clingfilm and let it chill in the refrigerator for the flavours to infuse for at least 3 hours, or overnight.

Next make the ssam jang sauce by mixing together all the ingredients in a bowl. Cover and chill.

Place the rice in a saucepan and add the same volume cup of water, plus an extra half a cup, then cook according to the packet instructions.

Meanwhile, heat a griddle pan or frying pan and drizzle with a little bit of vegetable oil. Drain the pork slices and griddle or char-grill until cooked through – about 1–2 minutes. Place on a plate and serve with the ssam jang sauce, lettuce, spring onions, sticky rice – and a cold beer.

To eat, grab a lettuce leaf, put in a small scoop of rice and a piece of pork, slather on some ssam jang sauce and top with a few thin slices of spring onion. Wrap and enjoy.

For the kebabs

1kg free-range pork belly, cut into 3cm chunks

1 tablespoon dried mint

1 tablespoon dried Greek oregano

juice of 1 lemon

100ml Greek extra virgin olive oil

2 garlic cloves, finely grated

1 tablespoon red wine vinegar

Maldon sea salt flakes and freshly ground black pepper

For the tzatziki

½ large cucumber, grated and drained

200ml plain Greek yoghurt

1 small garlic clove, crushed

1 tablespoon chopped fresh mint

5ml red wine vinegar

Maldon sea salt flakes and freshly ground black pepper

To serve

8 Greek flatbreads

Greek extra virgin olive oil, for brushing

2 tomatoes, sliced

½ red onion, thinly sliced

½ bunch of fresh mint, leaves picked and chopped

1 tablespoon chopped fresh Greek oregano

1 lemon

You will also need 8 wooden skewers, soaked in water for 30 minutes and a charcoal barbecue

While in hiding in the Cyclades Islands in my twenties, I discovered the joys of a late-night souvlaki -- the fast food of the islands, delicious and addictive, particularly after sampling the local ouzo or Metaxa. 'ένα σουβλάκι παρακαλώ!' If at all possible, do try to cook these over charcoal, as the flavour is incomparable.

SOUVLAKI Serves 4

Place the pork belly in a large non-reactive bowl and add the dried herbs, lemon juice, olive oil, grated garlic and red wine vinegar. Season, toss and refrigerate for a few hours.

Make the tzatziki by mixing all the ingredients in a small non-reactive bowl, seasoning to taste, and chill in the refrigerator.

Preheat either a charcoal barbecue to medium or a cast iron skillet. Whichever you use, it's important it is not too hot, as the pork belly will benefit from gentle cooking.

Thread the marinated pork belly on to the soaked wooden skewers – about 125g on each. Gently cook, turning frequently, for about 20 minutes, or even more slowly if possible.

When cooked, remove and let the skewers rest for a few minutes in a warm place.

Brush the flatbreads with olive oil and toast on your barbecue until just warm. Place 1 pork skewer in the centre of each, then close the bread around the outside, holding tightly on to the meat and pulling the wooden skewer free.

Top with tomato, red onion, tzatziki and more chopped herbs, then squeeze some lemon juice over the top and roll the flatbreads up in greaseproof paper, twisting the ends tightly. Serve immediately.

400ml cassis

200ml water

1 onion, quartered

3 garlic cloves, halved

1 strip of lemon peel, about 2cm wide and 8cm long

8 peppercorns

2 bay leaves

½ teaspoon dried thyme

3 strong liquorice sucking or chewing (soft or hard) sweets, or 2 teaspoons liquorice syrup

1.5–1.7kg piece of good fatty pork belly, rind removed

200g frozen blackcurrants

2 teaspoons red wine vinegar

2 tablespoons mustard powder

plenty of Maldon sea salt flakes

To serve

salad leaves

lemon

red wine vinegar

Maldon sea salt flakes and freshly ground black pepper

olive oil

boiled potatoes

Dijon mustard

capers

butter

red onion

You will also need a charcoal barbecue

BRAISED & CHARRED BLACKCURRANT PORK BELLY
Serves 4–6

BY VALENTINE WARNER

The belly pork was a present for a weekend invitation and the bottle of cassis happened to have been rolling around in the boot of my car for quite some time. My sister's freezer was chocker with blackcurrants and her kitchen has a large inglenook fireplace. Given the choice I would always prefer to cook over wood than on a hob. So there you have it! Good things come from a little scrape in the freezer, a quick scout of the surroundings and a vague knowledge of what lurks in a messy car.

Pour the cassis and water into a large saucepan and lay the pork belly in it. Around the pork add the onion, garlic, lemon peel, peppercorns, bay leaves, thyme and liquorice.

Put the pan on the hob and bring the liquid up to a gentle wobble, then cover the pan with some doubled-over foil and close it up around the edges, leaving one or two little airholes here or there. This will steam the meat while bringing up the temperature to a simmer. Cook the pork like this for 2–2½ hours. It should be tender to a deep prod with a knife, but on no account be falling apart. Remove the meat from the pan and allow to cool. The sauce should be the consistency of cough mixture. Pour the frozen blackcurrants into the pan, bring the sauce back to a simmer and when hot, press all the currants with a potato masher.

Put the onion quarters from the sauce into a non-reactive bowl and press the rest of the sauce through a sieve on top of the onions. Stir in the vinegar and allow to cool.

Light the charcoals of your barbecue – only when the embers appear whitish grey and orange are they ready to cook on.

In the meantime, divide the pork into 2 pieces and scatter the mustard over your work surface along with plenty of salt. Roll the pork in it.

Using a pastry brush or a new paintbrush, slap the blackcurrant lacquer over one side of each piece of pork and lay it, painted side down, over the coals. Paint the unpainted side now. Slap some around the edges and ends too. When the side that's cooking appears to be blistered and charring, turn it over and brush with more sauce.

Repeat the brushing and turning stages until all the sauce has been used up. Occasionally give the pork another good sprinkle of salt. Remember, too, that the sides of the pork will need attention with painting and charring, so stand them on their narrow sides.

All in all, the 2 pieces of belly want to cook for about 20 minutes over the embers, and by the time they are ready they should have built up many layers of sticky, charred, crusty, oozy and glistening deliciousness.

Very good eaten with a good salad of mustardy leaves, sharply dressed with lemon, red wine vinegar, salt and oil. I also like to accompany the pork with boiled potatoes, cooked to the point that they are crumbly at the edges, then mixed with Dijon mustard, capers, butter, finely chopped raw red onion, salt and pepper.

200g Basic Pork Sausages
(*see* page 146)

200g garlic (Toulouse)
sausages

150g smoked streaky bacon

600g dried haricot beans,
soaked in cold water
overnight

75g pork fat, from confit

1 celery stick, roughly chopped

1 small onion, roughly chopped

1 large carrot,
roughly chopped

6 garlic cloves, peeled
but left whole

1 bouquet garni

1.2 litres Master Pork Broth
(*see* page 335)

8 pinches of Maldon sea
salt flakes

2 pinches of freshly ground
black pepper

500g Pork Confit
(*see* page 97)

50g dried breadcrumbs

½ bunch of fresh flat-leaf
parsley, roughly chopped

Named after the deep, round, earthenware pot it's cooked in, cassoulet is the pinnacle of French comfort food and one of those dishes that tastes even better warmed up the next day. There are many versions in France, some with duck or goose, and some with mutton, but they all contain varying amounts of pork. My version is cassoulet at its simplest and most rustic.

PORK CASSOULET Serves 4

Cut the sausages into 1cm thick slices and the bacon into 1cm thick lardons.

Drain the soaked beans and tip them into a large saucepan, then add the bacon lardons and cover with fresh cold water. Bring to the boil and blanch for 10 minutes. Skim the surface of any skum. Drain the beans and lardons in a colander, discarding the cooking water.

Preheat the oven to 120°C/gas mark ½. Heat 25g of the pork fat in a large flameproof casserole over a low heat, add the celery, onion, carrot and 5 of the garlic cloves, and cook gently for 5 minutes. Add the bouquet garni, sausages, beans and lardons and pour in the pork broth. Bring to the boil, skimming as necessary, then season with the salt and pepper.

Transfer the casserole to the oven and cook, uncovered, for 2 hours, stirring every hour. The beans will be soft and the juice should have thickened. Remove from the oven and bury the Pork Confit in the beans. Crush and chop the remaining garlic clove, mix with the parsley and breadcrumbs and sprinkle over the cassoulet with the rest of the pork fat. Return to the oven and cook for a further 2 hours. Serve hot and bubbling.

1kg pork belly or shoulder, cut into 5cm pieces

100g interesting sugar (palm, maple or muscovado)

30ml sesame oil

3cm piece of fresh root ginger, peeled and sliced

3 garlic cloves, peeled

3 star anise

1 cinnamon stick

1 fresh red chilli

5 cloves

5g fennel seeds

50ml light soy sauce

50ml Worcestershire sauce

250ml Shaoxing wine

500ml Master Pork Broth (see page 335)

Red-cooking is a Chinese technique using caramel, soy sauce and occasionally fermented bean paste to impart a reddish-brown hue to slow-cooked meat. The Chinese are wizards with pork, and to my mind this is Chinese pork cookery at its absolute best.

RED-COOKED PORK (HONG SHAU ROU) Serves 4

Place the pork in a pan and cover with cold water. Bring to the boil, then reduce to a simmer for 5 minutes. Drain the pork and allow to dry.

Put the sugar into the same pan with a ladle of water and heat until a syrup forms and it just starts to caramelize. Add the blanched pork and coat with the syrup, continuing to caramelize for a few minutes. Remove from the heat and set aside.

Heat the oil in a wok or nonstick frying pan. Add the ginger slices and garlic and fry for 1 minute, then add the remaining spices. Fry for another minute, then add the light soy, Worcestershire sauce and Shaoxing wine. Add this mixture to the pork pan and pour over the pork broth. Bring to a simmer, then cover with a lid and cook for about 3 hours, or until the meat is tender. (This will vary according to cut.)

Remove the pork and sieve the sauce to remove all the spices. Return the sauce to the pan and reduce over a medium heat to a thick sticky syrup.

Return the pork to the pan and warm through gently. Serve with steamed green vegetables and rice.

- ½ bunch of spring onions
- 1 tablespoon chopped fresh thyme
- 1 tablespoon Maldon sea salt flakes
- ½ teaspoon freshly ground black pepper
- 1 tablespoon honey
- 1 tablespoon ground allspice
- 1 teaspoon grated nutmeg
- 1 teaspoon ground cinnamon
- 2 Scotch bonnet chillies
- 50ml soy sauce
- 50ml vegetable oil
- 50ml vinegar
- 1 onion
- 100ml orange juice
- 2 garlic cloves
- 3cm piece of fresh root ginger, grated
- ½ a pork belly, bones and skin removed
- ½ pork loin, bones and skin removed

You will also need disposable gloves, some butcher's string and a charcoal barbecue

For those of you for whom chicken is the jerk of choice, this recipe will be a revelation. It's likely that pork is the original jerk, and to my mind -- and that of many jerk practitioners -- it's the best.

JERK PORK Serves 10

In a high-powered blender mix all the ingredients except the pork to a smooth paste.

Place the pork in a large container, then, using a paring knife, make some stabs into the meat 2cm deep. Using gloves, massage the marinade into the meat and leave overnight in the refrigerator.

Remove the pork from the refrigerator and wrap the belly round the loin, then tie together with butcher's string spaced 2cm apart. Reserve the marinade for basting.

To slow-cook you can either grill on the top level of a barbecue or grill on your barbecue using indirect heat (the flame should be in one corner of the grill surface and the meat in the other, so as to avoid direct contact between the meat and the flame).

The pork belly allows the meat to self-baste the loin while cooking, so you don't get an overly dry dish because the loin is lean – you will notice that it will start going dark and look burnt, but this natural. It's just the sugars caramelizing – proper jerk is supposed to be that colour. But remember – no direct heat or it will actually burn.

Try to maintain an even 120°C. Keep the lid of your barbecue closed and brush with the marinade every 20 minutes or so for the next 3 hours.

Remove from the barbecue and allow to rest for 30 minutes before slicing. Serve with baked yams.

2 smoked ham hocks

1 litre Court-bouillon
(*see* page 335)

150g Blood Pudding, cut into
2cm dice (*see* page 174)

4 shallots, finely diced

¼ bunch of fresh parsley,
chopped

You will also need a
1.5 litre terrine mould

This terrine was made 'ad hoc' by Marcin Szott, one of my
senior chefs at Hawksmoor, and it's quite delicious, as simple
food so often is. The natural gelatine in the stock combined
with the overnight pressing holds everything together, and it's
very similar to a classic *jambon persillé* in construction.

HAM HOCK & BLACK PUDDING TERRINE Serves 8

Rinse the ham hocks under cold water, then place
in a saucepan and cover with the Court-bouillon.
Bring to a simmer and cook until soft and tender –
about 3 hours.

When the meat is ready, remove it from the pan
and reduce the remaining liquid by half. Remove
the bones, sinews and veins from the hocks and
flake the meat, then allow to cool down and mix
with the Blood Pudding, shallots, parsley and a
little of the reduced liquid.

Line a terrine mould with a double layer of clingfilm,
leaving enough overhanging to fold over the top,
and fill with your mixture. Fold over the clingfilm to
cover, then press with a heavy weight and refrigerate
overnight to set. Serve in slices, with mustard,
cornichons and a simple salad.

For the pastry crust

250g plain flour,
plus extra for dusting

1 teaspoon Maldon sea
salt flakes

50g lard

50ml cold water

For the pork & apple filling

680g pork belly,
cut into 2cm cubes

240ml water

100g onions, chopped

4 fresh sage leaves

1 teaspoon salt

100ml milk

50g flour

2 large tart apples,
peeled, cored and sliced

1 tablespoon sugar

For the glaze

1 egg yolk

a splash of milk

Ciste is a traditional Irish pork and apple pie with a suet pastry. The word 'ciste' means coffin in Gaelic, referring to the shape of the pie, one would assume.

IRISH CISTE Serves 4

To make the pastry crust, combine the flour and salt, mixing well. Cut in the lard with a knife until the mixture resembles coarse sand. Add water a splash at a time, while stirring with a fork, just until the mixture holds together. Form into a ball, wrap in clingfilm and refrigerate.

Brown the pork in large saucepan over a medium heat, stirring frequently. Add the water, onions, sage and salt, and mix well. Cover, then simmer over a low heat for 30 minutes, or until the meat is tender.

Combine the milk and flour, stirring to form a smooth mixture. Add to the pork mixture, stirring constantly to prevent lumps from forming. Cook over a low heat until thickened and bubbly. Pour half the pork mixture into a lightly greased 1.5 litre pie dish. Top with the apples and sprinkle with the sugar. Add the remaining pork mixture. Preheat the oven to 180°C/gas mark 4.

Roll out the dough on a lightly floured board until 2cm thick and cut out a shape to fit the pie dish. Place over the meat mixture. Turn under a small margin of pastry around the edge of the dish and crimp the edge. Cut several steam vents in the pastry.

Beat the egg yolk and milk together and brush over the crust. Bake for 30 minutes, then turn the oven off and allow to sit in the oven for a further 20 minutes. Serve with potatoes.

1 small cockerel or chicken

1 ham hock

1 onion, halved

1 carrot, halved

1 leek, halved

1 celery stick

1 head of garlic, split

400g suet crust pastry (*see* introduction on page 198)

200g button mushrooms, sliced

½ bunch of fresh curly parsley, chopped

Maldon sea salt flakes and freshly ground black pepper

steamed potatoes, to serve

You will also need a 2 litre pudding basin, kitchen string and a steamer

Steamed meat puddings are traditional British comfort food at its best. Save this for when the evenings are closing in and there's a chill in the air.

HOCK & COCK PUDDING Serves 8

Place the chicken and ham hock in a large flameproof casserole with the onion, carrot, leek, celery and garlic, and cover with cold water.

Bring to a gentle simmer and skim well, then continue cooking gently for 1 hour until the ham hock is tender and the small bone is easily removed and the chicken is cooked through. Take out the meats and vegetables and allow to cool.

Flake all the meats with your fingers and chop the vegetables. Put the bones, sinew and skin into the stock. Simmer the stock until reduced by three-quarters and pass through a fine sieve.

Add the flaked meat and chopped vegetables to the reduced stock and reserve.

Roll out the pastry until 2cm thick and use two-thirds of it to line a 2-litre pudding basin. Reserve the remaining third of the pastry to use as a lid. Fill the pastry-lined basin with layers of chicken, ham and mushrooms, sprinkling parsley on each layer and seasoning with salt and pepper.

Fill the basin to the brim with the remaining stock, then roll out the lid and stick it on top by moistening the edges with water. Cover the top with a cloth or foil secured with string and steam for 2 hours. Serve with steamed potatoes.

HOGTOPIA

Once you have tasted pork from a truly free-range, happy pig that has had freedom to root around, forage and socialize in a herd, you might never eat any other kind again. It is as far removed from your typical supermarket pork as Danish Bacon is to Pata Negra -- in fact, the analogy is apt, as Danish Bacon is from a deeply unhappy, intensively reared pig while a Pata Negra pig has a right old time of it in the Spanish hills. This chapter is a brief insight into what makes pigs happy, from social conditions to living area.

Pigs are social creatures. At a bare minimum, three or four pigs kept together is best, but they thrive in small herds of up to a dozen. Happy pigs make the very best pork, and if kept in groups of more than three pigs they have the opportunity to socialize, form bonds and lead as content a life as possible.

THE PASTORAL PIGGERY

Most rare breeds are bred to be kept outdoors and as such are quite hardy. They can cope with extremes of weather, and many thrive under conditions that might not suit intensively reared pigs. The choice of an appropriate site for free-range pig keeping is important to both the production efficiency and the welfare of the pigs. Actually, the very best land for pig keeping is often the cheapest: slopes, copses and rough ground being perfect for pigs but of little use for anything else. However, outdoor piggeries, just like any other livestock operation, can impact on the environment if not managed correctly.

Ideally, a free-range piggery should consist of at least two paddocks sited in an area receiving less than 80cm (31in) of rain per year. Areas of greater rainfall may be acceptable, depending on soil type, but will require a higher standard of management. Flat areas prone to flooding should be avoided, and the soil must be free-draining to prevent the pigs and their shelters from becoming waterlogged. While pigs like mud, they need to have a dry area to retire to at all times.

The maintenance of ground cover is important. Although grazing a paddock until bare can be an excellent tool if the intention is to crop that area, it is undesirable to over-graze paddocks in normal pasture rotations. Ground cover will slow the movement of water, provide additional drainage and help prevent damage to wet soils. It also acts as an insulator, keeping the ground cooler in hot weather. To this end, a paddock rotation system is a good idea, as it will minimize environmental damage and give land the chance to recover when the pigs are moved to the next paddock, once the ground cover is down to 30 per cent of the original level. If the paddocks remain constantly bare it is likely to be a sign of overstocking, which could lead to long-term damage to the land.

Some woodland or scrub along one end of the paddocks is desirable, allowing pigs good foraging and rooting and providing some shade in summer. Indeed some pigs like Mangalitsas and Tamworths often eschew their shelter in favour of digging scrapes under fallen trees in which to bed down and nest. If woodland contains mast trees like beech, oak, chestnut and other forest trees capable of producing food for pigs, then it really will be hogtopia.

HOME SWEET HOME

Less hardy pigs need somewhere dry, warm and draught-free to sleep. While they care little for aesthetics, a sturdy permanent brick sty remains cooler in summer and warmer in winter than a movable wooden ark with a corrugated sheeting roof. Where a sty is not an option, the best and largest ark possible is a good alternative. The height is particularly a consideration for the keeper's comfort, as pigs need cleaning out, which involves entering the ark! (While pigs are clean animals, I prefer to be standing at this time than on my hands and knees.) The ark should be positioned so that the entrance faces away from the prevailing wind, with burlap sacking suspended from the entrance to cut down on draughts. Inside, dry, clean bedding is important – good straw changed regularly will provide warmth in cooler months, plus the pigs will eat some of it and it will break down quickly when removed during cleaning.

Farmers of free-range pigs should be stewards of the land, ensuring that pigs do not cause permanent harm to their environment. Pasture management that includes the even spread of manure is a vital part of this. Manure build-up and run-off should be avoided; a carefully planned system can actually be of benefit to the land when fertilized by pigs over several months, before they are moved to a neighbouring paddock to allow the first paddock to recover and a new covering of vegetation to grow.

Wallowing is in a pig's nature and is good for them: it cools them down in summer, helps to prevent sunburn and keeps insects at bay. A wallowing hole, which is simply a dip in the ground filled with water daily, must be included in one in the paddocks. Pigs drink a lot of water, so ideally an automatic water system should also be used to maintain peak condition.

Pigs are excellent escape artists and will spend time trying to work out a path to freedom, so fencing is important. Because they will put it to the test, the first criterion is that it must be strong and sound – it is amazing how small a gap a piglet can squeeze through in search of adventure, often squeezing back through at feed time with noone the wiser. Ringlock with electric fencing works well, but the mesh needs to be very well strained and the posts have to be closer together than with fencing for other farm animals. A mains energizer unit to power electric fencing is preferable to battery because it is stronger and will not run flat. Pigs know when an electric fence is no longer electric and will take full advantage.

AS NATURE INTENDED

In its natural state, a pig will take from seven months to a year to mature fully. In the unnatural state of modern agricultural production, it will take from three to six months, primed with a cocktail of scientifically formulated foods, antibiotics, chemicals and husbandry designed to make it as big as possible as quickly as possible. There is no way a year-old pig can be produced for the cost of a three-month-old pig, and there is no way a three-month-old pig can taste like, or have the nutritional value of, a year-old pig.

Ultimately the secret to top-quality, tasty pork, the likes of which will have your family in rapturous silence at the table, is simple: happy pigs make tasty pigs. If they are given enough room to range freely and plenty of balanced food supplemented with fresh vegetables and forage (*see* Feeding, page 140), are kept clean and in groups, and are treated with respect, pigs will grow as nature intended – more slowly than an intensively farmed pig, but all the better for it.

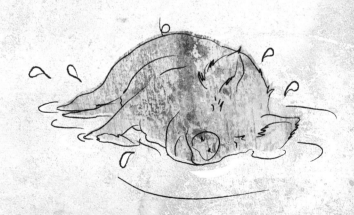

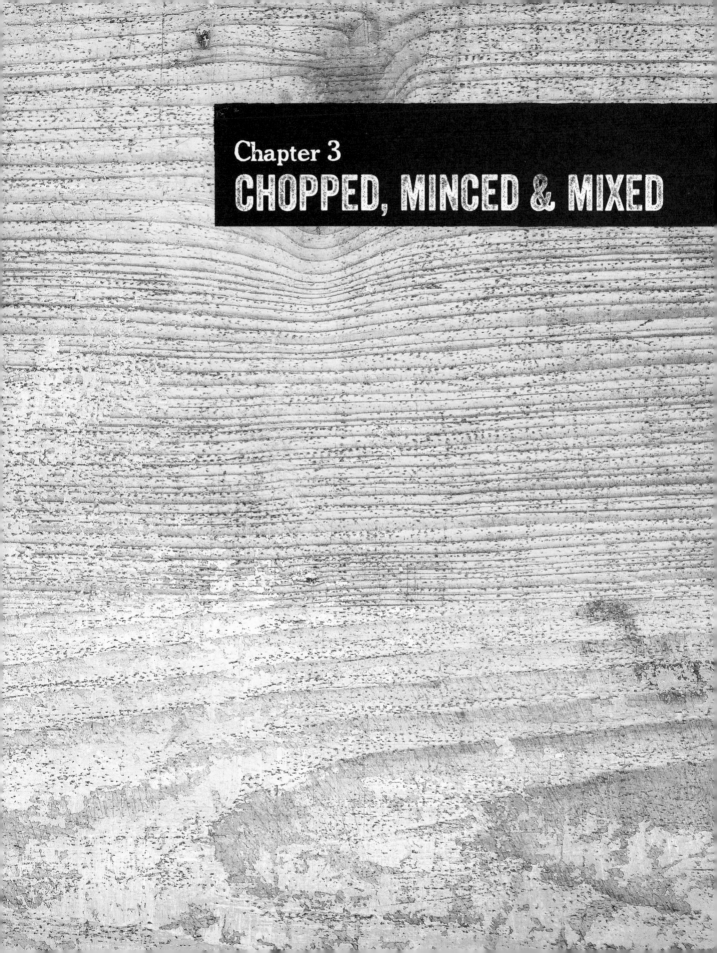

Chapter 3
CHOPPED, MINCED & MIXED

250g pork fat, cut into 1cm dice

500g pork shoulder,
cut into 2cm dice

250g pork belly,
cut into 2cm dice

Maldon sea salt flakes

freshly ground white pepper

100ml dry white wine

100ml water

1 garlic clove, peeled
but left whole

1 small celery stick

1 small onion

1 small carrot

1 faggot of fresh herbs, made
with sage, thyme, rosemary
and bay

toasted sourdough bread or
baguette, to serve

You will also need
a kilner jar and
ice cubes

Foie gras and truffles are all well and good, but for everything
you need to know about France, look no further than rillettes --
to my mind this is French cooking at its absolute best.
It really does behove you to let your rillettes mature before
eating, as a strange and peculiar transformation takes place
that you shouldn't miss.

PORK RILLETTES Serves 6–8

Put the pork fat and meats into a large bowl,
season with salt and pepper, then cover and
refrigerate overnight.

The following morning, preheat the oven to 160°C/
gas mark 3.

Remove the meat from the refrigerator and place
in a large ovenproof casserole with the remaining
ingredients. Cover with a lid and bake for 2 hours.

Remove from the oven and transfer everything to
a bowl and allow to cool. Prepare an ice bath (fill a
baking tray with ice cubes) and place the bowl on
top of the ice to cool and set. Remove the faggot

of herbs and the vegetables and flake the meat
with your fingers. As the mixture cools it will start
to go white – at this point adjust the seasoning.
Remember that when cold the seasoning will fade,
so be generous.

Transfer the flaked meat to a sterilized Kilner jar
and cover with a circle of greaseproof paper, then
seal the jar.

Refrigerate untouched for at least 1 week to allow
the flavours to develop. When ready, allow to reach
room temperature before eating. Serve with toasted
sourdough or a crunchy baguette.

1kg pork belly (the thick end), skin on and boned, cut into 4cm cubes

50g Maldon sea salt flakes

a pinch of hot smoked paprika

300g lard

200ml dry white wine

1 bay leaf

2 garlic cloves, halved

1 large sprig of fresh thyme

1 sprig of fresh rosemary

8 white peppercorns

200ml water

Similar to *confit* in cooking technique, these meaty snacks hail from the Touraine region of France and are ever so slightly addictive. Forget bowls of nuts in front of the television – a bowl of these and a glass of wine is the way forward.

RILLONS Serves 4–6 as a snack

Sprinkle the pork belly cubes with the sea salt and smoked paprika, cover and refrigerate overnight.

The next day, preheat the oven to 150°C/ gas mark 2. Rinse the salt from the pork and pat dry with kitchen paper.

Heat a frying pan over a high heat, add a little of the lard and fry the pork until brown all over.

Place in one layer in an ovenproof dish, add the wine, bay leaf, garlic, thyme, rosemary, peppercorns, the remaining lard and the water and bake in the oven for 1½ hours.

Once tender, remove from the oven and leave the pork to cool in the fat.

Refrigerate for a few days before using. To use, fry the rillons in their own fat until crisp.

50g bread

20ml olive oil

300g young dandelion leaves

200g Rillons (see opposite)

4 free-range eggs

40ml cider vinegar

fresh parsley leaves, to garnish

For the dressing

50ml olive oil

15ml cider vinegar

1 teaspoon clear honey

1 teaspoon Dijon mustard

Maldon sea salt flakes and freshly ground black pepper

The bitterness of the dandelion leaves and the sweetness of the dressing are a great contrast to the rich porky flavour of the rillons. This is a substantial and classic salad.

FRIED RILLON, EGG & DANDELION SALAD Serves 4

Preheat the oven to 200°C/gas mark 6.

Tear the bread into pieces, drizzle with a little olive oil and bake for 15 minutes. Remove, then set aside.

Wash the dandelion leaves in cold water, then dry them and put them into a salad bowl.

Fry the rillons until crisp. Take them out of the pan with a slotted spoon and leave to drain, then fry the pulled bread croutons in the pork fat until golden and crispy.

Poach the eggs in water acidulated with the vinegar for about 3 minutes, or until they are cooked to your taste.

Mix all the dressing ingredients, and season to taste, then pour over the dandelion leaves and toss well.

Put the eggs, rillons and croutons on top of the salad and garnish with the parsley. Serve while still slightly warm.

1 free-range egg beaten with a pinch of Maldon sea salt flakes and 1 tablespoon water, for glazing

Master Pork Broth (see page 335)

mustard and cornichons, to serve

For the filling

400g pork shoulder

100g unsmoked bacon belly

1 teaspoon chopped fresh sage

1 teaspoon anchovy essence, or 2 anchovy fillets crushed to a paste

a pinch of ground allspice

a pinch of freshly grated nutmeg

a pinch of ground cinnamon

Maldon sea salt flakes and freshly ground black pepper

For the hot water crust pastry

400g strong plain white flour

¼ teaspoon fine sea salt

50ml milk

50ml water

130g lard, cut into small pieces

You will also need 6 x 10cm diameter pork pie moulds

Hot water crust pies are not the easiest of things to make, but practice is key here and once you've got your head round it there are myriad permutations: gala pies, game pies, terrines en croute, to name but a few.

PORK PIES Makes 6

Roughly chop the meats, then combine all the filling ingredients and season well. Preheat the oven to 180°C/gas mark 4.

Sift the flour and salt into a bowl. Put the milk and water into a small saucepan and add the lard. Place the pan over a gentle heat and when the fat has completely melted in the liquid, turn up the heat to bring it just to the boil. Pour it on to the flour and, using a wooden spoon, mix everything together.

Turn the dough out on to a work surface and knead briefly and quickly – it's important that the pies go into the tin while the dough is still warm. Take two-thirds of the dough and cut it into 6 equal pieces. Roll each of these into a ball and put one of them into each of the moulds. Using your thumb, quickly press each ball flat on to the base and up the sides of the mould. Press the pastry over the rim of the top edge to overlap by 1cm.

Now divide the pork mixture between the lined moulds. Roll out the remaining pastry and cut out six 10cm rounds for the lids. Eggwash round the edge of each lid and gently press a lid on each pie, eggwash

side down. Using a fork, press the lids to seal the pies, then glaze the tops with the rest of the eggwash and make a small hole in the centre of each one.

Place the moulds on a baking sheet and bake for 30 minutes on the middle shelf, then remove them from the oven.

Using a small, round-bladed knife, carefully remove the hot pies from the tin and place them directly on the hot baking sheet. Bake for a further 20–25 minutes, or until the sides and base of the pies are crisp, then remove from the oven and leave to cool on a wire rack.

Meanwhile, place the pork broth in a saucepan over a medium-high heat and let it reduce by half. When reduced, allow to cool to room temperature.

Using a funnel, pour the still-just-liquid pork broth into the holes in the tops of the cooled pies – you may need to do 2 fills, letting the broth settle in between fills, to make sure it is evenly distributed. Refrigerate uncovered, to allow the jelly to set, then serve with mustard and cornichons.

500g shoulder of wild boar, diced

250g wild boar belly, diced

250g smoked streaky bacon

250g wild boar or pork liver, trimmed and diced

2 large shallots, roughly chopped

2 garlic cloves

100ml red wine

50g breadcrumbs

Maldon sea salt flakes and freshly ground black pepper

50ml pork dripping

100g pork caul

½ bunch of fresh sage

You will also need a mincer and a 1.5 litre loaf tin or terrine mould

The ancestor of the modern domesticated pig, wild boar makes for great terrines. Since it is leaner and darker than pork, it consequently benefits from a little additional fat to lubricate it -- in this recipe I've used bacon.

WILD BOAR TERRINE Serves 10–12

Combine all the meats with the shallots, garlic and wine in a non-reactive bowl, then cover and refrigerate overnight.

The following morning, mince all the meat mixture through the coarse plate on your mincer and place in a bowl.

Add the breadcrumbs and mix thoroughly, then season heavily with salt and pepper. Fry a small amount of the mixture and taste it, adjusting the seasoning bearing in mind it will fade when it cools.

Preheat the oven to 170°C/gas mark 3½. Brush a loaf tin or terrine mould with pork dripping, line with pork caul (leaving enough overhanging the tin to wrap over the top) and place sage leaves intermittently along the base.

Pack the meat mixture into the mould, pressing it down firmly. Wrap the pork caul over the top, then cover tightly with foil and place in a roasting tin. Pour in hot water from the kettle to come halfway up the sides of the mould, then bake for 1½ hours, or until the terrine has come away from the sides of the tin and a metal skewer pressed into its centre for a few moments comes out piping hot.

Place another mould on top and fill that with weights, then leave the terrine weighted-down until completely cool. Remove the weights and refrigerate for 48 hours to allow the flavour to develop.

To turn the terrine out, run a small knife around the edges to release it, then invert on to a board or plate. Slice and serve with cornichons, a good chutney or fruit ketchup (see page 338–9) and a simple salad.

1 large Savoy cabbage

150g lean pork shoulder, chopped

150g lardo or pork fat, chopped

50g pork liver, trimmed and chopped

1 garlic clove, crushed

10g fresh flat-leaf parsley, chopped

10g fresh breadcrumbs

25ml dry white wine

2 teaspoons brandy

1 small free-range egg, beaten

Maldon sea salt flakes and freshly ground black pepper

250ml Master Pork Broth (*see* page 335)

250ml tomato passata or canned tomatoes

You will also need a mincer, some heat-resistant clingfilm and a steamer

Variations of stuffed cabbage are found all over Europe, and this one is based on the classic French family dish *chou farci*.

STUFFED CABBAGE Makes 4

Remove 12 unblemished leaves from the cabbage – 4 large, 4 medium and 4 small. Wash them thoroughly, then blanch for 1 minute in boiling water to soften. Remove, refresh in iced water and set aside.

To make the stuffing, mix together the pork, lardo, liver, garlic, parsley, breadcrumbs, wine, brandy and egg. Combine thoroughly, then season with salt and pepper and mince through the coarse plate on your mincer. Test the stuffing by frying a small portion, then tasting. Adjust the seasoning if necessary.

Take 1 of the large cabbage leaves and spread it with a good layer of the stuffing, leaving a gap around the edge. Cover with a medium cabbage leaf and spread with some more stuffing, followed by a small leaf, and finally top with a small ball of stuffing. Transfer to a square of double-layer ovenproof clingfilm. Pull the 4 corners of the large cabbage leaf tightly

together, then twist the clingfilm so that it closes into a ball. Repeat with the remaining leaves, to make 4 balls in total.

Place the cabbage balls, in their clingfilm, in a steamer over boiling water. Cover with a lid and steam for 20 minutes.

Preheat the oven to 180°C/gas mark 4. Unwrap the cabbage balls from the clingfilm and place in a clean baking dish. Mix the pork broth and passata in a saucepan and bring to a gentle simmer. Pour over the stuffed cabbage and bake for 20 minutes, or until bubbling, then serve.

800g pork shoulder, diced

400g pork liver, trimmed and sliced

¼ teaspoon quatre épices

35g Maldon sea salt flakes

½ teaspoon freshly ground black pepper

100g breadcrumbs

1 small onion, chopped

2 garlic cloves, crushed

1 teaspoon vegetable oil

50ml apple brandy

100ml double cream

2 eggs

25g chopped fresh parsley

1 teaspoon chopped fresh thyme leaves

1 teaspoon chopped fresh rosemary leaves

about 300g sliced back fat, lardo or bacon, enough to line your terrine

You will also need a mincer, a 1.5 litre loaf tin or terrine mould, heat-resistant clingfilm, a piece of cardboard and a meat thermometer

A rough French-style terrine that's great for a light supper with chunks of bread, some pickles and a glass or two of your favourite red. A whole terrine will keep for a week in the refrigerator if looked after properly.

COUNTRY PÂTÉ Serves 8

Put the meat, quatre épices, salt and pepper into a large bowl and toss together, then cover and refrigerate overnight. Chill your coarse plate and mincer attachments.

Next day, put the breadcrumbs into a large bowl. In a nonstick frying pan sweat the onion and garlic gently in the oil until softened, then add the apple brandy and flame to burn off the alcohol. Stir in the double cream, then pour the mixture over the breadcrumbs, stir and allow to cool.

Take the marinated meat from the refrigerator and add it to the breadcrumb mixture, along with the eggs and herbs. Mix well, then mince through the coarse plate on your mincer. Test the mixture by frying a small portion and tasting it. Adjust the seasoning if necessary. Preheat the oven to 160°C/gas mark 3.

Line a terrine mould with heat-resistant clingfilm leaving enough overhanging to wrap over the top, and then line again with sliced back fat, lardo or bacon (whichever you have chosen to use), leaving enough overhanging to wrap over the top. Pack the pâté mix into your mould and fold the back fat, lardo or bacon over the top, followed by the clingfilm.

Line the base of a roasting tray with a sheet of cardboard (this moderates the heat on the top of the terrine). Place the terrine on top of the cardboard, then pour in hot water from the kettle to come two-thirds of the way up the sides of the terrine. Bake for 1½ hours, or until an internal temperature of 70°C is reached.

Remove from the oven and allow to cool, then refrigerate for 48 hours before eating.

30ml vegetable oil

1 garlic clove, finely chopped

20ml hot chilli paste, such as sambal oelek

500g minced pork

zest and juice of 2 limes, plus extra lime wedges to serve

20ml fish sauce, such as nam pla or nuoc mam

20g palm sugar

1 small red onion, half finely chopped and half sliced

1 bunch of fresh mint leaves, half chopped and half left whole

1 head of butter lettuce, leaves separated

1 cucumber, thinly sliced

½ bunch of fresh coriander

A fresh and vibrant pork salad in the style of a laab; the authentic versions I've had have all packed a formidable chilli punch and this is no exception. This salad might be a tad challenging for the non-chilli-head, so do reduce the hot chilli paste if that's you.

SPICY PORK SALAD   Serves 4

Heat half the oil in a large skillet over a medium-high heat. Add the garlic and half the chilli paste and cook until the garlic is softened – about 1 minute.

Add the minced pork and cook, breaking up with a spoon, until it is cooked through. Transfer the mixture to a plate and allow to cool.

To make the dressing, whisk the lime zest, lime juice, fish sauce, palm sugar, the remaining oil and the remaining chilli paste in a small bowl. Pour half this dressing into a small plastic container and reserve.

Add the chopped onion, chopped mint and the pork mixture to the remaining dressing and toss to combine.

Put the lettuce, cucumber and sliced onion into a large bowl and toss with the rest of the dressing.

Arrange the salad on a plate, top with the pork mixture, and garnish with the coriander, whole mint leaves and the remaining lime.

250g canned chopped tomatoes

25g chipotle chilli, from a jar

400g minced pork

1 free-range egg

1 large Spanish onion, chopped

2 garlic cloves, chopped

1 bunch of fresh coriander, chopped

Maldon sea salt flakes and freshly ground black pepper

A simple spicy meatball recipe that has many applications -- sandwiches, tacos or burritos perhaps, or served simply with rice and beans.

ALBONDIGAS MEXICANAS Serves 4

Preheat the oven to 160°C/gas mark 3.

In a food processor or blender, blend together the tomatoes and chipotle chilli. Pour into a large saucepan over a medium heat and leave to simmer.

Place all the other ingredients in a mixing bowl and combine well. Roll the mixture in the palms of your hands to make meatballs, each weighing about 30g. Place them on a baking tray and bake in the oven for 20 minutes.

Remove the meatballs from the oven and add them to the simmering sauce. Cook for a further 45 minutes, seasoning with salt and pepper to taste.

Serve with the sauce, a wedge of lime and your accompaniment of choice.

100g fresh breadcrumbs

500g minced pork

2 good-quality anchovy fillets, mashed, or 1 teaspoon of anchovy essence

1 onion, finely chopped

1 garlic clove, roughly chopped

½ small bunch of fresh parsley, chopped

1 tablespoon chopped fresh oregano

4 tablespoons grated Parmesan cheese

1 free-range egg, beaten

8 slices of Air-cured Ham (*see* page 206)

mixed salad and pickles, to serve

You will also need a 1.5 litre loaf tin

The name 'picnic meatloaf' sells this cold larder star somewhat short -- it could just as easily be called terrine of pork. Cooking one during testing, it was bloody lovely and singularly failed to last a weekend in my house.

PICNIC MEATLOAF Serves 10

Preheat the oven to 190°C/gas mark 5.

Thoroughly mix all the ingredients except the Air-cured Ham.

Line the loaf tin with the ham leaving enough overhanging to wrap over the top, then spoon in the meatloaf mix and press down well. Flip the overhanging ham over the top, then put the loaf tin into a roasting tray. Pour hot water from the kettle into the roasting tray to come halfway up the sides of the loaf tin to make a water bath, and bake for 50 minutes until the loaf shrinks from the sides of the tin.

Remove from the oven and cool in the water bath for 15 minutes. Remove from the water, allow to cool, then chill.

When needed, turn out on to a board and cut into thick slices. Serve with a salad and pickles.

100ml pork lard

200g minced pork

100g pork belly,
cut into 1cm dice

50g spicy chorizo sausage,
cut into 1cm dice

100g Spanish onions,
chopped

2 green chillies, deseeded
and finely chopped

1 tablespoon cider vinegar

1 teaspoon dark brown sugar

1 teaspoon ground cumin

200g canned chopped
tomatoes

2cm piece of cinnamon stick

2 bay leaves

1 teaspoon dried oregano

2 teaspoons chilli powder

Maldon sea salt flakes and
freshly ground black pepper

100g black beans

To serve

soft flour tortillas

100g guacamole

25g pickled shallot, sliced

100g white cabbage, sliced

1 lime

150ml soured cream

¼ bunch of fresh
coriander leaves

Traditionally *carnitas* are small chunks of pork covered in lard and cooked low and slow in a thick-bottomed copper pot for hours before being fried until crisp, much like a confit. They would then be cooled, shredded and served with tacos and garnishes. The method below is easier and produces just as good a result; but if you'd prefer to try the traditional method, just replace the meats with an equal amount of shredded crispy Rillons (*see* page 122).

CARNITAS Serves 4

Heat the lard in a large skillet and gently brown all the meats, then add the onions and cook gently until soft.

Add all the remaining ingredients except the beans and bring to a gentle simmer, stirring regularly.

Cook for 1 hour, then add the beans and cook for a further 30 minutes. Remove the bay leaves and cinnamon stick and adjust the seasoning if necessary. Serve with tortillas, guacamole, pickled shallot, white cabbage dressed with lime juice, soured cream, coriander leaves and season with pepper.

FEEDING

Like us, pigs are omnivores and will eat a wide variety of foods. Also like us, they need a balanced diet of fibre, energy, protein, vitamins and minerals to thrive. Feed is the largest expenditure in pig keeping, so it pays to get it right. Pigs have the ability to grow at an incredible pace. In a nine-month period, piglets of 1.2kg (2lb 10oz) could typically increase in weight by as much as 3,000 per cent, and this growth translates into a higher return on feed than for any other domesticated animal. The simplest way to ensure adequate nutrition is to use a ready-mixed feed, but good pig keepers will often mill and mix their own in consultation with an animal nutritionist.

An advantage to pig rearing is pigs' omnivorous nature: they eat a wide range of foods that are plentiful and cheap. For example, surplus crops, such as wheat, barley and beets in Europe, corn in the United States, sweet potatoes in New Guinea and coconuts in Polynesia can all be used as pig feed. The type and quality of feed is the most important contributing factor to producing good-quality, tasty pork, and getting it right makes the difference between success and failure. It really is that important.

As mentioned earlier, extensive farming techniques take a long, slow path in the rearing of rare-breed pigs in the belief that ethics and quality of pork are everything. Feed is supplemented by foraging, which gives the animals room to range, socialize and root about as well as eat grass and soil which provide nutrients and minerals – all of this makes for a happy and consequently tasty animal. Foraging is an important part of a pig's welfare and cannot be adequately replaced by feed alone.

Supplementing feed and forage with fruit, vegetables and salads is also important, as long as these are not catering waste from a kitchen, private or commercial, or from anywhere that sells meat. Pigs should never be fed meat products of any kind. This is not only potentially risky but also illegal in Europe, North America, Australia, New Zealand and elsewhere. In addition, there are laws against feeding pigs swill or indeed anything that has been through a kitchen.

Pigs love milk and milk products, and many countries have herds of pigs where cheese whey is a major factor in the final flavour of their pork and charcuterie. Pigs prefer their feed wet, so adding surplus milk or whey to their feed will be appreciated, as long as the milk has not entered a kitchen (in which case it would be deemed as catering waste). Government guidelines suggest that a pig's diet should not consist of more than 80 per cent milk products.

FEED MANAGEMENT

Pigs are usually fed twice a day, with the amount and type of feed depending on the age and the reproductive state of the pig. Up to 40kg (88lb) in weight, piglets should be allowed to eat as and when they like from a self-service hopper – despite their reputation they will rarely overeat. From 40 kg (88lb) onwards, however, they are more prone to running to fat, and their feed should be restricted to 1.8kg (4lb) per pig per day and, from 70kg (154lb), it should be restricted to 2kg (4½lb) per pig per day.

Commercial feed comes in several varieties. Creep pellets are tiny pellets that are high in protein and are fed to piglets in an area accessible only to them. Grower pellets are larger, with even more protein, and are used just before weaning until pork weight, if desired. Finisher pellets are used after three to four months and are used if the animals are becoming too fat. Sow and weaner nuts can be used instead of grower pellets or for gilts that are in pig (pregnant), and pig nuts are fed to adults that are not in pig.

In cold weather, pigs use up energy to keep warm, so in autumn their feed is increased, depending on their condition or level of fat cover. This is regularly checked by running a hand along the spine. If the spine can be felt clearly, the pig is a bit thin; if it can be felt only with firm pressure, it is fine; and if it cannot be felt at all, the pig is too fat. Counter-intuitively, a fat pig is neither happy nor healthy. Excessively fat pigs have trouble breeding, and ultimately too much fat makes for unappetizing pork. While fat indeed provides flavour, there really is only so much fat we can eat without nausea.

Pigs that eat a lot of carbohydrates produce saturated fat, while pigs that eat a lot of polyunsaturated fats produce more polyunsaturated fat. The double bonds that form the structure of the polyunsaturated fats are softer, making for softer, creamier fat. Pigs fed a diet high in carbohydrates and low in polyunsaturated fats convert the carbs to fat internally. Whether the fat is deposited on the pork or converted from a carbohydrate, it is the presence of fat that affects the flavour.

We know this matters for texture and mouth feel, but does it matter when it comes to taste? After all, grass-fed beef has a distinctly different flavour from corn-fed beef, but the meat does not actually taste like grass. There is, however, strong evidence that feed directly influences the flavour of pork – just look at the acorn-fed pigs in Spain or the whey-fed pigs in Italy. The characteristics of their meat and of the resulting charcuterie are directly and clearly informed by their feed. Feed really is that important!

INTENSIVE VS EXTENSIVE: THE RESULTS

Intensive farming techniques aim to get hybrid pigs to porker weight of 60kg (132lb) in around three months on a diet of high-protein pig nuts, whereas a free-range, rare-breed pig with access to good foraging land and fed a varied diet, might take six months or longer. The high-protein diet fed by intensive farmers helps hybrid piglets to grow and fatten faster, but this would not be a good thing for a free-range, rare-breed pig, which is unsuited to such practice.

Keeping pigs in one spot and bringing food to them is, by definition, creating a more consistent product – the more variables that are cut out, the more consistent the pork. The problem is that when animals are fed a consistent diet in the same spot, without needing to exercise to get their food, and are not allowed to forage, the result is a flavour deficit – as found in the majority of pork sold today. The pork you see in the supermarket has been bred with money in mind, and the pigs are grown as fast as possible to maximize profit. But anything tasty takes time – it is the guiding principle of the Slow Food movement – and anything worth eating is worth waiting for.

Chapter 4
SAUSAGES

1 recipe sausage mix of your choice (see below)

You will also need 1 length of large sausage casing, and a mincer with a sausage stuffer attachment

The cuts of meat you use for sausages will depend on the fat content of the pork. Sausages from traditional breeds with a very good covering of fat, such as Tamworth, are probably best made from the shoulder. With less fatty pigs it will be better if you use half shoulder and half fat belly pork. If the meat is too lean the sausage will be dry, while a fatter sausage can be cooked in a way that renders much of its fat.

SAUSAGES 10 WAYS All recipes make 1kg sausages

TO PREPARE THE SAUSAGE MIX

Choose your filling from pages 146–8. The meat should be kept as cold as possible, so work in a cool room and return the meat to the refrigerator until it is needed, and chill your mincer and attachments.

Begin by roughly cutting the meat so that is easy to feed through the mincer.

Soak the casing in cold water for about 1 hour, to soften it and loosen the salt in which it is packed. Place the wide end of the sausage stuffer up against the tap and run cold water through the inside of the casing to remove excess salt.

Fit the coarse plate into your mincer and mince the meat into a large mixing bowl (for very coarse sausages, dice by hand). When you have minced all the meat, follow with the filler (such as any breadcrumbs or rice), if using. Sprinkle over salt, fresh herbs, spices and other flavourings or liquids as required, and mix thoroughly.

Test the mixture by frying a small portion and tasting it. Adjust the seasoning if necessary before making into sausages.

TO MAKE THE SAUSAGES

Cut the casing into 2 lengths and tie a small knot in one end of each. Fit the open end over the tip of the sausage stuffer and slide it on until the tip of the stuffer touches the knot – this stops excess air from getting into the casing. Fit the stuffer on to the meat grinder according to the manufacturer's instructions, or hold the wide end of the stuffer against or over the opening by hand.

Fill the hopper with the sausage mixture. Turn the machine on and feed the sausage gradually into the hopper – for a manual machine the sausage casing will fill and gradually inflate. Smooth out any bumps with your fingers, being careful not to push the stuffing out of the casing, and tie off the open end of the sausage tightly by making a knot in the end.

To form the links, hold the entire casing up by its middle and twist it to form the first link. Then twist at the required intervals, going in opposite directions for each sausage to prevent the links unravelling. Hang for at least a few hours in the refrigerator to dry out before cooking (see page 148).

Continued...

This is a pork sausagemeat for stuffing or sausages. The lack of any filler here makes for a very meaty sausage indeed.

BASIC PORK SAUSAGES

20g fine sea salt

1 teaspoon ground white pepper

½ teaspoon grated nutmeg

½ teaspoon ground mace

1 teaspoon ground coriander

700g pork shoulder

300g pork belly

Mix together the salt, white pepper, nutmeg, mace and ground coriander.

Mince the meat on the coarse plate of your mincer and place in a non-reactive bowl. Thoroughly mix in the seasonings, then mince again through your desired plate. Use as a stuffing, or *see* page 145 to make into sausages.

Sage is a very English herb and these sausages are its finest moment.

LINCOLNSHIRE SAUSAGES

1kg pork shoulder

150g fresh breadcrumbs

20g fine sea salt

3 teaspoons chopped fresh sage

To prepare the sausage mix and make into sausages, *see* page 145.

Effectively the Cambridge sausage is the standard British sausage, flavoured with sage, thyme, cayenne, mace, nutmeg, pepper and salt.

CAMBRIDGE SAUSAGES

1kg pork shoulder

150g cooked rice

20g fine sea salt

1 teaspoon chopped fresh sage

½ teaspoon chopped fresh thyme

¼ teaspoon ground mace

¼ teaspoon grated nutmeg

¼ teaspoon freshly ground black pepper

To prepare the sausage mix and make into sausages, *see* page 145.

Cumberland sausage uses no breadcrumbs, only meat. It is also formed as one coiled, continuous sausage.

CUMBERLAND SAUSAGE

1kg pork shoulder

20g fine sea salt

½ teaspoon chopped fresh sage

½ teaspoon chopped fresh rosemary

½ teaspoon chopped fresh thyme

a good pinch of cayenne pepper

¼ teaspoon grated nutmeg

½ teaspoon freshly ground white pepper

To prepare the sausage mix and make into sausages, *see* page 145.

These are made with equal parts of lean pork and veal together with beef suet. Old recipes suggest that this should be in the same proportion as each of the meats, but modern tastes will prefer half this. Unusually they are never put into skins.

OXFORD SAUSAGES

350g pork shoulder

350g lean veal

150g beef suet

150g fresh white breadcrumbs

20g fine sea salt

grated zest of 1 small lemon

1 teaspoon chopped fresh sage

1 teaspoon chopped fresh thyme

1 teaspoon chopped fresh marjoram

freshly ground black pepper

Mince the pork and veal together. Coarsely grate the beef suet and mix with the meat and the remaining ingredients. Place on a lightly floured surface and form into sausages with your hands. Leave overnight in the refrigerator to firm up and develop their flavour before cooking (see page 148).

One of our biggest sellers at Turner & George.

PEPPER PIG SAUSAGES

800g pork shoulder

200g pork fat

20g fine sea salt

½ teaspoon freshly ground white pepper

½ teaspoon mild chilli powder

½ teaspoon fresh oregano

⅛ teaspoon ground nutmeg

2g garlic, crushed

20ml sweet white wine

To prepare the sausage mix and make into sausages, see page 145.

James George's favourite sausage!

SUPPER PIGS

800g pork shoulder

200g pork fat

50g breadcrumbs

12g fine sea salt

1 tablespoon freshly ground black pepper

a pinch of fresh thyme

a pinch of fresh rosemary

a pinch of herbes de Provence

1 tablespoon water

To prepare the sausage mix and make into sausages, see page 145.

Continued...

An old English recipe revived from history.

THE VICTORIAN

400g pork shoulder

200g pork fat

170g beef flank

170g mutton breast

100g bone marrow

50g breadcrumbs

15g fine sea salt

a pinch of marjoram

a pinch of nutmeg

a pinch of fresh thyme

a pinch of mace

8g freshly ground black pepper

50ml gravy or jus

To prepare the sausage mix and make into sausages, *see page 145.*

The breakfast sausage, to which all others must bow.

BREAKFAST PIGS

800g pork shoulder

200g pork fat

50g breadcrumbs

16g fine sea salt

a pinch of freshly ground white pepper

a pinch of chopped fresh sage

a pinch of nutmeg

a pinch of mace

1 tablespoon water

To prepare the sausage mix and make into sausages, *see page 145.*

Wild boar is too lean to use exclusively. Pork fat and bacon provide the much needed lubricant.

WILD BOAR SAUSAGES

700g wild boar shoulder

200g bacon belly

100g pork fat

50g breadcrumbs

15g fine sea salt

freshly ground black pepper

pinch of fresh thyme leaves

pinch of fresh rosemary leaves

50ml red wine

To prepare the sausage mix and make into sausages, *see page 145.*

HOW TO COOK SAUSAGES

Assuming you are using natural casings, which of course you should be, you do not need to prick sausages – this is an old wives' tale and allows precious juices to escape along with the fat, which is the flavour. Use a heavy-based frying pan to diffuse the heat over a low heat. Fry the sausages low and slow, turning occasionally, for about 30 minutes. If the sausages are colouring too quickly, reduce the heat even further and sprinkle with a little water.

If you are barbecuing sausages, blanch them in boiling water for 10 minutes at 80°C before cooking, and only cook over smouldering charcoal, low and slow.

800g Basic Pork Sausage mix
(*see* page 146)

100g fresh breadcrumbs

1 teaspoon finely chopped
fresh sage

1 free-range egg

50g chopped prunes (optional)

For the rough puff pastry
(makes 800g)

325g strong plain flour

1 teaspoon fine sea salt

325g unsalted butter, diced

150ml cold water

There are sausage rolls and there are sausage rolls. Eaten from a refrigerated cellophane packet you'd be forgiven for wondering why anyone would bother, but when made well, using great pork and still warm from the oven, it's easy to see the attraction.

SAUSAGE ROLLS   Makes 6 large rolls

First, make the pastry. Sift the flour and salt into a large mixing bowl and add the diced butter. Rub together to mix, but leave a few visible lumps of butter. Pour in the cold water and mix to combine and form into a firm dough, but do not overmix. Cover with clingfilm and rest in the refrigerator for 30 minutes.

Turn the pastry dough on to a floured board and roll out into a square – there should be small streaks of butter running through the pastry. Fold the right-hand third halfway into the middle and repeat with the remaining left-hand side, roll out again and repeat the folding process. Cover with clingfilm and rest in the refrigerator for 30 minutes, or until needed.

Preheat the oven to 180°C/gas mark 4.

Place the sausagemeat in a mixing bowl and add the breadcrumbs, sage and 100ml of water. Mix with your hands until evenly blended, then set aside. Roll out the pastry dough to about 40 x 25cm. Work the sausagemeat into a long, even roll and place along the length of the pastry. Brush the exposed pastry with beaten egg, then roll over and crimp the join together with a fork.

Cut the roll into 6 smaller rolls and brush the pastry with egg. Place on a baking sheet and bake for 45 minutes until golden brown and cooked through. Serve warm.

100ml milk

100g breadcrumbs

500g Basic Pork Sausage mix
(see page 146)

50g Parmesan cheese, grated

2 banana shallots, split in half

Maldon sea salt flakes and
freshly ground black pepper

200g seedless black grapes

2 sprigs of fresh rosemary

2 sprigs of fresh thyme

2 bay leaves

100ml Master Pork Broth
(see page 335)

100ml olive oil

100ml red wine

100ml good-quality balsamic
vinegar

I have an old recipe for *Polpette al forno* that reads
something like: ground meat, breadcrumbs, egg, milk,
Parmesan, salt, ground black pepper. It's that simple --
and my kind of recipe. I've fleshed it out a bit here and
added some acidity to offset the richness of the meat.
I'm not sure this is an improvement, just a variation.

POLPETTE AL FORNO Serves 4

Pour the milk over the breadcrumbs and allow to
absorb, then mix with the sausagemeat and Parmesan.
Form the mixture into 12 equal-sized meatballs and
allow to firm up in the fridge for 20 minutes.

Preheat the oven to 180°C/gas mark 4.

Place the shallots in the bottom of an ovenproof dish
that will hold the grapes and meatballs in a single
layer. Season with salt and pepper, and lay the

meatballs and grapes on top. Using a wooden spoon,
crush about a third of the grapes to release their juice.
Scatter over the herbs, season again, then add the
pork broth, olive oil, red wine and balsamic vinegar
and roast for 45 minutes, or until cooked through,
turning the meatballs from time to time.

4 red onions

25g pork dripping

Maldon sea salt flakes and
freshly ground black pepper

1 large sprig of fresh thyme

1 head of garlic

200ml Master Pork Broth
(*see* page 335)

50g stale breadcrumbs

50ml milk

200g Basic Pork Sausage mix
(*see* page 146)

25g Parmesan cheese, grated

200ml double cream

A rustic Italian vegetable dish stuffed with a large portion of
pork sausagemeat, as all vegetables should be. Serve these with
any pork roast instead of stuffing on the side. The sauce makes
an excellent gravy.

SAUSAGE-STUFFED ONIONS Makes 4

Preheat the oven to 180°C/gas mark 4.

Peel the onions, taking off the outside dark skins
plus one layer of soft inner skin. Trim a couple of
centimetres off the top of the onion but keep the
root end intact.

Rub the onions with pork dripping, season with salt
and pepper and place in a casserole with a lid.

Remove the leaves from the thyme and set aside.
Smash the head of garlic, then add to the casserole
with the thyme stalks and pork broth.

Cover the casserole and bake for 1 hour, or until a
knife pierces the onions easily. Remove from the
oven and leave to sit for 30 minutes, then remove
the onions and gently scoop out (and reserve) the
centres, making sure to leave several layers and
keeping the onion shape intact.

Soak the breadcrumbs in the milk, then mix with the
sausagemeat and Parmesan.

Fill each onion with the sausage mixture and return
to the casserole with the scooped-out centres of
the onions and the double cream. Scatter with
the reserved thyme leaves and return to the oven,
uncovered, for 30 minutes, basting the tops of the
onions every 5 or so minutes to allow the sauce
to seep in.

Remove the onions to a serving dish, then pass the
sauce through a fine sieve. Serve the onions with
the sauce poured over the top.

200g Basic Pork Sausage mix (*see* page 146), shaped into a patty

1 burger bap (preferably brioche), split

2 teaspoons mustard mayonnaise (50/50 mix)

1 teaspoon Apple Ketchup (*see* page 339)

1 Bibb lettuce leaf

1 slice of onion

2 thin slices of gherkin

1 thin slice of beef tomato

100g Pulled Pork (*see* page 312)

1 thin slice of cheese (Ogglesheild for preference, or Comté)

2 rashers of candied streaky bacon (*see* method on page 237 but omit the popcorn and pecan nuts)

50ml Sausage & Onion Gravy, for dipping (*see* page 227)

There's very little that can compete with a well-made beefburger, but I'm prepared to stick my neck out and say this chap has a damn good go.

HOGBURGER Serves 1

Without seasoning (as the sausage is ready seasoned), grill the sausagemeat patty until charred and just cooked through. Set aside to rest in a warm place.

Toast the insides of the bap and spread the mustard mayonnaise on the bottom and the ketchup on the top. Place the lettuce leaf, onion, gherkin and sausage patty on the mayonnaise side of the bun and the tomato on the ketchup side.

Warm the pulled pork and place on top of the sausage patty. Top with cheese and place under the grill to melt. Place the candied bacon on top of the melted cheese and close the sandwich.

Serve with the Sausage & Onion Gravy on the side.

5 large free-range eggs

50g plain flour, seasoned with Maldon sea salt flakes and freshly ground black pepper

300g Basic Pork Sausage mix (*see* page 146)

100g fresh breadcrumbs

vegetable oil, for deep-frying

Scotch eggs were first seen at Fortnum & Mason in London, but it's possible that they were inspired by the Moghul dish *nargisi kofta*, made with hard-boiled eggs wrapped in spicy kofta meat. Much-abused versions can now be found in shops, supermarkets and garages across the country, but homemade they really are delicious. Try eating them hot, with a pork gravy.

SCOTCH EGGS Makes 4

Place 4 of the eggs in a pan of cold water, bring to the boil and cook for exactly 3 minutes. Turn off the heat and allow to cool in the water, then peel and set aside.

Dust the boiled eggs with seasoned flour and divide the sausagemeat into 4 equal portions. Form each portion into a flat cake large enough to fit around an egg, then work the sausagemeat around the egg as evenly as possible while keeping the egg shape and making sure there are no cracks. Place the Scotch eggs in the refrigerator for 20 minutes to firm up.

Beat the remaining egg. Remove the Scotch eggs from the refrigerator and roll them in more of the seasoned flour, then dip them into the beaten egg and finally roll them in the breadcrumbs, making sure to coat well at each stage.

Preheat the oven to 200°C/gas mark 6.

Heat the oil to 180°C in a deep-fat fryer or a large, deep heavy-based saucepan and fry the Scotch eggs, turning them frequently, for 3 minutes. Remove the eggs and place them in the preheated oven for 5 minutes, or until golden brown all over.

2kg sauerkraut, drained

100ml pork dripping

1 large onion, sliced

4 large garlic cloves,
lightly crushed

10 juniper berries

3 large bay leaves

½ teaspoon caraway seeds

1 teaspoon black peppercorns

a few cloves

600ml Master Pork Broth
(*see* page 335)

300ml Riesling

1kg bacon belly,
cut into large chunks

1kg mixed pork sausages

1kg potatoes, peeled

1kg boneless boiled ham,
sliced 1cm thick

assorted mustards, to serve

Choucroute was born in Germany, but grew up in France. Not the prettiest of dishes, it makes up for its lack of looks with character and *bonhomie*. Legendary food critic Jeffrey Steingarten once catalogued the ingredients in an authentic choucroute, and this version follows his lead.

CHOUCROUTE Serves 6–8

Preheat the oven to 150°C/gas mark 2.

Rinse the sauerkraut in cold water and squeeze dry. Heat a large roasting tray and melt the pork dripping. Add the onion and garlic and cook over a low heat, stirring, until softened. Stir in the sauerkraut, juniper berries, bay leaves, caraway seeds, black peppercorns, cloves, pork broth and wine and bring to the boil.

Place the pieces of bacon belly randomly into the sauerkraut and bring back to the boil over a moderately high heat, then cover with foil and bake for 1½ hours. Remove from the oven and nestle in the sausages and potatoes. Cover and bake for a further 30 minutes.

Pile on a large plate and serve with assorted mustards.

250ml pork gravy

250ml tomato passata

½ small light beer of choice

hot sauce or Sriracha, to taste

4 fresh sausages, such as Supper Pigs or Breakfast Pigs (*see* pages 147-8)

4 smoked sausages

4 thin steaks, beef or pork

Maldon sea salt flakes and freshly ground black pepper

8 slices of white bread

4 slices of ham

24 small slices of cheese (Portuguese for preference)

A big messy sandwich from Porto in Portugal that requires a knife and fork, *francesinha* means 'Frenchy', referencing its probable origins in the croque monsieur sandwich of France.

FRANCESINHA Makes 4

To make the sauce, pour the pork gravy, passata and beer into a saucepan and bring to a gentle simmer. Reduce to a thickish sauce consistency and season with hot sauce to taste.

To assemble the sandwiches, first you have to get the meats ready. Split the fresh sausages and the smoked sausages in half lengthways and cook on a hot griddle until cooked.

Season the steaks with salt and pepper and griddle until cooked.

Meanwhile, preheat the oven to a low setting.

Lightly toast or griddle the sliced bread and place 4 of the slices in 4 wide, ovenproof soup dishes.

Place the ham, grilled steaks, grilled fresh sausages and smoked sausages on top, and follow with the remaining slices of bread.

On top of this put the slices of cheese, covering the whole sandwiches, and divide the sauce between each, pouring it over the top. Place in the oven for 10 minutes, to heat through, then serve.

VARIATIONS

Francesinha especial, with egg and chips
Francesinha à barcarola, with prawns or shrimp
Francesinha de carne asada, with roast pork
Francesinha à cascata, with creamed mushrooms
Francesinha em forno a lenha is cooked in a wood-fired oven

200g pork shoulder

200g pork fat, diced

200g oats, soaked
in 200ml water

100g white of leek, chopped

200g potato flour (farina)

20g fine sea salt

½ teaspoon freshly ground
white pepper

a pinch of ground coriander

a pinch of ground pimento

a pinch of ground mace

You will also need
beef runners
(sausage casing), and
a mincer with a
sausage stuffer
attachment

Once a regional speciality, white pudding has been overtaken in favour by its now more common sibling, blood pudding. This is a shame, as they each have their place at the English breakfast table.

WHITE PUDDING Makes 4 large sausages

Combine everything in a large mixing bowl and stir until it's all thoroughly mixed.

Slowly feed the mixture through the mincer on the smallest mincing plate on your mincer. Keep feeding the mixture through until all your ingredients are minced before returning it to the mixing bowl.

Now you have your white pudding mix made up, the next step is to turn it into sausages by stuffing it into casings (*see* method on page 145).

When you're ready to poach your puddings, set a large covered pan of water on the stove and bring it to a gentle simmer. Poach the puddings for 20 minutes, then lift them out of the water and leave to cool.

The puddings are now ready to fry for breakfast, or spread them on toast with a caper and onion salad.

2kg smoked pork shoulder, diced

500g pork fat, diced

40g chopped onion

20g garlic, crushed

40g fine sea salt

1 teaspoon pink salt

⅓ teaspoon cayenne pepper

⅓ teaspoon hot smoked paprika

⅓ teaspoon ground mace

⅓ teaspoon ground cloves

⅓ teaspoon ground allspice

⅓ teaspoon mustard powder

⅓ teaspoon freshly ground black pepper

⅓ teaspoon fresh thyme leaves

You will also need 2m runners or sausage casing, a mincer with a sausage stuffer attachment, a charcoal barbecue or smoker and a meat thermometer

Andouille is a heavily spiced smoked sausage popular in Cajun cookery, and is often double-smoked. Although it originated in France, this version is closer to the American version used in gumbo and jambalaya.

ANDOUILLE Makes 25–30

Soak the casing in cold water for about 1 hour to soften it and loosen the salt in which it has been packed. Place the wide end of the sausage stuffer against the tap and run cold water through the inside of the casing to remove excess salt.

Pass the meat once through the coarse plate on your meat mincer. In a large bowl, mix the minced pork and fat with the rest of the ingredients.

Cut the casing into 2 lengths and tie a small knot in one end of each. Fit the open end over the tip of the sausage stuffer and slide it on until the tip of the stuffer touches the knot – this stops excess air from getting into the casing. Fit the stuffer on to the meat grinder according to the manufacturer's instructions, or hold the wide end of the stuffer against or over the opening by hand.

Fill the hopper with the sausage mixture. Turn the machine on and feed the sausage gradually into the hopper – for a manual machine the sausage casing will fill and gradually inflate. Smooth out any bumps with your fingers, being careful not to push the stuffing out of the casing, and tie off the open end of the sausage tightly by making a knot in the end.

To form the links, hold the entire casing up by its middle and twist it to form the first link. Then twist at the required intervals, going in opposite directions for each sausage to prevent the links unravelling.

Hang the sausages for a couple of hours in the refrigerator to dry out, then smoke them on the barbecue at 90°C for 1 hour, or until an internal temperature of 70°C is reached. Eat immediately or refrigerate until needed.

2 metres of runners or
sausage casing

750g pork shoulder, diced

250g pork fat, diced

20g fine sea salt

½ teaspoon pink salt

1 tablespoon hot smoked
paprika

1 tablespoon crushed garlic

1 tablespoon water

1 tablespoon cider vinegar

All fresh sausages are actually semi-cured, despite the name, and this is no exception. Use it in the migas and tortilla (*see* pages 166 and 169) or on its own as a tapas dish.

FRESH COOKING CHORIZO Makes 1kg

Soak the casing in cold water for about 1 hour, to soften it and loosen the salt in which it is packed. Place the wide end of the sausage stuffer up against the tap and run cold water through the inside of the casing to remove excess salt.

Pass the meat once through the coarse plate on your mincer. In a large bowl, mix together the minced pork and fat with the remaining ingredients.

Cut the casing into 2 lengths and tie a small knot in one end of each. Fit the open end over the tip of the sausage stuffer and slide it on until the tip of the stuffer touches the knot – this stops excess air from getting into the casing. Fit the stuffer on to the meat grinder according to the manufacturer's instructions, or hold the wide end of the stuffer against or over the opening by hand.

Fill the hopper with the sausage mixture. Turn the machine on and feed the sausage gradually into the hopper – for a manual machine the sausage casing will fill and gradually inflate. Smooth out any bumps with your fingers, being careful not to push the stuffing out of the casing, and tie off the open end of the sausage tightly by making a knot in the end.

To form the links, hold the entire casing up by its middle and twist it to form the first link. Then twist at the required intervals, going in opposite directions for each sausage to prevent the links unravelling.

Hang for a couple of hours in the refrigerator to dry out before cooking (*see* page 148).

500g stale bread

25ml pork dripping

200g Fresh Cooking Chorizo (*see* page 164), crumbled

4 garlic cloves, halved

smoked sea salt flakes

a large pinch of hot smoked paprika

1 tablespoon chopped fresh parsley

fried eggs, to serve

Making migas is a traditional Spanish way of using up leftover bread, and while the ingredients will vary from province to province, this version is close to that of Teruel in Aragon, Eastern Spain. I've long been fascinated by migas; in the right hands it's a comforting dish that is a perfect way to start the day.

CHORIZO MIGAS Serves 4

Cut the stale bread into cubes and put them into a bowl. Sprinkle water evenly over the bread – it should be moist, but not soaking wet. Cover the bowl and leave to stand for 20 minutes.

Put the pork dripping into a frying pan over a medium heat and add the crumbled chorizo, stir, then after 2 minutes add the garlic and cook until the chorizo is lightly brown on all sides. Remove the garlic and chorizo and set aside.

Add the moistened bread to the fat in the frying pan and begin to stir with a large wooden spoon or a spatula, moving it around constantly and breaking it into smaller pieces. The bread should form small clumps, fried and golden on the outside and soft on the inside.

Return the chorizo and garlic to the pan and season to taste with smoked salt and hot smoked paprika. Stir in the chopped parsley, then serve with fried eggs.

200ml olive oil

150g Fresh Cooking Chorizo
(*see* page 164), diced

1 small jar of piquillo peppers,
julienned

1 small onion, sliced

1kg Maris Piper potatoes,
peeled and sliced 5mm thick

Maldon sea salt flakes and
freshly ground black pepper

6 large free-range eggs, beaten

The mighty Jose Pizarro introduced me to this dish when we opened Tapas Brindisa in Borough Market, London. My version makes use of the amazing piquillo peppers, available in good supermarkets or online; I hope it's worthy.

CHORIZO TORTILLA Serves 4

Heat 50ml of the olive oil in a frying pan over a medium heat and cook the chorizo until lightly golden. Add the peppers and onion and cook for a minute or two, then transfer to a bowl.

Wipe out the pan and heat another 75ml of the oil, then add the potatoes and cook for 30 minutes over a low heat until tender. Stir them frequently so they don't stick. Pour off the excess oil and season the potatoes with salt and pepper. Tip the potatoes into the bowl of peppers and onions and, while they are still hot, stir in the eggs.

Heat the remaining oil in a large frying pan. Add the potato mixture and stir for 1 minute. Smooth the mixture down and cook over a very low heat for 10 minutes, or until the underneath has set to a brown crust.

Place a plate on top of the frying pan, then turn the pan over so that the tortilla rests on the plate. Slide the tortilla back into the pan, uncooked side down. Cook until browned on that side, too.

Slide the tortilla back on to a large plate and let it cool for at least 1 hour before serving.

250g pork meat, from the shoulder, belly and jowl

750g pork back fat

0.5g acidophilus (bactoferm, find it in health food stores)

20ml water

100g hot smoked paprika

50g fresh red chillies, chopped

50g Korean chilli powder

30g Maldon sea salt flakes

You will also need some ice, a mincer with a sausage stuffer attachment, a free-standing mixer with a paddle or dough hook and 1 length of large sausage casing

This spicy, spreadable Italian sausage (pronounced 'un-do-yah') -- typically made from shoulder, belly and jowl, roasted hot peppers and spices -- originates from Spilinga in Calabria, where it is served with slices of bread or with cheese. It also makes excellent pasta sauces.

N'DUJA Makes 1.25kg

Chill your mincer attachments.

Soak your sausage casing in running water for 15 minutes, making sure the clean water is running through the skins as well as around them.

Cut the meat and fat into 1cm cubes for grinding, then freeze until nearly solid.

Add the acidophilus to the water and combine with the paprika, chillies, chilli powder and salt.

Set up a bowl sitting in a tub of ice with some water in it for grinding the meat into. The meat needs to remain as cold as possible throughout the process. Mince the almost frozen meat and fat twice, through the smallest plate on your mincer, into the chilled bowl – this is important.

A free-standing food mixer works best for the next stage. Add the spices and salt to the pork mince, put into the mixer then, using a paddle or dough hook attachment, beat the meat for 5 minutes until completely bound. Stuff the mixture into the soaked sausage casing (see page 145) and tie off the individual sausages.

Leave the n'duja to hang at 25°C for 24 hours, then hang for a further 24 hours at 12°C. At this point the n'duja needs to be hung in a dry, cool place for 6 weeks until matured and ready to eat.

75g N'duja (*see* opposite)

20ml Dijon mustard

2 free-range egg yolks

1 garlic clove, crushed

20ml water

20ml lemon juice

250ml neutral olive oil

Maldon sea salt flakes and
freshly ground black pepper

A great addition to sandwiches, this is equally good served as a side to grilled pork, especially where that pork might lack a little lubricating fat, as is so often the case nowadays.

N'DUJA MAYONNAISE Makes 400ml

Remove the N'duja from its casing and blend with the mustard, egg yolks, garlic, water and lemon juice to a paste, then very slowly whisk in the olive oil until incorporated.

Season with salt and pepper and refrigerate for up to 4 days.

3 red onions, finely sliced

2 garlic cloves, crushed

2 tablespoons olive oil

1 fennel bulb, trimmed and finely sliced

200ml cider

100ml cider vinegar

100ml apple juice

500g N'duja, chopped (*see* page 170)

N'duja is damned spicy stuff and not for the faint-hearted. This treatment tames it somewhat and gives it a little sweetness to balance the fire.

N'DUJA MARMALADE Makes 1kg

In a large skillet over a medium heat, cook the onions and garlic in the oil until caramelized and golden brown – about 10 minutes. Add the fennel and cook for a further 2 minutes. Add the cider and cook until dry and starting to caramelize again, then add the cider vinegar and apple juice. Lastly add the N'duja and cook for 2 minutes, stirring and scraping up any browned bits from the skillet.

Reduce the heat to a bare simmer and cook uncovered, stirring occasionally, until the liquid almost completely evaporates and the marmalade becomes thick – about 30 minutes.

Let the mixture cool slightly, spoon into sterilized jars, seal and refrigerate. Use to spread on toast or use as a garnish. Refrigerate for up to 2 weeks.

500g smoked bacon belly,
cut into strips

4 onions, very finely sliced

2 garlic cloves, crushed

120ml strongly brewed coffee

120ml cider vinegar

120ml bourbon whiskey

120ml orange marmalade

There seems to be an invasion of bacon jams, pickles, cakes and conserves at the moment, some of which can only be described as spurious. This pimped-up burger relish relies on good bacon paired with slow-cooked sweet onions to deliver a much-needed bacon hit in a spreadable form. You could probably make this with just bacon, onions and some liquid if you were feeling purist.

BACON MARMALADE Makes 700g

In a large skillet over a medium heat, cook the bacon, stirring occasionally, until the fat is rendered and the bacon is lightly browned – about 20 minutes. Transfer the bacon to plates lined with kitchen paper and leave to drain.

Pour off most of the bacon fat and reserve for another use. Add the onions and garlic to the skillet and cook until the onions have cooked down and caramelized – about 12 minutes. Add the coffee, vinegar, bourbon and orange marmalade and bring to the boil. Cook, stirring and scraping up any browned bits from the skillet, for 2 minutes. Add the bacon strips and stir to combine.

Reduce the heat to a bare simmer and cook uncovered, stirring occasionally, until the liquid almost completely evaporates and the mixture becomes thick – about 1 hour.

Let the mixture cool slightly, then spoon into individual sterilized jars, seal and refrigerate. Use to spread on toast or use as a garnish. It will keep for up to 2 weeks in the refrigerator.

2 litres fresh pig's blood or 750g dried pig's blood mixed with 1.25 litres water

100g rolled oats

1 onion, finely diced

4 garlic cloves, crushed

250g sugar (any type)

250ml cider vinegar

a few fresh thyme leaves, chopped

a few fresh rosemary leaves, chopped

¼ teaspoon crushed mace

¼ teaspoon crushed allspice

¼ teaspoon crushed black peppercorn

50g Maldon sea salt flakes

250g pork back fat, diced

You will also need either sausage casing and a mincer with a sausage attachment, or pudding sleeves or a terrine mould

It's not at all easy to acquire fresh pig's blood, but if you do, you must work fast to prevent the blood coagulating and becoming unusable. That said, there is no doubt fresh pig's blood produces superior results, so if you get the opportunity don't be squeamish.

BLOOD PUDDING Makes 3kg

In a bowl, mix together the blood and the oats.

Put the onion, garlic, sugar and vinegar into a pan and bring to the boil, then cook until the mixture becomes thick.

Add the blood mixture, herbs, spices and salt and stir over a very low heat until the mixture thickens enough to stop the back fat from sinking when you add it. Add the back fat and stir. Adjust the seasoning to taste (fry off a small piece if you are feeling at all squeamish about tasting the mixture as it is), then remove from the heat and leave to cool.

Stuff the mixture into sausage casings (see page 145), black pudding sleeves or terrine moulds.

If using casings or black pudding sleeves, poach gently at the barest simmer for 40 minutes, then remove from the pan, allow to cool and chill until needed.

If using terrine moulds, cover with ovenproof cling film and place in a roasting tray with water to come halfway up the sides of the terrines, with a cloth in the bottom of the pan. Cook in a preheated oven at 150°C/gas mark 2 for 1 hour. Remove and allow to cool in the moulds, then refrigerate.

When needed, cut into slices and grill or fry until hot and crispy. Keep refrigerated for up to 4 days or store in the freezer.

500g mashing potatoes, peeled and diced

150g unsalted butter

Maldon sea salt flakes and freshly ground black pepper

4 onions, finely sliced

25g pork dripping or lard

100g bacon lardons

100g cooking apple, peeled and diced

500g Blood Pudding, diced (see opposite)

50g fresh breadcrumbs

You will also need a 1.5 litre pie dish

This is based on a lovely side dish I ate some years ago, in a posh Lancashire restaurant that had two twinkly Étoiles Michelin, at a time when such things meant something.

BLOOD PUDDING COTTAGE PIE   Serves 4

Preheat the oven to 180°C/gas mark 4.

Cook the potatoes in boiling salted water for 20 minutes until just tender. Drain and allow to steam dry, then add the butter and mash, adjusting the seasoning.

Cook the onions gently in the dripping for 10 minutes until golden and sweet. Add the bacon lardons and apple and continue cooking until the bacon is cooked through. Stir in the blood pudding and remove from the heat.

Fill a 1.5 litre pie dish with the blood pudding mix and spread or pipe the mashed potato over the top.

Sprinkle with the breadcrumbs and bake in the oven for 30 minutes, or until hot and golden brown on top.

1 large beetroot

1 large apple

400g Blood Pudding
(*see* page 174)

40g unsalted butter

2 teaspoons sugar (any type)

Maldon sea salt flakes and
freshly ground black pepper

2 teaspoons cider vinegar

4 slices of white country bread

springs of fresh thyme,
to garnish

Baking beetroots concentrates their inherent sugars, making them deliciously sweet, and when paired with apple they provide an excellent contrast to a rich blood pudding.

BLOOD PUDDING, APPLE & BEETROOT ON TOAST Serves 4

Preheat the oven to 180°C/gas mark 4.

Wrap the beetroot in foil and bake for 40 minutes until tender, then allow to cool in the foil. Peel the beetroot and cut into 8 wedges, then do the same with the apple, removing the core.

Slice the Blood Pudding into larger chunks and set aside.

Heat half the butter in a nonstick frying pan or skillet and sauté the apple and beetroot until the apple is just cooked. Add the sugar, salt and pepper and allow to caramelize – the apples should be a lovely golden-red colour by now.

Deglaze the pan with a splash of cider vinegar and remove from the heat. Transfer the apple and beetroot to a plate and keep warm. Clean the pan or skillet, then heat the remaining butter, add the blood pudding and fry until hot and slightly crispy.

Toast the bread and place on 4 plates. Top with the Blood Pudding, followed by the apple and beetroot mixture. Serve garnished with thyme sprigs.

200g uncooked rice

1 lemon grass stick, split

3 garlic cloves, crushed

200g minced pork

250ml pig's blood

2 teaspoons Maldon sea salt flakes

20g palm sugar

4 large banana leaves

To serve

50g sliced shallots

50g cucumber julienne

8 dry-fried bird's-eye chillies

30g fried chopped garlic

You will also need a steamer

Every pork-loving nation has a way of using pork blood and this is a steamed Thai parcel that uses blood to hold everything together. Unlikely to be seen in your local Thai restaurant, this is worth making -- providing you have a ready supply of pig's blood, of course.

KHAO KANCHIN   Serves 4

Cook the rice with the lemon grass and garlic cloves, then spread on a tray while still warm and remove the lemon grass. Add the minced pork and pig's blood, mix well and season with the salt and sugar.

Lay out the banana leaves and spoon some of the rice mixture on to each. Fold them into tight parcels and secure with bamboo skewers.

Steam the parcels for 20 minutes, then serve with sliced shallots, cucumber julienne, fried bird's-eye chillies and fried chopped garlic.

400ml Sausage & Onion Gravy (*see* page 227)

200g sautéed potatoes

8 roasted field mushrooms

8 roasted tomatoes

200g Baked Beans (*see* page 282)

4 smoked bacon chops, about 200g each

8 Sausages (*see* page 146)

4 slices of Scrapple (*see* page 276)

4 slices of Blood Pudding (*see* page 174)

4 slices of sourdough bread

1 tablespoon pork dripping

8 eggs

A Bacchanalian frenzy of porcine indulgence, the full English breakfast is to be treated with utmost respect -- eat too many and life will be enjoyable but short, but then who wants to live forever anyway?

THE FULL ENGLISH BREAKFAST Serves 4

You should cook a number of the elements of the breakfast ahead: the Sausage & Onion Gravy, the sautéed potatoes, the mushrooms, tomatoes and the Baked Beans. Keep them warm while you cook the rest of the breakfast in order of the time the various elements take to cook, starting with the chops and finishing with the eggs.

Preheat the oven to 180°C/gas mark 4.

Place a large griddle pan over a high heat and sear the bacon chops, sausages, Scrapple and Blood Pudding on both sides, then transfer to a hot oven for 10–15 minutes until cooked through.

Toast or grill the sourdough as you're frying the eggs and spread the toast with the pork dripping.

Assemble all the ingredients on 4 plates and serve with a jug of sausage gravy on the side.

Finally loosen your belt and take a nap, assuming you haven't been foolhardy enough to attempt this on a school day.

400g Wild Boar Sausagemeat (*see* page 148)

1 small onion, diced

2 garlic cloves, crushed

200ml red wine

2 anchovy fillets, chopped

200ml tomato passata

200ml Master Pork Broth (*see* page 335)

Maldon sea salt flakes and freshly ground black pepper

1 faggot of fresh herbs, made with thyme, bay, oregano and rosemary

1 small spice bag, made with 1 dried chilli, ½ cinnamon stick and 2 cloves

200ml water

400g fresh pappardelle pasta

grated Pecorino cheese, to serve

This is a little like the Bolognese found up and down the country in its preparation, but leagues ahead in flavour. The trick is to cook low and slow until the sausage is broken down and the flavours are deep and rich. It's equally good made with pork sausagemeat -- just substitute Parmesan for the Pecorino at the end. The use of a little pasta water when finishing is an essential touch, it brings the sauce together and improves the overall flavour.

WILD BOAR SAUSAGE PAPPARDELLE Serves 4

Preheat the oven to 140°C/gas mark 1.

In a nonstick pan, cook the sausagemeat, onion and garlic slowly, stirring with a wooden spoon – it should take 10 minutes to gently cook down. Add the red wine and simmer for a few minutes to reduce.

Add the anchovies, passata and pork broth and cook for a few minutes, seasoning gently with salt and pepper.

Transfer the mixture to an ovenproof lidded casserole and add the faggot of herbs, spice bag and water. Cover and place in the oven for 2 hours, stirring from time to time.

Bring a pan of salted water to the boil and cook the pappardelle until al dente. Drain, reserving a little of the pasta water, then toss with the hot ragù and serve with plenty of freshly grated Pecorino.

BREEDING

Pigs are highly prolific, with a gestation period of only four months. A typical sow gives birth to an average of ten piglets (though litter size may be as large as thirty), and can breed twice a year. The world record for the number of piglets born to one sow is 37!

Pigs used for breeding are carefully selected because inferior pigs produce inferior piglets, which in turn make for mediocre meat – so it is important to start with the best genes possible. The pigs must be in peak condition to breed to best results, and this means not too fat. For breeding, leaner is better.

MAKING BABIES

A young female pig, known as a gilt, will reach sexual maturity at around six months of age, but will not be large enough to breed until nine months. Gilts are 'receptive', or ready to mate, for three days of each subsequent three-week cycle and can be identified as being in oestrus (heat) by various signs. These include having a swollen vulva or a slight vaginal discharge, acting restless, urinating frequently, twitching her tail or holding her ground rather than moving off when pressed down on her hindquarters. Gilts should be mated on their first day of heat, and sows (who have had at least one prior litter) should be mated on the second day, as ovulation occurs slightly later in the cycle for older females. Both gilts and sows should receive a second mating 24 hours after their first.

As for the boars, an eight- to twelve-month-old can usually service twelve extensively kept sows in pasture, and an older boar can service thirty-five or so. It is important that the boar is the right size – a nine-month-old gilt is in physical danger from a fully grown boar just because of his weight and size, and a young boar may not be able to cover an older sow. There is a saying that the boar is half the herd, which means that there is no point being selective in choosing the gilts and sows if they are going to mate with a scrawny boar.

When pigs mate, there is a brief courtship consisting of the boar sniffing the female under her tail and pushing her flanks while he snorts and froths at the mouth. Eventually he will mount, or 'cover', the female and after some brief activity will rest, remaining in position over her for some time. He will repeat the process several hours later and again the following day.

The gestation period for a pregnant female is around three months, three weeks and three days (about 114 days on average).

PREPARING FOR PIGLETS

The ideal farrowing house for the birth of piglets is a stable with a split door and a partially divided, solid concrete floor facing away from the door so as to avoid draughts, with an outer area for eating, drinking and defecating and an inner area for the nursery. Piglets need a warm environment: they will thrive at 30°C (86°F), suffer at 20°C (68°F) and die at 10°C (50°F). The sow, on the other hand, has 10cm (4in) of lard around her middle and so is more likely to suffer from overheating. While the piglets will try to cuddle up against her to stay warm, she will just as likely be trying to cool off by continually standing up and sitting down. And every time she settles back down, she runs the risk of landing on and perhaps killing a piglet.

To avoid disaster, a farrowing house should incorporate separate heat lamps for the piglets so they won't need to scramble up to their mother for warmth. It should also have piglet 'guard rails' that stand around 25cm (10in) off the floor and extend around 25cm (10in) from the walls, adjacent to the heat lamps. By crawling under the rails, the piglets can curl up and sleep safely in their own heated spot and still reach the sow to feed. A week before the piglets are due, the expectant female should be moved into the farrowing house so she can adjust to her new surroundings, and let out for two fifteen-minute periods of exercise every day.

Important steps must be taken in advance to help keep diseases from striking the fragile newborns. Each female should be wormed and sprayed for parasites about two weeks before her due date. The expectant mother should be immunized against erysipelas to strengthen both her own resistance and the piglets' to this common and often fatal disease. And because good sanitation is a vital part of preventive health care, the farrowing house must be thoroughly cleaned and the pregnant female washed with a mild detergent and warm water before being penned up for delivery. Enough straw should be provided so that she can nest and be ready to bear her young when she gets restless.

THE NEW ARRIVALS

As each piglet is born, they should be dried with clean rags and their navels painted with iodine before they hit the ground. The newborn piglets are best kept in a box under their heat lamps, away from their mother while she finishes her labour. Once they are all born and the afterbirth has been disposed of, each newcomer is given the chance to nurse and obtain some of its mother's precious colostrum. This 'first milk' is high in nutrients, vitamins, minerals and antibodies. Finally, the soiled bedding is cleaned away, and the new mother and her piglets are made comfortable.

A sow's milk is naturally deficient in iron, so one piglet-caretaking task is to supplement the newborns' supply of that mineral by providing a boxed supply of soil in the farrowing pen so the piglets can get all the iron they need by rooting in the earth. Iron deficiency can result in anaemia, which is potentially fatal.

Water is now even more important to the piglets and especially the sow. In order to produce endless supplies of milk she will need endless supplies of water and food, so it has to be constantly refreshed.

WEANING

The piglets' main diet from birth until they are weaned will be their mother's milk, or 'suckle', but they are also provided after the first week with a supply of high-quality creep feed containing at least 18 per cent protein and essential amino acids, vitamins and minerals. Sow milk yield typically plateaus at about 12 to 16 days of lactation, so creep feeding is recommended from about 10 days of age. Freshness is important, because piglets must be attracted to the feed. Limited amounts of feed (from a supply stored in a facility or room separate from the pigs) should be offered to the piglets several times daily, and positioned so that the sow cannot get it. Stale or uneaten feed should be removed daily. It is also still important to have fresh water available – piglets that have access to fresh water eat more feed than those who do not.

Any males that are not going to be raised for breeding stock are usually castrated while young, to prevent uncontrolled mating and to keep their meat from developing an 'off' or 'boarish' flavour and odour called boar taint. The best time to castrate a piglet is when it is four to fourteen days of age.

The piglets' suckle is supplemented at three weeks of age with grower pellets. They are weaned when they are from four to eight weeks old – the later the better, to make best use of the mother's milk and all the goodness that provides. Once the piglets are weaned, the mother's milk is dried up by reducing her food and water. This is important because continued lactation can cause problems.

Complete records are kept on each sow's productivity, including the weights of her litters when weaned, so the poor producers can be culled from the herd and overall breeding efficiency promoted. Happy, healthy and well-kept sows can produce happy, healthy and strong litters for up to ten years or more.

Chapter 5
CURED

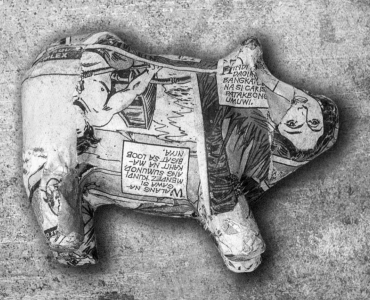

950g fine sea salt

500g light brown muscovado sugar

50g curing salt, such as Instacure No. 2 or Prague powder No. 2

1 whole fresh pork leg, about 8kg, aitchbone removed

You will also need disposable gloves and a piece of muslin large enough to wrap the ham

Ham curing was once an integral part of pig-rearing; pre-refrigeration it would have been impossible to eat a whole pig before it spoiled, so various preservation methods were essential to utilize every part of the animal. Over the centuries ham has become a staple, and a delicacy that has survived the advent of modern-day preservation methods. Dry-curing is the oldest method of ham curing, and by far the best.

BASIC HAM (DRY-CURED) For a 10kg ham

Wash your hands well and don disposable plastic gloves – cleanliness is paramount when handling your ham.

Mix the sea salt, sugar and Instacure No. 2, then rub the ham with this mix, taking care to cover every exposed part, flesh and bone.

Place skin side down in an immaculately clean plastic tray or tub and cover with clingfilm. Place another tray on top and place a heavy weight on top of that, at least 4kg, preferably more.

Refrigerate for up to 2 weeks, checking every day and pouring off any liquid, and re-rubbing with fresh curing salt mix. When the ham is firm to touch, with little give, it's time to wash it thoroughly in cold water, then dry and wrap it in muslin to store in the refrigerator.

Before use the ham will need to be soaked in cold water for several hours, to purge some of the salt.

2kg fine sea salt

1kg light brown
muscovado sugar

50g curing salt, such as
Instacure No. 2 or Prague
powder No. 2

3 litres good-quality
cider or beer

5 litres water

aromatics of choice:
peppercorns, cloves, juniper
berries and star anise all
work well

1 whole fresh pork leg, about
8kg, aitchbone removed

You will also need
a piece of muslin
large enough to
wrap the ham

Wet-curing is a modern way of making ham — the method
has its pros and cons, and is a halfway house to industrial
ham curing that uses saline injections to speed up the process.
We all love ham, and a wet-cured ham has its place, provided
the quality is there in the animal.

BASIC HAM (WET-CURED) For a 10kg ham

Bring the sea salt, sugar, Instacure No.2, cider, water
and aromatics to the boil in a large stainless steel
saucepan. Allow to cool, then chill.

Place your chilled pork leg in a large plastic container
large enough to take it, then pour over the chilled
brine and cover with clingfilm to exclude any air.
Weight down with a large, heavy non-metallic
weight to keep the ham submerged.

Place the container in the fridge or a very cool cellar
for 1 week, turning the ham halfway through the week.

Remove the ham from the brine and dry, then wrap
in 1 or 2 layers of muslin and refrigerate until needed.

Before use the ham will need to be soaked in cold
water for several hours, to purge some of the salt.

NB: cider and beer will produce two very different
results, and good beer means ale, not lager.

glaze recipe of your choice

1 Basic Ham (*see* pages 188–9), soaked in cold water for a few hours

300ml water

300g fresh breadcrumbs (optional)

Cola Glaze

1 litre cola

100g dark brown muscovado sugar

50g hot mustard

Honey Glaze

100ml water

100ml orange juice

100ml clear honey

100g light muscovado sugar

Spice Glaze

200ml water

200g dark brown muscovado sugar

10g fresh root ginger, finely grated

5g cinnamon sticks, crushed

5g star anise

5g cloves

5g fennel seeds

Treacle Glaze

100g light brown muscovado sugar

100ml black treacle

100ml golden syrup

100ml water

Citrus Glaze

100ml orange juice

100ml lemon juice

100ml lime juice

100ml water

100g light brown muscovado sugar

Apple Glaze

200ml apple juice

200ml cider

100ml water

100g light brown muscovado sugar

Raisin Glaze

100g seedless raisins

100ml Pedro Ximénez sherry

100ml water

100ml clear honey

100g light brown muscovado sugar

I'll have no truck with turkey at Christmas; a proper ham from a proper pig is truly a sight to behold, and will last for days in even the largest of houses. Don't feel you have to slavishly follow the glaze recipes above -- mix them up and be creative. A little bourbon in the cola glaze might be a good addition, for instance.

ROAST GLAZED HAM
Serves: depends on weight of your ham

Place all the ingredients for your choice of glaze in a saucepan and bring to a simmer. Remove from the heat and blend to a smooth paste in a blender.

Preheat the oven to 160°C/gas mark 3.

Note the weight of your ham. Put the ham into a roasting tray, add 300ml of water and roast in the oven for 20 minutes. Remove from the oven, pour half the glaze over the ham, then return it to the oven and roast for a further 45 minutes per kilo. Halfway through the roasting time, take it out again and pour over the other half of the glaze.

Coat generously with breadcrumbs, if using, then put back into the oven to finish cooking.

When the time is up, remove the ham from the oven, transfer to a clean dish and leave to rest for 30 minutes.

Pour off the glaze from the roasting tray and pass through a fine sieve into a saucepan. Simmer until reduced to a sticky syrup and serve alongside the ham.

a large bundle of organic hay

1 Basic Ham (*see* pages 188–9)

1 bunch of fresh mint

Cooking in hay is an old-fashioned method of slow-cooking that imbues the ham with a lovely summer farmyard character. You can use other herbs and even spices, but there's something very English about mint with ham that I really like.

HAM IN HAY Serves 12–15

Preheat the oven to 140°C/gas mark 1.

Make a base layer of hay in a large lidded flameproof pot. Place half the mint on top of the hay, then lay the ham on top. Put the rest of the mint on top of the ham, then cover with more hay.

Pour in water to cover and bring to the boil, then turn down to the gentlest simmer. Put a lid on the pot and place in the oven. Bake for about 4 hours, or until the ham is tender all the way through. Check that it's ready by probing with a thin, sharp knife.

Remove all the skin and as much of the fat as your conscience dictates.

Present the cooked ham on a platter in a nest of cooked hay (do not eat the hay).

1kg Basic Ham (*see* pages 188–9)

200g carrots, peeled

200g onions, peeled

400g potatoes, peeled

100g unsalted butter

25g fresh curly parsley, chopped

Maldon sea salt flakes and freshly ground black pepper

This is a simple boiled ham served with 'liquor' in the Old English sense of the word, with no alcohol involved. Keep any alcoholic liquor for washing it down.

BOILED HAM & LIQUOR   Serves 4

Place the gammon, carrots and onions in a large flameproof pot and cover with water.

Bring to a gentle simmer, then skim and cook for 1 hour. Skim again, add the potatoes and cook for a further 30 minutes until the ham is cooked through.

Remove the ham, vegetables and potatoes to another dish and boil the cooking liquor to reduce by half. Crush one of the cooked potatoes and whisk into the liquor, followed by the butter.

Pass the now thick liquor through a sieve, pressing any potato bits through, then return it to the pan and add the chopped parsley. Adjust the seasoning only if absolutely necessary – this will depend on the saltiness of the gammon.

Slice the ham and arrange on a platter with the carrots, onions and potatoes. Pour the parsley liquor over the top and serve with your favourite mustard.

4 x 250g Basic Ham steaks (*see* pages 188–9), each 3cm thick

500ml Master Pork Broth (*see* page 335)

4 sprigs of rosemary

4 garlic cloves, crushed

¼ freshly grated nutmeg

25g tinned anchovies, chopped

pinch of cayenne pepper

250g cooked spinach, drained and roughly chopped

125ml double cream

Maldon sea salt flakes and freshly ground black pepper

8 free-range eggs (Burford Browns for preference)

50ml white wine vinegar, for poaching

In 19th-century Britain, the word 'spinach' also meant nonsense and Dickens uses the phrase 'gammon and spinach' in this sense with Miss Mowcher in *David Copperfield*: 'What a world of gammon and spinnage it is though, ain't it!'

POACHED GAMMON STEAKS WITH POACHED EGGS & CREAMED SPINACH Serves 4

Place the gammon steaks in a shallow baking tray and pour over the pork broth to cover.

Add the rosemary, garlic, nutmeg, anchovies and cayenne pepper to the tray, cover with kitchen foil and bring to the barest simmer – at no point should it boil – so your lowest hob setting would be ideal. Cook for 10 minutes, turning over halfway through, then remove from the heat and allow to stand for a further 10 minutes.

Drain the gammon cooking liquid through a fine sieve into a saucepan. Add the double cream and cooked spinach to the liquid and heat through. Taste and adjust the seasoning if necessary. At this point the creamed spinach could be blended to a smooth purée if so desired, or kept as is.

Bring a deep saucepan of water to a rolling boil and add the vinegar, then poach the eggs until just cooked – about 2 minutes.

When ready to serve, place the gammon on 4 warm serving plates, top each with 2 hot poached eggs and pour the creamed spinach over the top.

2 x 1kg ham hocks (*see pages 188–9*)

200g carrots

200g onions

Court-bouillon, to cover (*see page 334*)

400g potatoes, peeled

½ small bunch of fresh curly parsley, chopped

2 tablespoons Dijon mustard

Maldon sea salt flakes and freshly ground black pepper

1 x recipe Rough Puff Pastry (*see page 149*)

1 free-range egg, beaten, (or use milk)

This is one of my absolute favourite pies. I used to make it with an old-fashioned suet crust pastry, which I love, but others prefer it with rough puff and I eventually caved in. If you want to make it with suet crust, blend two parts flour with one part suet and a pinch of salt in a food processor until there are no lumps. Keeping the motor running, spoon in a tablespoon of milk at a time until the pastry starts to come together, before finishing it with your hands.

HAM, ONION & POTATO PIE   Serves 4

Place the ham hocks, carrots and onions in a large flameproof pot and cover with court-bouillon. Do not season. Bring to a gentle simmer and cook for 1 hour, then add the potatoes and cook for a further 20 minutes.

Remove the ham and vegetables to another dish and simmer the cooking liquid until reduced by half. Crush one of the potatoes and whisk into the liquid. Pass the now thick liquid through a sieve, pressing any potato bits through, then return it to the pan and add the chopped parsley and the mustard, adjusting the seasoning carefully and only if necessary.

Flake the ham, crush the carrots and cut the onions and potatoes into chunks. Pour the parsley liquid over the top and pour into a suitable pie dish.

Roll out your pastry on a floured surface to 1cm thick. Cut a pastry strip the same width as the lip of the dish, then wet the edge of the dish with egg and fix the strip around it. Brush with more egg and lay the remaining pastry over the top. Trim the pastry to the edge of the dish, then pinch the cut edges and cut a slit to let the steam escape. Brush all over the top with egg.

Bake for 30 minutes, or until hot, golden and risen, and eat with mustard on the side.

1 ham hock (*see* pages 188–9), soaked in cold water overnight

200g dried green peas, soaked in cold water overnight

1 onion

1 leek

1 carrot

1 tablespoon unsalted butter

50ml extra thick double cream, to serve

Maldon sea salt flakes and freshly ground black pepper

In Victorian London a combination of geography, weather and coal heating frequently resulted in a thick green smog. An 1871 *New York Times* article referred to 'London, particularly, where the population are periodically submerged in a fog of the consistency of pea soup...' London particular, then, became the name for a thick pea and ham soup.

LONDON PARTICULAR (PEA & HAM SOUP) Serves 4

Drain the soaked ham hock and dried peas, discarding the soaking liquid.

Peel the vegetables and cut them into chunks, then place in a large saucepan cook them gently in the butter until soft. Add the peas and ham hock, cover with fresh water and bring to a simmer, then cover the pan with a lid and cook gently for about 1 hour until the peas are soft and the ham shank is cooked.

Take the ham shank out of the pan and pull it into nice chunks, discarding any fat, sinew or skin. Put the meat back into the pan, stir well and adjust the seasoning, but only if needed.

The ham should be tender and the peas mushy. Serve hot, with a dollop of extra thick double cream.

20g unsalted butter, plus extra for spreading

20g plain flour

100ml hot milk

8 slices of Comté cheese, plus 50g grated Comté

grated nutmeg

Maldon sea salt flakes and freshly ground black pepper

8 slices of white bread

Dijon mustard, for spreading

4 thick slices of really good cooked ham

I first ate this classic French sandwich as staff food in the iconic restaurant Le Gavroche in London. I've gone for Comté cheese here because I prefer it, but use your favourite. Variations on this theme are legion, but I've included a few below that I quite like the sound of.

CROQUE MONSIEUR Makes 4

Melt the butter in a saucepan and stir in the flour to make a roux. Cook for 1 minute, then gradually whisk in the hot milk, a little at a time, until smooth. Simmer for a few minutes until thickened, then add the grated Comté cheese and stir until melted. Grate in a little nutmeg and season lightly.

Preheat the grill.

Brush one side of each slice of bread liberally with butter, then toast. Spread the untoasted sides of the bread with Dijon mustard and put the ham on top, followed by the Comté slices. Place under the grill for 1 minute, or until the cheese has melted.

Top with the rest of the bread, with the toasted side uppermost, and spread with the cheese sauce. Grill until golden and bubbling, then serve immediately.

VARIATIONS

Croque madame, with fried egg

Croque provençal, with tomato

Croque auvergnat, with bleu d'Auvergne cheese

Croque gagnet, with Gouda cheese and andouille sausage

Croque norvégien, with smoked salmon instead of ham

Croque tartiflette, with sliced potatoes and Reblochon cheese

Croque Bolognese, with Bolognese sauce

Croque señor, with tomato salsa

Croque Hawaiian, with a slice of pineapple

Monte Cristo Sandwich, *see* page 204

2 free-range eggs

Maldon sea salt flakes and freshly ground black pepper

4 slices of sturdy white bread (or other white bread of preference)

2 tablespoons mustard

2 tablespoons mayonnaise

200g thick-sliced baked ham

50g shredded Comté cheese

2 tablespoons butter

icing sugar (optional)

The daddy of them all, the Monte Cristo Sandwich, is courtesy of the good old U S of A! Trust the Americans to take a classic sandwich to the next level and beyond.

MONTE CRISTO SANDWICH Makes 2

Beat the eggs in a shallow dish (large enough to fit a sandwich), along with a few pinches of salt and pepper. Set aside.

Assemble your sandwiches as you like them, with the sliced bread, mustard, mayonnaise, ham, cheese, salt and pepper. Slightly compress each sandwich.

Melt the butter in a skillet over a medium heat. Dip each sandwich in the beaten egg, then cook for 2–3 minutes on each side until browned to your liking and the cheese has melted.

Dust with icing sugar, if you like, and serve.

250g cooked ham, chopped

125g unsalted butter

125ml double cream

a splash of brandy or bourbon

1 teaspoon Worcestershire sauce

a pinch of cayenne pepper

a pinch of black pepper

a pinch of ground cinnamon

a pinch of grated nutmeg

50g melted butter, for sealing

This is an old-fashioned, homely picnic spread that's really quick and easy to make. Use a proper cooked ham of the kind seen on the bone in good delis or old-school butchers' shops.

POTTED HAM Makes 2 x 250ml jars

Put all the ingredients into a food processor and pulse-blend to a paste. Scrape down the sides to make sure it's well mixed, and process again.

Pot in sterilized glass jars and pour over the melted butter to seal. Place in the refrigerator to set.

Remove from the refrigerator 1 hour before use and serve at room temperature with toast or biscuits.

950g fine sea salt

50g curing salt, such as Instacure No. 2 or Prague powder No. 2

1 whole fresh pork leg, about 12kg, aitchbone removed

950g pork lard

50g rice flour

You will also need disposable plastic gloves, a 2m-square piece of muslin and some butcher's string

AIR-CURED HAM (PROSCIUTTO) For 1 ham

Air-curing your own ham is a long, involved, but ultimately rewarding process. Be warned, though -- it's by no means easy, and even following the recipe to the letter and practising scrupulously clean methods will occasionally result in failure.

While some traditional air-cured hams, such as San Daniele or Parma, use pure salt as a curative agent, most modern air-cured hams also use nitrites, which help prevent bacterial growth and in reaction with the meat's myoglobin give the ham its dark red colour. They are, however, toxic in excess, so clearly they should be used sparingly and judiciously. Fortunately, there are several ready-made mixes available to de-risk the process somewhat.

The dry-curing of ham involves a number of biochemical reactions caused by enzymes, which cause a breakdown of proteins in the muscle tissue, creating large numbers of small peptides and free amino acids, while the lipids in the muscle and connective tissue break down and create free fatty acids. Baffled? Yes, me too, but fortunately you don't need a science degree to make your own air-cured ham -- just patience, persistence and fastidious kitchen practice.

Wash your hands well and don disposable plastic gloves – cleanliness is paramount when handling your ham. Mix the sea salt and Instacure No. 2 and rub the pork with this mix, taking care to cover every exposed part, flesh and bone.

Place the pork skin side down in an immaculately clean plastic tray or tub and cover with clingfilm. Place another tray on top and put a heavy weight on top of that, at least 4kg, preferably more.

Refrigerate for up to 2 weeks, checking every day, pouring off any liquid and re-rubbing with fresh curing salt mix. When the ham is firm to touch, with little give, it's time to wash it thoroughly in cold water, then dry.

Mix the pork lard with the rice flour and rub your ham with this mixture, taking care to cover it everywhere. Lay your muslin on a sterile table and place the ham at one end. Roll the ham in the muslin so there are at least 4 and as many as 6 layers of muslin, then tie securely with butcher's string.

Hang your ham in a large (preferably walk-in) refrigerator at about 5°C with 60–70 per cent humidity, for around 6 months.

When your ham is ready, at around the 6-month mark, it will have lost about a third of its original weight and be about 8kg in weight. Remove the muslin and pork lard and rub it down thoroughly. Keep it cool, and slice off thin slivers as required.

The success of air-curing your own ham depends in equal parts on the quality of the meat you start with, on cleanliness, the environment you hang the ham in and a portion of luck.

200ml milk

200ml Master Pork Broth
(see page 335) or ham
bone broth

freshly grated nutmeg

Maldon sea salt flakes and
freshly ground black pepper

50ml extra virgin olive oil

1 large banana shallot,
finely diced

1 leek, white part only,
finely diced

100g Ibérico ham, finely diced

50g plain flour

100g plain flour, seasoned
with Maldon sea salt flakes
and freshly ground black pepper

1 free-range egg, beaten,

fresh or dried breadcrumbs,
to coat

vegetable oil, for deep-frying

A classic tapa found all over Spain; croquettes can be,
and are, made with different hams, but here I've chosen
Ibérico, the king of hams. I've also eaten a delicious version
made with both chicken and ham -- just substitute half the
ham for chopped cooked chicken.

HAM CROQUETTES Serves 4

Put the milk and broth into a saucepan, season with
nutmeg, salt and pepper, and put on the stove to
heat up to just below boiling point.

In a separate saucepan, heat the olive oil and gently
fry the shallot until soft. Add the diced leek, then the
ham, and finally the 50g plain flour, stirring as you go.
Continue cooking for 3–4 minutes.

Stir the hot milk and broth into the ham mixture a
ladleful at a time. Keep stirring for 8 minutes or so,
until the mixture thickens. Taste and adjust the
seasoning, then set aside to cool.

Line a baking tray with clingfilm. When the ham
mixture is cool, take dessert spoonfuls of mixture and
place in balls on to the prepared baking tray until all
the mixture is used up. Cover with more clingfilm
and refrigerate for 1 hour until firm.

Place the seasoned flour, beaten egg and
breadcrumbs in 3 separate bowls and remove the
firmed-up croquettes from the refrigerator. One at a
time, dust them with the flour, then dip into the egg
and finally coat with the breadcrumbs. Return them
to the refrigerator for 30 minutes.

Heat the oil to 180°C in your deep-fat fryer on in a
deep, heavy-based saucepan and fry the croquettes
in small batches for 3 minutes, or until golden. Drain
on kitchen paper, then serve hot.

1 whole large pork belly, about 5kg, ribs and skin on

malt vinegar

vegetable oil

freshly ground black pepper

For the dry cure mix

500g fine sea salt

75g light brown muscovado sugar

2 teaspoons cracked black pepper

2 teaspoons fennel seeds, toasted and crushed

You will also need a 2m-square piece of muslin and some butcher's string

Bacon is easy to make, and once you have made it a few times you will be able to tweak the recipe and become a complete bacon master. Additions such as spices or sugar change the character, making for a more interesting flavour. Curing for 5 days gives fresh and soft bacon, but with good air circulation the bacon will begin to air-dry and get firmer. It can be wrapped and refrigerated as soon as it reaches the desired texture, and kept for up to a week.

BACON Makes 5kg

Mix all the ingredients for the dry cure together in a bowl until they are thoroughly combined.

In a non-reactive container, rub the dry cure mix all over the belly. The belly will need to cure for 5 days – turn it daily and pour away any liquid in the container.

Remove the belly after 5 days, lightly rinse off the cure and dry thoroughly.

Mix equal quantities by weight of malt vinegar, vegetable oil and black pepper and bring to the boil.

Allow to cool, then paint it all over the bacon belly with a pastry brush.

Wrap the belly in muslin and tie securely, then hang in a cool place, out of sunlight, at below 10°C and leave to dry for up to a further 5 days before cooking and eating or cold-smoking (see page 212) as desired.

1 whole large pork belly,
about 5kg, ribs and skin on,
ready-cured and chilled

You will also need
a smokebox or
container that will
hold smoke for long
enough, and half a
bucket of wood
shavings or chippings

Apple, cherry and oak wood chips can all be used to cold-smoke bacon for as little as 8 hours and as long as 24 hours.

SMOKED BACON

Cold-smoking is a useful preservation tool, in combination with curing and drying, and the smoking time also serves to dry the bacon further. The curing and drying makes the interior of the bacon inhospitable to bacteria, while the smoking gives the vulnerable exterior surfaces an extra layer of protection. Cold-smoking temperatures should typically be maintained between 10°C and 20°C – in this temperature range the food will not cook and will take on a rich, smoky flavour and develop that deep colour.

Cold smoking is a bit trickier than hot smoking because it's important that the smoking temperature is under 20°C. This is achievable, but it usually means that any heat source used to get the wood to smoulder must be kept separate from the smoking chamber. If you get this wrong, the food can start to cook and will lose its preserving qualities. Higher temperatures will also provide exactly the conditions on which bacteria thrive.

Lay a trail of wood chips in the bottom of your smoker in a horseshoe shape about 15cm high and wide. You can expect a trail of woodchips that reach halfway around the smoker to burn for about 8 hours. Three-quarters of the smoker circumference should burn through the night. The burning time will be shorter if there is significant draught. Light one end

of the trail and allow the chips to reach a steady state of smoke production and burn around the ring. The wood chips can ignite and burst into flames if you are not careful, which will greatly reduce the smoking time and smoke density. The more compacted the shavings or chips are, the slower they will burn.

Once the smoker is producing lots of smoke, the bacon can be placed in the smoker on a rack or hung from a special bacon hanger or even a meat hook. Make sure you leave sufficient space around the food for the smoke to circulate. Check the temperature and monitor the smoker occasionally to make sure it remains lit.

I suggest you smoke the bacon until you get the colour you like and the smokiness you are after – you can achieve a lovely mahogany colour and more smoke than that found in commercial bacon. When you are satisfied with the smoked bacon, take it out of the smoker, wrap it in greaseproof paper or foil, and store it in the refrigerator for 24 hours to allow the flavour to permeate the meat fully. The bacon can be kept in the refrigerator for up to 2 weeks if kept wrapped up.

350g Maldon sea salt flakes

50g pink salt

150g maple sugar

150ml maple syrup

1 whole large pork belly,
about 5kg, ribs and skin on

If you live in the States or have spent any time there, the
marriage of maple syrup and bacon will be obvious and clear,
akin to pork and apple sauce in the UK. It just works.

MAPLE-CURED BACON Makes 5kg

Combine the salts, sugar and
maple syrup thoroughly and rub
this mixture all over the pork belly.

Place the belly in a non-reactive
container. The belly will need to
cure for 5 days – turn it daily and
pour away any liquid in the
container.

Remove the belly after 5 days,
lightly rinse the cure off and dry
thoroughly.

The bacon can now be cooked
and eaten, or cold-smoked if so
desired (*see* opposite).

1 teaspoon Dijon mustard

20ml cider vinegar

60ml olive oil

1 banana shallot,
finely chopped

8 cornichons, finely chopped

10g Lilliput capers

Maldon sea salt flakes and
freshly ground black pepper

400g sprouting broccoli

4 free-range eggs

400g bacon belly, roasted or
poached until falling apart

As this has the word 'salad' in the title, it's technically health food...

BACON, EGG & BROCCOLI SALAD Serves 4

To make the dressing, whisk together the
mustard, vinegar and olive oil. Add the chopped
shallot, cornichons and capers and season with
salt and pepper.

Bring a pan of salted water to the boil and cook
the broccoli until tender – about 3 minutes.
Drain and set aside.

Place the eggs in cold water and bring to the boil.
Time them for 3 minutes after they come to the boil,
then remove from the heat and allow to cool in the
water. Peel, cut in half and set aside.

Shred the bacon belly roughly and toss with the
broccoli and dressing. Serve the salad garnished
with the eggs.

For the bacon mincemeat

2 apples, peeled, cored and chopped small

120g bacon, cut into small lardons and cooked

all the reserved bacon fat from the pan

75g sultanas

25g dried cherries

1 tablespoon soft dark brown sugar

40ml Eagle Rare bourbon

zest of ¼ orange

zest of ¼ lemon

pinch of ground cloves

pinch of ground nutmeg

For the kouign amann pastry

7g fresh yeast

125ml water

250g plain flour

a pinch of fine sea salt

180g cold salted butter

For the bacon and cinnamon sugar

2 bacon rashers, cooked and dried in a low oven (100°C/gas mark ¼) overnight

100g caster sugar

1 teaspoon ground cinnamon

For the bourbon butterscotch

125g butter

125g soft light brown sugar

125ml double cream

125ml bourbon

icing sugar, to serve

BACON, BOURBON & BUTTERSCOTCH MINCE PIES Makes 13

BY NEIL RANKIN

These pies are everything your doctor told you not to eat. There really is no goodness in them at all, as all the room is taken up by bad. The bacon adds a saltiness and the bourbon adds acidity but in reality none of the ingredients should be there -- but bloody hell, they taste so good you may never want to eat anything else again.

Mix all the mincemeat ingredients together, put into a jar and keep for at least 24 hours – 3 days is better.

To make the pastry, the night before add the yeast to the water (warm from the tap) and mix with the flour and salt. Divide in half and leave overnight in the refrigerator in a oiled bowl, covered with clingfilm.

Blitz all the ingredients for the bacon and cinnamon sugar in a blender, then pass through a sieve and set aside.

To make the bourbon butterscotch, melt the butter with the sugar then mix in the cream and the bourbon. I recommend lots of bourbon.

When ready to make the pies, beat out and flatten the butter between two sheets of greaseproof paper.

Take the dough out of the refrigerator and quickly knock it back, then roll it out to a flat rectangle. Lay the butter in the middle, sprinkle with a quarter of the bacon and cinnamon sugar and fold it in like a book. Roll it out to the length of the board and fold again. If it's warm, cool it in the refrigerator for 10 minutes.

Take the pastry out of the refrigerator and roll it once again. Sprinkle with another quarter of the bacon and cinnamon sugar. Fold. And repeat this twice more. Refrigerate it again for 10 minutes.

Preheat the oven to 170°C/gas mark 3.

Roll the pastry into a large rectangle and sprinkle with the mincemeat – enough to cover, but not completely – you should still see a lot of pastry. Cut into strips 2.5cm wide and roll them up.

Butter the holes of a muffin tray, insert the coils of dough and bake for 15–20 minutes, or until golden brown. Transfer to a wire rack to cool, and baste with the bourbon butterscotch at least every 20 minutes while cooling, the last time when cold. Dust with icing sugar to serve.

1 sub roll

3 Country Fried Bacon rashers
(*see* page 227)

2 free-range eggs

25ml Smoked Baconnaise
(*see* page 340)

10ml Sriracha or other
hot sauce

1 large light green romaine
lettuce leaf

30g thinly sliced tomato

100g hot shredded smoked
bacon rib

25ml hot Barbecue Baste
(*see* page 337)

150g sliced smoked ham

A ridiculous 'dude food' take on the classic club sandwich, this really is as unhealthy as it looks -- so maybe have a defibrillator at the ready.

CLUB SUB Serves 1

Slice the roll in half and lightly grill each exposed side.

Fry the Country Fried Bacon and the eggs.

Spread the Smoked Baconnaise on the base of the roll, then spread the hot sauce evenly across the lid.

Top the bun base with the romaine leaf, followed by the sliced tomato and the hot shredded bacon. Lightly brush the shredded bacon with the hot Barbecue Baste, and put the sliced smoked ham on top. Top this with the fried eggs and Country Fried Bacon, add the lid, and serve immediately.

12 small potatoes, scrubbed and dried

6 streaky bacon rashers

20g unsalted butter, melted

a few dashes of Sriracha or other hot sauce

100g grated cheese

To garnish

a handful of pickled jalapeños, sliced

3 spring onions, sliced

Most often served in sports bars and at sporting events, potato skins have many claimants to the title of inventor, but in the UK it's safe to say these were introduced by T.G.I. Friday's in the '80s. Trashy snack food at its very best.

LOADED BACON POTATO SKINS Serves 4

Preheat the oven to 180°C/gas mark 4.

Bake the potatoes in the oven for 30 minutes, or until they can be pierced easily with a knife.

Sauté the bacon until crispy, then drain on kitchen paper and roughly chop.

Cut the potatoes in half and scoop the insides out, leaving a 1cm-thick layer of potato. Brush the insides with the butter and a dash of hot sauce, then fill with cheese, top with bacon and put back into the oven until golden. Scatter with pickled jalapenos and sliced spring onions to serve.

4 streaky bacon rashers

10g pork fat or lard

1 small onion, diced

1 red pepper, diced

2 garlic cloves, minced

a few fresh thyme leaves

250g lima (butter) beans

250g sweetcorn

100ml Master Pork Broth (*see* page 335)

100ml double cream

Maldon sea salt flakes

Sriracha or other hot sauce, to taste

My first introduction to the name 'succotash' was when the words 'sufferin' succotash' were used by Sylvester the Cat and Daffy Duck as a cuss in lieu of 'suffering saviour' in the cartoons of my childhood. Originally a Native American dish, succotash is often served at Thanksgiving in the States, and due to its cheap ingredients, variations proved popular sustenance during the Great Depression of the 1930s.

BACON SUCCOTASH Serves 4

Heat a large nonstick pan over a medium heat and cook the bacon in the pork fat until crisp – about 5 minutes. Leaving the drippings in the pan, use tongs to transfer the bacon to a plate lined with kitchen paper.

Add the onion, red pepper, garlic and thyme leaves to the pan and cook, stirring, until softened, then stir in the beans, sweetcorn, pork broth, cream and salt. Bring to a simmer, then reduce the heat to medium-low and cook for 5 minutes.

Adjust the seasoning with salt and hot sauce, then crumble the bacon and sprinkle it on top.

1 Earl Grey tea bag

50ml brandy

Maldon sea salt flakes and
freshly ground black pepper

5ml Sriracha, or other
hot sauce

6 Agen prunes, pitted

6 rock oysters, shucked

18 proper dry-cured streaky
bacon rashers

6 good chipolata sausages
(don't be tempted to use
inferior sausages)

oil, for frying

Pigs on horseback are really pigs in blankets, but I like the idea
that the three might ride together. Another great ingredient that
suits this treatment is scallops, but the truth is you can improve
anything by wrapping it in bacon.

DEVILS, ANGELS & PIGS ON HORSEBACK Makes 18

Make a cup of black tea with the teabag and allow to cool. Add the brandy, a pinch of sea salt, the hot sauce and the prunes and allow to steep for a few hours.

Drain the oysters on kitchen paper, then season with black pepper and wrap each one in a slice of streaky bacon. Wrap the sausages the same way and then the soaked prunes.

Heat a little oil in a frying pan and fry the wrapped chipolatas or 'pigs' seam side down, turning to colour them all over, then set aside in a warm place. Repeat this process with the wrapped prunes or 'devils', and

finally with the oysters or 'angels' on horseback; these should be just cooked when you eat them, hence leaving them until last.

Serve all three as a canapé, a starter or a savoury at the end of the meal in the manner of an Old English menu.

1 free-range egg, beaten

250ml buttermilk

10 smoked streaky bacon rashers

120g plain flour

a pinch of dried oregano

a pinch of dried sage

a pinch of dried basil

a pinch dried marjoram

a pinch of chilli powder

a pinch of freshly ground black pepper

¼ teaspoon smoked paprika

¼ teaspoon dried garlic

¼ teaspoon dried onion

a pinch of salt

vegetable oil, for frying

For the sausage & onion gravy

300g Basic Pork Sausage mix (*see* page 146), broken into small chunks

300g onions, sliced

10g butter

200ml cider

500ml Master Pork Broth (*see* page 335)

100ml double cream

There's no small amount of 'country' or 'southern' fried in this book, mostly because I'm an avid consumer of anything fried, particularly this way. I recommend this stuff for breakfast any day of the week, as here with sausage gravy, but also with pancakes and maple syrup.

COUNTRY FRIED BACON WITH SAUSAGE & ONION GRAVY Serves 4

First make the gravy: put the onions into a large saucepan and sweat in the butter until caramelized and golden in colour – about 20 minutes. Add half the cider and continue to sweat until the onions start to darken a little more, then add the remaining cider and reduce down.

Add the sausagemeat to the pan and continue sweating down. Add the pork broth and continue to cook until reduced by half. Add the double cream and cook at a bare simmer for 10 minutes. Reserve until needed.

Combine the egg and buttermilk in a large bowl. Soak the bacon in this mixture.

Blend the flour with all the herbs and spices and flavourings to a fine sandy mixture. Remove the bacon from the buttermilk and roll in the seasoned flour until completely covered.

Heat the oil to 200°C in a deep-fat fryer or a large heavy-based saucepan.

Use tongs to carefully lower 5 pieces of the bacon into the hot oil, then fry for 5 minutes until golden brown and thoroughly cooked. Transfer the bacon to a plate lined with kitchen paper.

Repeat with the remaining 5 pieces of bacon. Serve with the gravy on the side for dipping.

100g cornmeal or polenta

Maldon sea salt flakes and freshly ground black pepper

2 dozen large oysters, freshly shucked

100g butter

12 smoked streaky bacon rashers

4 small French sticks

100g garlic butter, softened

100ml mayonnaise

10ml cider vinegar

Sriracha or other hot sauce, to taste

Green Sauce (see page 341)

In 1764 Elizabeth Moxon, in her book *English Housewifery*, described oyster loaves thus:

'To make OYSTER LOAVES.
Take half a dozen French loaves, rasp them and make a hole at the top, take out all the crumbs and fry them in butter till they be crisp; when your oysters are stewed, put them into your loaves, cover them up before the fire to keep hot whilst you want them; so serve them up.
They are proper either for a side-dish or mid-dish.
You may make cockle loaves or mushroom-loaves the same way.'

Over a hundred years later versions started appearing in Louisiana, and this is a homage to those.

LOUISIANA BACON & OYSTER LOAVES Makes 4 loaves

Preheat the oven to 200°C/gas mark 6.

Season the cornmeal with salt and pepper and toss the oysters in it to coat.

Heat the butter and gently fry the bacon until crisp, taking care not to let the butter burn. Remove the bacon and drain on kitchen paper, then chop roughly and set aside.

Add the cornmeal-coated oysters to the pan and fry in the bacon-flavoured butter until just crispy. Remove, drain and reserve.

Cut the tops off across the French sticks horizontally and hollow them out. Brush the insides with the garlic butter and fill with the fried oysters and bacon. Put the tops on the loaves and bake in the oven for 8 minutes.

Meanwhile, mix together the mayonnaise, cider vinegar and hot sauce.

Remove the baked loaves from the oven and serve with the Green Sauce and spicy mayonnaise.

200g streaky bacon

4 large free-range eggs

250ml milk

150g plain flour

zest of 1 lemon

55g butter

To serve

icing sugar, for dusting

lingonberry preserve

whipped cream

This light and luscious bacon pancake is a billowy cloud of goodness that looks much like the English Yorkshire pudding. It's served with lingonberry preserve, called cowberries in the UK or mountain cranberries in the US. In Scandinavia, where this dish hales from, lingonberries are also served with blood pudding, a most excellent idea.

FLASKPANNKAKA Serves 4–5

Preheat the oven to 200°C/gas mark 6.

Cut the bacon into small cubes and cook in a large skillet until crisp, then drain on kitchen paper.

In a food processor, combine the eggs, milk, flour and lemon zest and process until blended.

Put the butter into a low-rimmed ovenproof frying pan and place in the oven until the butter melts. Remove the pan from the oven and tilt until the butter evenly covers the bottom. Pour the batter into the pan and sprinkle the bacon evenly over it. Return the pan to the oven and bake until golden and fluffy – about 20 minutes.

Serve at once, dusted with icing sugar and with preserves and whipped cream alongside.

200g smoked bacon rashers

50g smoked sea salt

20g light brown muscovado sugar

½ teaspoon fennel seeds

¼ teaspoon black peppercorns

Great with chips, or just as a seasoning where the mighty talents of bacon are needed!

SMOKED BACON SALT   Makes about 250g

Preheat the oven to 180°C/gas mark 4.

Take 2 heavy metal trays and 2 sheets of greaseproof paper. Sandwich the bacon between the greaseproof sheets and the 2 heavy metal trays. Bake in the oven for 30 minutes, or until brown and crispy.

Remove from the oven and lay the bacon on kitchen paper to cool and dry out.

In a food processor or blender, pulse-blend the dry bacon to a fine powder with the remaining ingredients. Sprinkle over a clean tray and leave to dry further. When completely dry, blend once more and keep in airtight jars to use as needed.

free-range bantam eggs

Smoked Bacon Salt
(see above)

On gastro-pub bars you occasionally see boiled eggs served with celery salt, a lovely bar snack based on a classic gull's egg preparation. Bantams or 'banties' are miniature hens known for their feisty nature. I've teamed their eggs, lightly boiled, with smoked bacon salt.

BANTAM EGGS WITH SMOKED BACON SALT

Place your bantam eggs in cold water straight from the tap and bring to the boil. Boil for 2 minutes, then turn off the heat and allow to cool in the water.

When cool, peel the eggs and dip into the bacon salt before eating.

1kg chipping potatoes, peeled, rinsed and dried

1 quantity Smoked Bacon Salt (*see* page 233)

100ml mayonnaise

20g chipotle chillies en adobo, from a jar

vegetable oil, for frying

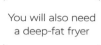

You will also need a deep-fat fryer

These fries are what we call triple-cooked in restaurants, and the trick here is to roughen the edges of the fries as much as possible without breaking them. This process is called 'chuffing' in the kitchen, but when I Googled the word to check, it came up with 'used for emphasis or as a mild expletive', as in 'Chuffing hell!'

FRIES WITH SMOKED BACON SALT & CHIPOTLE MAYONNAISE Serves 4

Preheat the oven to 180°C/gas mark 4.

Cut the potatoes into chips and place in a large pan of salted cold water. Bring to a simmer and cook until almost tender – about 10 minutes. Remove the chips from the water and drain thoroughly, then give them a good shake to roughen the edges. Allow to air-dry as they cool.

Line a baking tray with baking paper, then lay each slice of bacon on the tray and bake for 15–20 minutes until crisp and dry.

Transfer the bacon to a plate lined with kitchen paper and allow to cool. Crumble, then put into a food processor with the salt and sugar and pulse-blend to a fine consistency.

Turn out on to a plate lined with fresh kitchen paper and allow to air-dry in a low oven at 120°C/gas mark ½ for an hour or so, then blend once more to a fine salt-like crumb.

In a food processor or blender, blend the mayonnaise with the chipotle in adobo until smooth, and set aside.

Heat the oil to 140°C in a deep-fat fryer and blanch the chips until light golden – about 3 minutes. Remove from the fryer and air-dry until cool. Increase the temperature of the oil to 180°C and fry the chips once more, until golden brown. Transfer to a plate lined with kitchen paper.

Put the fries, in batches, in paper bags with portions of the smoked bacon salt and shake to coat. Serve with the chipotle mayonnaise on the side.

200g bacon lardons
100g popcorn kernels
200g pecan nut halves
400g caster sugar

50ml groundnut oil
100g liquid glucose
100ml water
20g Maldon sea salt flakes

I had an outstanding caramel popcorn at April Bloomfield's The Breslin in New York, and this is my riff on it. You might think the addition of bacon is superfluous, but it proves my long-held belief that almost everything can be improved by bacon...

CANDIED BACON PECAN POPCORN Serves 4

Preheat the oven to 160°C/gas mark 3.

Fry the bacon lardons over a medium heat until crisp, then set aside.

Pop the popcorn according to the packet instructions, then place on a large lipped baking tray. Add the pecans and bacon lardons.

Put the sugar, groundnut oil, glucose and water into a saucepan and bring to the boil. Continue to cook until the mixture turns a honey colour, then add the salt.

Pour the hot caramel over the popcorn mixture and toss to coat.

Bake for 5 minutes, then toss again and turn out on to a sheet of greaseproof paper. Using a spoon, move the popcorn around as it cools, to prevent it sticking together. When cool, serve.

250g Rough Puff Pastry (*see* page 149)

1 free-range egg, separated, plus 1 extra egg yolk

100g streaky bacon, cut into lardons

150ml double cream

150ml milk

freshly grated nutmeg

2 eggs

Maldon sea salt flakes and freshly ground black pepper

You will also need a 20cm diameter 3cm deep tin

Quiche Lorraine is an open-topped egg and bacon pie from the Lorraine region of France. We've all seen cold, flaccid versions in the refrigerator aisle at our local supermarket, but eaten freshly baked and warm it is a marvellous thing indeed.

QUICHE LORRAINE Serves 4–6

Preheat the oven to 180°C/gas mark 4 and put a baking tray in to warm.

Grease a 20cm diameter 3cm deep tin and line it with the pastry, leaving an extra few centimetres overhanging to minimize shrinkage. Line with a cartouche (a circle of greaseproof paper) and fill with baking beans or rice. Place on the warmed baking tray and blind-bake in the oven for 30 minutes, then remove the foil and beans and patch up any holes with the extra pastry if necessary. Bake for a further 10 minutes, then brush the base with egg white and put back into the oven for 5 minutes.

Fry the bacon in a nonstick frying pan for 4 minutes, or until cooked through, but not crisp. Drain and spread half over the hot pastry base.

Put the cream, milk, nutmeg, whole eggs and the extra 2 egg yolks into a large bowl, season with salt and pepper and beat together slowly until combined and frothy. Pour over the pastry base, then sprinkle over the rest of the bacon.

Bake for 25 minutes – it's done when it's slightly puffed but still a bit wobbly. Allow to rest for 20 minutes, then carefully trim the overhanging pastry to neaten before serving.

VARIATION

50g of grated Comté cheese could be added to the quiche – not classic, but tasty.

4 heads of corn, husks and silk removed

200ml water

200ml double cream

1 teaspoon sugar

Maldon sea salt flakes and freshly ground black pepper

75g bacon lardons

2 teaspoons baking powder

220g yellow cornmeal

180g rendered bacon fat

2 eggs, gently beaten

220ml buttermilk

1 onion, grated

75g good Cheddar cheese, grated

You will also need a 23cm diameter cake tin

Cornbread is a cornerstone of Southern US cookery and can be traced back to the European settlers, who were taught to cook with corn by the Native Americans. Be warned, this cornbread contains a big old holy trinity hit of salt, sugar and fat and is dangerously addictive, so go easy on it.

CHEESE & BACON CORNBREAD Serves 8

First remove the kernels from the corn: cut off the tip of each cob and stand it in a wide shallow bowl. With a sharp knife, slice downward to remove the kernels, then, with the edge of a soup spoon, scrape downwards to remove the pulp.

In a medium saucepan, heat the corn kernels, pulp and the water. Bring to the boil, then reduce to a simmer, cover the pan and cook until the corn is tender – about 10–15 minutes. Add the cream and sugar, then bring to a gentle boil to reduce and thicken, uncovered – about 8 minutes. Season with salt and pepper and set aside.

Meanwhile, fry the bacon lardons until crisp, then set aside.

Preheat the oven to 170°C/gas mark 3½ and grease the cake tin.

Mix the baking powder, cornmeal and 1 teaspoon of salt in a large bowl and set aside. In another bowl, mix together the bacon fat, eggs, buttermilk and creamed corn. Mix the grated onion into the wet ingredients, then stir the dry ingredients into the wet ingredients.

Pour half the batter into the cake tin and sprinkle over half the bacon lardons and half the Cheddar. Pour in the remaining batter and top with the rest of the bacon and cheese.

Bake in the oven for 45 minutes, then remove from the oven – a knife inserted into the centre should come out clean. Allow to cool for 10 minutes, then cut into wedges and serve warm (see photo overleaf).

300g polenta

300g plain flour

100g light brown sugar

7g baking powder

20g Maldon sea salt flakes

200g whole free-range eggs (about 4 large eggs)

480ml milk

30g butter, melted and cooled

100g good-quality pork lard

For the honey butter

50ml clear honey

50g butter, melted

I was given this recipe by Brad McDonald from The Lockhart restaurant in London after an excellent lunch starring, for me at least, this cornbread. I've taken a small liberty with the name, but the recipe remains faithful. Do try it served hot, straight from the oven.

LARDY CORNBREAD WITH HONEY BUTTER Serves 6

Preheat the oven to 180°C/gas mark 4.

Mix all the dry ingredients together. In a separate bowl, mix together the eggs, milk and melted butter. Combine the 2 mixtures.

Heat a cast iron skillet and pour in the pork lard to a shallow depth. Add the cornbread mixture. Let it sizzle and start to cook at the sides, then put into the oven for 20 minutes, or until a skewer comes out clean when inserted into the cornbread.

Remove from the oven, turn over and moisten with honey butter, made by combining the honey and butter.

Left above: Cheese & Bacon Cornbread (*see* page 239)
Left below: Lardy Cornbread with Honey Butter

1kg pork shoulder, diced

250g Lardo, diced
(*see* page 247)

30g Maldon sea salt flakes

3g curing salt, such as
Instacure No. 2 or Prague
Powder No. 2

30g dried milk powder

15g dextrose

3g black peppercorns, crushed

3g fennel seeds, crushed

3g paprika

3g crushed garlic

10g acidophilus (Bactoferm)

30ml boiled water

70ml dry red wine

You will also need a mincer with a sausage stuffer attachment, large sausage casing (soaked and rinsed), and some butcher's string

Salami is a cured, fermented and air-dried sausage made from a variety of meats, including pork. Historically, salami was popular in southern Europe because it can be stored at room temperature for periods of up to a month once cut, supplementing an inconsistent supply of fresh meat. Making your own is not too difficult, and the results are softer and altogether better than that bought from a shop. Just remember that cleanliness is absolutely paramount.

SALAMI Makes 1kg

Place the meats and your coarse plate mincer attachments in the freezer for a couple of hours to chill to almost frozen.

Remove the meats from the freezer and mix together with the salt and Instacure No. 2. Remove the mincer attachments from the freezer and set up. Fit the coarse plate into your mincer and mince the meat into a chilled bowl.

Mix together all the dry ingredients.

Dissolve the acidophilus in the cooled boiled water and add to the meat with the dry ingredients and red wine. Mix well, preferably with a cold spoon or in a free-standing food mixer.

Stuff the mixture into your sausage casings (*see* page 145), tying both ends with butcher's string. Using a sterile needle, stab the sausage to remove any air pockets and to help drying.

Keep at 25°C for 12 hours to start the beneficial bacteria producing lactic acid, then hang in a cool place at around 15°C, with 60 per cent humidity, for 3–4 weeks to dry. The sausage should lose a third of its weight over this time. After drying it can be refrigerated for up to 6 weeks.

5 garlic cloves, crushed

15g pink salt

50g Maldon sea salt flakes

25g light brown muscovado sugar

50g black peppercorns, crushed

1 teaspoon fresh thyme leaves

1 teaspoon fresh rosemary leaves

1 bay leaf, chopped

2.5kg pork belly, skin removed

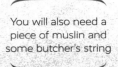

You will also need a piece of muslin and some butcher's string

An Italian bacon made from salt-cured pork belly, there are two types of pancetta, *arrotolata* -- rolled -- and *stesa* -- flat. This is a rolled version and can be sliced like ham for frying or diced for use in Italian dishes.

PANCETTA Makes 2.5kg

Combine all the ingredients except the pork belly in a bowl, keeping half the crushed black peppercorns to one side. Rub this mixture all over the pork belly, taking care to cover every part.

Place the pork belly on a plastic tray lined with clingfilm, cover with clingfilm and place another plastic tray on top. Refrigerate for 1 week, turning the 2 trays over every day.

After 7 days the belly should be firm to the touch – if not, return it to the refrigerator for another day or so.

When firm, remove from the refrigerator and wash under cold running water. Dry thoroughly and rub the remaining crushed black pepper all over the meat.

Lay the belly on a clean table and roll it lengthways very, very tightly indeed, then wrap it in muslin and tie it tightly with butcher's string. Skewer a hole through one end of the rolled pork and thread with butcher's string, then hang at 10°C, between 40–60 per cent humidity, for 2 weeks.

Once dried, the pancetta can be unwrapped, cut into 500g portions, then wrapped in clingfilm and refrigerated for up to 6 weeks.

400g watermelon

100ml cider vinegar

herb stalks, from the garnish herbs (see 'For the garnish')

2 shallots, sliced

20ml honey

Maldon sea salt flakes and freshly ground black pepper

100ml water

30ml lime juice

400g Rillons (*see* page 122)

flour, for dusting

For the garnish

lime wedges

3 spring onions, sliced

a handful of fresh parsley, mint and coriander

Ah, the many uses of rillons – here paired with juicy watermelon to make a lovely summer salad. Do take the time to pickle the rind, as it helps offset the rich, fatty qualities of the meat.

CRISPY RILLON & PICKLED WATERMELON SALAD Serves 4

To make the salad, cut the watermelon flesh into 2.5cm dice, discarding the seeds and reserving the rind. Refrigerate the flesh until ready to use. With a sharp knife, remove the outer green skin of the rind, reserving the white part. Dice the white rind into 1cm cubes and transfer to a heatproof bowl.

In a saucepan over a medium-high heat, combine the cider vinegar, herb stalks, shallots, honey, 1 teaspoon salt and the water, then bring to the boil. Strain the liquid over the white watermelon rind and allow to cool, then chill for at least 1 hour. Add the lime juice and refrigerate until needed.

Lightly dust the Rillons with flour, shaking off the excess. Working in batches, fry in their own fat until dark golden brown and crispy – about 4 minutes. Transfer to a plate lined with kitchen paper and season with salt and pepper if necessary.

In a mixing bowl, toss the watermelon flesh with just enough of the pickling liquid to coat, then divide between 4 serving plates. Add a few cubes of pickled rind to each plate and top with the pork. Garnish with a lime wedge, spring onions and herb leaves and drizzle with extra pickling liquor.

1kg pigs' jowl

100g Maldon sea salt flakes

100g interesting sugar
(I love maple sugar, jaggery or
failing these, muscovado)

2 garlic cloves, crushed

1 teaspoon black peppercorns,
crushed

1 large sprig of fresh thyme

You will also need
a piece of muslin and
some butcher's string

Akin to jowl bacon in America, guanciale is its Italian originator. Its name is a derivative of *guancia*, meaning 'cheek'. Bacon is almost unsurpassed in its ability to make me happy, but then there is this ... über bacon.

GUANCIALE Makes 1kg

Wash and dry the pork jowl thoroughly and remove any veins or glands.

Combine the salt, sugar, garlic, peppercorns and thyme leaves. Place the jowl on a plastic tray and rub thoroughly with the salt/sugar mixture. Make sure there is plenty of this mix underneath and over the jowls, then cover with clingfilm and refrigerate for up to a week.

Turn the jowls every day, spreading the cure each time. When the jowls are firm, which could take 5 days, or if from large animals as long as 7 days, remove them and wash and dry thoroughly.

Wrap in a single layer of muslin and hang at 10°C with 40–60 per cent humidity for 2 weeks, then unwrap, cover with clingfilm and refrigerate for up to 6 weeks. To use, slice and fry like bacon.

250g Maldon sea salt flakes

25g pink salt

50g black peppercorns

5 bay leaves

1 bunch of fresh thyme, chopped

1 bunch of fresh rosemary, chopped

125g granulated sugar

1.5kg free-range pork back fat, skin removed

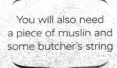

You will also need a piece of muslin and some butcher's string

I discovered lardo late in life, on a trip to meet Dario Cecchini, the butcher of Panzano in Italy. One of the best things about my chosen métier is the people I meet, and Dario is a shining example. Driven and passionate, he fed me lardo and his trademark burro del Chianti, a memorable experience. Lardo can only be made from free-range beauties with their many layers of deep creamy fat, not intensively reared pigs.

LARDO Makes about 1.2kg

Mix the salts, peppercorns and herbs with the sugar and rub the pork back fat with this mixture.

Layer half the remaining seasoning mix on a large plastic tray and lay the pork back fat on top, then layer the rest of the seasoning mix on top of the fat. Cover with clingfilm, then wrap in foil.

Place in a refrigerator for 2 weeks with a large heavy weight on top, the heavier the better. The pork fat needs to be turned and rubbed with the seasoning daily, redistributing the seasoning mix every time.

After 10 days, remove the pork and rinse under cold water. Dry thoroughly and wrap in muslin, skewering a hole in one corner. Thread the hole with butcher's string and hang at 10°C, somewhere between 40–60 per cent humidity, for 2 weeks before using. Refrigerate for up to 6 weeks.

Swedish crispbreads
(Peter's Yard, for preference)

thinly sliced Lardo
(*see* page 247)

salted (Cantabrian, for
preference) anchovy fillets

thinly sliced shallot rings

Hardly a recipe at all, but delicious nonetheless. I could eat a dozen of these washed down with pre-dinner drinks, no bother.

LARDO, ANCHOVY & SHALLOT CRISPBREADS
Makes as many as you like

Lay thin slices of lardo on the crispbreads,
with anchovies and shallot rings on top. Enjoy.

5kg frozen pork shoulder, diced

50g freshly ground black pepper

100ml cider vinegar

1 tablespoon cloves

3 heads of garlic, peeled and crushed

300g ground red pepper flakes

100g Maldon sea salt flakes

10g curing salt, such as Instacure No. 2 or Prague powder No. 2

60g hot smoked Spanish paprika

You will also need sausage casing, a mincer with a sausage stuffer attachment, ice cubes and some butcher's string

Like all cured meat recipes, but perhaps even more so, cured sausages rely on the quality of the meat, on cleanliness, the environment you hang it in and a bit of trial and error.

CURED CHORIZO Makes 5kg

Wash the sausage casing in cold water and chill the pork shoulder and your mincing attachments separately.

Mince the frozen pork shoulder through a 9mm plate on your mincer into a large bowl over ice, then wash the attachments and put them into the refrigerator along with a 6mm plate.

Add all the other ingredients a little at a time, kneading the meat as if you were making bread. Test the mixture by frying a small portion and tasting it. Adjust the seasoning if necessary

Set up the mincer again with the re-chilled attachments and the 6mm plate, then attach the sausage casing and start to fill with the meat (see page 145), making sure to avoid air pockets. Leave about 5cm of unfilled casing on each side to tie the openings closed. Tie each end with butcher's string and prick each sausage a few times.

Hang the chorizos to dry in a very cool, dry place below 10°C, or in a walk-in refrigerator, for 2 weeks, or until they harden.

If a white coat begins to form on the casings, moisten a piece of kitchen paper with vegetable oil and rub them to remove it. After you have rubbed them with oil, dry them with another piece of kitchen paper. They are ready to eat when they are solid all the way through and firm to the touch. Keep refrigerated for up to 6 weeks.

250ml Master Pork Broth
(*see page 335*)

1 teaspoon ground coriander

1 teaspoon freshly ground
black pepper

1 teaspoon grated nutmeg

10g curing salt, such as
Instacure No. 1 or Prague
powder No. 1

250ml iced water

200g pork back fat

4.5kg lean pork shoulder

75g Maldon sea salt flakes

125g skimmed milk powder

You will also need
a mincer with 10mm
and 6mm plates and
a sausage stuffer
attachment, 3m beef
runners, a smoker or
charcoal barbecue
and a meat
thermometer

Mortadella hails from Bologna in Italy, and among the many pork sausage products made in this region it is the most celebrated. Mortadella has been made for at least 500 years, and may even have origins in Roman times, when it was flavoured with myrtle berries and prepared using a mortar and pestle. The method below is more akin to that used to make hot dogs.

MORTADELLA Makes 5kg

In a saucepan, bring the pork broth to a gentle simmer and add the spices. Continue to simmer for a further 5 minutes, then set aside until completely cooled. Meanwhile, chill all your mincer attachments.

Add the Instacure No. 1 to the iced water, stirring to ensure it has dissolved, and set aside. Cut the pork back fat into 1cm dice and place in the refrigerator.

Mince the pork meat through a 10mm plate on your mincer into a large bowl. Sprinkle the salt and milk powder over the meat and massage gently through. Add the cooled broth, then the iced water. Blend thoroughly to ensure that all the ingredients have been evenly distributed, then mince the whole mixture again through a chilled 6mm plate.

Evenly distribute the diced fat over the sausagemeat and mix carefully, making sure the fat doesn't get too broken up and squashed. When mixing the meat and fat, ensure that the meat temperature is kept very low to avoid the fat softening. Once mixed, place in a plastic container, cover and chill for 6 hours.

Soak the beef runners in cold water for 1 hour, then rinse them well inside and out. Thread on to the sausage stuffer attachment, then put it on to a plate and keep in the refrigerator.

Set up and sanitize the sausage cannon. Fill the bowl of the cannon with the forcemeat, being careful not to leave any air pockets in the mixture, as this will create air pockets in the sausage. Attach the nozzle to the end of the sausage cannon.

Remove the mixture from the fridge. Start to pump the mixture out of the end of the nozzle before you tie off the end to avoid air pockets forming. Slowly start to crank the cannon and fill the sausage.

Guide the casing out of the cannon as it fills, using your whole hand, on to a clear sterilized work surface. Once it has reached the desired length, stop and tie off the end. Repeat the process until you've used up the mixture.

Place the sausage in the smoker once the temperature has reached 50°C. Smoke it heavily, raising the temperature gradually to about 75°C, and hold until the internal temperature of the mortadella reaches about 65°C, measured with a meat thermometer – this will take about 3 hours. Remove from the smoker and refrigerate overnight before using. Slice as required and use within 6 weeks.

4 slices of white bread, crusts removed, cut into 1cm cubes

250ml milk

120g Mortadella, chopped (*see* page 250)

120g Air-cured Ham (*see* page 206) or prosciutto, chopped

120g minced pork

120g Parmesan cheese, grated, plus extra to serve

2 large free-range eggs, beaten

1 teaspoon freshly grated nutmeg

Maldon sea salt flakes and freshly ground black pepper

50ml extra virgin olive oil

1 onion, halved

1 carrot, halved

1 chilli, halved

5 garlic cloves, very thinly sliced

1kg canned tomatoes

1 faggot of herbs, made with thyme, rosemary, bay and oregano

pasta, to serve

These are from Italy by way of Little Italy, by which I mean that while the ingredients might be Italian, these are more likely American. There's a great scene in *The Godfather* where Clemenza teaches Michael to make meatballs with spaghetti sauce... 'Come over here, kid, learn something. You never know, you might have to cook for twenty guys someday. You see, you start out with a little bit of oil. Then you fry some garlic. Then you throw in some tomatoes, tomato paste, you fry it; you make sure it doesn't stick. You get it to a boil, you shove in your sausage and your meatballs, huh? And a little bit of wine. And a little bit of sugar, and that's my trick.'

MORTADELLA & PROSCIUTTO MEATBALLS Serves 4

In a small bowl, combine the bread and milk and leave to stand for 10 minutes. Drain, discarding any milk that hasn't been absorbed by the bread.

In a food processor, combine the mortadella and prosciutto and pulse until the meat is coarsely ground. Transfer to a large mixing bowl and combine with the minced pork, Parmesan, eggs and bread. Add the nutmeg and season well with salt and pepper. Mix gently by hand until just combined, then let the mixture rest in the refrigerator for 1 hour. Form into 12 golfball-sized meatballs and return them to the refrigerator.

Preheat the oven to 180°C/gas mark 4. Heat half the olive oil in a large lidded flameproof casserole.

Add the onion, carrot, chilli and garlic and fry until the garlic is translucent – about 5 minutes. Add the canned tomatoes and the faggot of herbs, cover with the lid and place in the oven for 30 minutes.

In a large, nonstick skillet, heat the rest of the oil over a medium-high heat. Add the meatballs and fry, turning occasionally, until browned on all sides – about 10 minutes. Remove the tomato sauce from the oven, add the meatballs, and return the casserole to the oven, uncovered, until the meatballs are cooked through – about 20 minutes.

Remove from the oven, discard the onion, carrot and herbs, and serve with pasta and grated Parmesan.

SLAUGHTER

Dear reader, due to the content of this chapter, vegetarians, the very young and the squeamish should look away. This is an explanation of the slaughter process; read no further if you don't want to know. There will be blood.

Most countries have adopted the principle of a two-stage process for the non-ritual slaughter of animals. This is to ensure a rapid death with minimal suffering. The first stage of the process, usually called stunning, renders the animal unconscious, but not dead. In the second stage, the animal is killed. Pigs are slaughtered and consumed at every stage of life, as piglets from one to three months old, as fattening pigs intended for pork and bacon at four to twelve months old, or as older pigs, such as sows and boars.

When the time finally comes to slaughter the animals, there are two critical factors that must inform the process. First and foremost, we owe it to our livestock to make this process as quick, painless and humane as possible – in today's meat production, ethics should be paramount.

It is in nobody's interest to have a stressed animal at slaughter. The acclaimed professor of animal science Dr Temple Grandin has designed slaughterhouses specifically with the animals' sensibilities in mind: there are only natural curves, natural light and matt surfaces, and classical music plays throughout the process. The refrigeration is also exceptional. The carcasses are not simply taken to a giant walk-in fridge after slaughter for rapid chilling (which can create 'cold shortening' whereby the muscles contract, producing dry and tough meat). Instead, they are taken through a gradual process in which carcasses take 24 hours to chill fully. The post-slaughter chill is, from a culinary perspective, the most important moment in the whole process. It is unlikely that you will be able to know these things when buying from your butcher, but do look for the signs of stress in the meat, and avoid it when you find them.

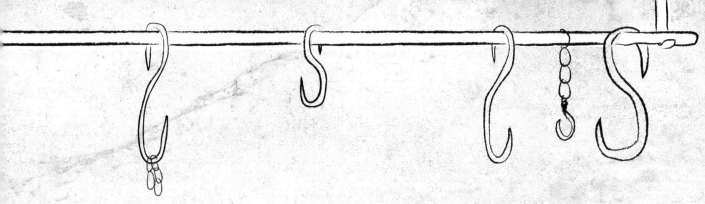

TRADITIONAL SLAUGHTER

Once upon a time, communal pig killing was a time for celebration, and a great social occasion in many rural areas. Slaughter traditionally took place in the autumn and early winter, and the timing had several practical considerations. It could start as soon as it got cold, to help preserve the relatively large quantities of meat during the butchering.

Traditionally, slaughter was the job of the butcher – a trade passed from father to son. It required numerous preparations, not to mention pots and sharp knives, troughs, large quantities of boiling water, and large wooden barrels for storing meat, and it could last for as long as three days. Because people were stocking up on supplies before winter, it became customary to slaughter more than one pig, which increased the amount of time necessary for the meat to be processed – and the number of helpers required. Very little mechanization was used, with meat being cut manually. Any grinding of meat was done with relatively small, manually operated meat-grinding machines.

The standard of hygiene recommended by veterinarians included rigorous requirements for the people, tools and space used in the process. Everyone involved in the slaughter and butchering had to be healthy and wearing a hat, apron and boots, and their hands had to be clean. The tools (knives, axes, saws and so on) were sharpened, scoured and disinfected before use, and were kept in a hygienic place throughout the process, preferably in a toolbox on the butcher's belt. The location of the killing had to be a clean concrete surface with a drainage canal, so the space could be easily washed. The trough had to have a zinc surface, which was easy to scrub and disinfect.

SMALL-SCALE SLAUGHTER TODAY

Today, almost anyone so inclined can afford to slaughter. In most countries, the law requires a registered slaughterer or veterinarian to be present, but it is otherwise similar to the long-standing traditional practice. The process can be physically demanding, and pig slaughter is not a process to be attempted alone, which is one of the main reasons it is traditionally a communal event. It will take all day – so it makes sense for more than one pig to be slaughtered at a time. Certain equipment and scrupulous hygiene are, of course, required. Meat from an animal slaughtered privately cannot be sold; it is for personal use only. The key stages are described here, but it is essential that professionals are involved in the actual process.

The day before

Animals for slaughter must be in top condition. They should be separated from the rest of the herd in a gentle, calm manner and moved gently to a quiet and familiar environment. Stressing and bruising of the animals must be avoided at all costs. It is important that they are comfortable and have adequate bedding to encourage urination, which helps clear the digestive system. Feed is withheld and plenty of water provided. This lowers the risk of contamination as there is less waste in the entrails, and it reduces the weight of the animal, making it easier to work afterwards. Hydrated animals are also easier to eviscerate and clean.

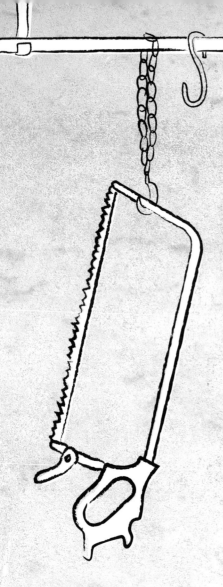

On the day

The first step is preparing a scalding barrel and heating enough water to cover the pig to around 63°C (145°F), ready for the slaughtered animal.

It is critical that the pig is unconscious before slaughter, so the next step is to stun the animal. Known as percussive stunning, this is usually done with a bolt to the head using a captive bolt pistol aimed just between and behind the eyes and to the front of the ears, on what is best described as the animal's forehead, producing immediate unconsciousness by brain trauma. Dr Temple Grandin's list of conditions to confirm the animal is properly stunned is the gold standard for humane practice.

Once it has been absolutely confirmed that the pig is unconscious and is insensible, it is 'stuck', or stabbed through the main arteries in order to bleed out as quickly as possible. Sticking a pig is no easy task, and certainly not for anyone of less than stoic constitution. The aim is to make as small an incision as possible while allowing for the blood to exit after severing blood vessels. If done properly, blood will immediately start gushing from the animal, so a large bowl is positioned ready to catch it, and in which the warm blood is continually stirred to prevent coagulation. The animal will kick as it bleeds out – a normal reflex action. When the pig stops moving, the last of the blood is pumped out by moving the front leg while placing pressure on the chest. I did say there would be blood...

The next stage is the scalding and scraping of the carcass. The pig is hung upside down and placed headfirst into the scalding barrel, where it is rotated and occasionally removed from the water so that the hairs can be checked. When these pull easily from the flanks behind the shoulders, the pig is removed and turned the other way up in the scalding water. While the rear of the pig is scalding, the front half is thoroughly scraped, and the front toenails and claws are removed. Then the pig is taken from the water so that the same can be done to the rear parts. Finally, a blowtorch is used to singe any remaining hairs and any areas that resisted scraping.

Once the carcass is clean, it is broken down or 'eviscerated'. The skin of the belly is severed from the rectum to the snout, then the abdomen is split all the way to the sternum. The bung (entrails) is very carefully removed to prevent breakage of the bladder, digestive tract or lower intestines, which would lead to contamination of the flesh. Next, the viscera (stomach, upper intestines, spleen and liver) are pulled out. The caul fat is separated from around the stomach, and the liver, spleen and bile sac are removed with great care. The sternum is then split and the pluck (heart and lungs) removed.

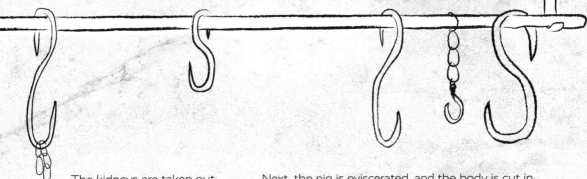

The kidneys are taken out next, or are sometimes left attached to the carcass, according to the butcher's preference. All the removed offal is rinsed, wrapped separately and refrigerated or frozen for future use.

Finally it is time to split and cool the carcass. First, it is rinsed thoroughly with cold water. A meat saw is used to cut down through the pelvis to the ribs, and a cleaver to cut down through the spine and between the shoulders, veering off to one side to leave the head attached to one half. The two halves are rinsed once more with cold water and hung in a refrigerator or cold cellar to cool down and age for up to two weeks, ready for butchery.

INDUSTRIAL SLAUGHTER

Commercially, pork is slaughtered in an industrial process, which is usually much more mechanized. In most countries, slaughterhouses have a veterinarian on site to witness the arrival and unloading of animals and to ensure they are in good health. The veterinarians also monitor how the animals are handled and whether they are properly stunned before slaughter. Misdemeanours, cruelty and incompetence can all be reported, and ultimately a veterinarian has the authority and power to shut production down. Another responsibility of a veterinarian is to manage meat inspections and health and hygiene.

Typically, pigs are first rendered unconscious by stunning using electric current applied with electrodes, a captive bolt pistol or inhalation of carbon dioxide. They are then hoisted on to a rail where they are bled out via the carotid artery and the jugular vein. After they have been bled, the carcass is drenched in hot water in a pig scalder. This helps with the removal of hair, which is subsequently completed by using scissor-like devices and if necessary a torch.

Next, the pig is eviscerated, and the body is cut in two, one half with the head attached. The halves are washed to remove any remaining blood, bacteria or remains of bone, and are then chilled in a temperature-controlled environment. This is done to bring the carcass temperature down, which reduces bleeding, as well as to firm up the carcass for cutting. During this first phase of 'becoming meat', each carcass will shrink through loss of moisture by about one to two per cent. Pig carcasses are usually chilled for one day. After that, the facility needs to move the carcasses out, because chill rooms can hold only a set number of carcasses at any one time, and the profitability of a slaughtering facility is determined by its throughput.

Most pig keepers are likely to send their pigs to slaughter rather than do it themselves, and this is probably prudent – it is very hard not to get attached to animals you have raised and cared for yourself.

WHY IT MATTERS

The process of slaughter directly affects the flavour and taste of the resulting meat, and after all this effort to produce tasty animals ethically, we really should not fall at the last hurdle. If an animal is stressed at time of slaughter, be it from a long journey or from unsympathetic handling at the slaughterhouse, it produces adrenalin, which floods the muscles and gives the meat an unpleasant taste and texture. It is important to seek out the best facility available, which is as close to the animals as possible, in order to finish the job in good conscience.

Chapter 6
SNOOT TO TAIL

4 medium pigs' kidneys
(core removed), sliced

milk, to cover

1 teaspoon mustard powder

1 teaspoon cayenne pepper

1 teaspoon plain flour

Maldon sea salt flakes and
freshly ground black pepper

10g unsalted butter

80g thick-cut bacon lardons

1 shallot, finely diced

50ml Madeira

50ml Master Pork Broth
(*see* page 335)

1 teaspoon Worcestershire
sauce

50ml double cream

10g chopped fresh parsley

toasted bread, to serve

An Edwardian dish, this was often prepared with lambs'
kidneys in gentlemen's clubs. The trick here is to cook them
quickly in a hot pan and allow the residual heat to finish the
cooking process once the sauce is finished.

DEVILLED KIDNEYS Serves 4

Soak the kidneys in the milk for 30 minutes, then drain.

Mix together the mustard powder, cayenne and flour,
and season with salt and pepper, then dust the
kidneys in the seasoned flour.

In a frying pan, melt the butter, then sauté first the
bacon, then the kidneys and finally the shallot.

Deglaze the pan with the Madeira and add the pork
broth, Worcestershire sauce and double cream. Finish
with the chopped parsley and adjust the seasoning.
Serve immediately, on toast to soak up the sauce.

500g pork shoulder,
cut into large dice

Maldon sea salt flakes and
freshly ground black pepper

100g pork dripping

2 onions, sliced

750g Snoots & Foots
(see page 336)

200g bacon lardons

6 pigs' kidneys, split and cored

200g Blood Pudding
(see page 174),
cut into large chunks

12 Agen prunes, pitted

buttered mashed potatoes,
to serve

There's a lot going on here, and for those non-offal-lovers among us this might be entirely too piggy, but as you've bought this book I hope you are on board.

STICKY PORK WITH PRUNES Serves 4

Preheat the oven to 160°C/gas mark 3, and heat a large cast iron skillet on the stove until hot.

Season the pork shoulder with salt and pepper. Add half the pork dripping to the hot skillet, then add the pork and sauté until golden brown. Remove and place in a large lidded casserole.

Sauté the onions in the same skillet and add to the pork, then cover the pork with the Snoots & Foots mix, cover and place in the oven for 1 hour.

After 1 hour has passed, reheat the skillet and sauté the bacon and kidneys. Add these to the casserole along with the Blood Pudding and prunes. Return to the oven for a further hour, or until the pork shoulder is tender. Taste and adjust the seasoning, then serve with buttered mashed potatoes.

100g pork shoulder, roughly chopped

100g pig's liver, roughly chopped

250g fatty belly pork, roughly chopped

100g bacon

75g kidneys, cored

100g breadcrumbs

1 medium onion, finely chopped

2 tablespoons chopped fresh parsley

2 fresh sage leaves, finely chopped

a pinch of ground mace

a pinch of ground allspice

Maldon sea salt flakes and freshly ground black pepper

caul fat

For the onion gravy

500g onions, sliced

oil, for frying

500ml Master Pork Broth (*see* page 335)

You will also need a mincer

Faggots are an old-fashioned British food that has sadly fallen out of favour in recent years. Traditionally, faggots are made from pork offal and the bits of the animal that are generally discarded, making them a cheap and nutritious dish, much like scrapple on the other side of the Atlantic (*see* page 276). The home of faggots is considered to be the Midlands, where they are eaten with mushy peas or mashed potatoes.

FAGGOTS Serves 4

Preheat the oven to 170°C/gas mark 3½.

To make the onion gravy, cook the sliced onions gently in a little oil over a low heat for 20 minutes, stirring from time to time. Add the pork broth and continue simmering gently over a low heat.

Mince all the meats through the coarse plate on your mincer. If you don't have a mincer, pulse-chop them in a food processor. Place the minced meat in a large bowl, add the breadcrumbs, chopped onion, herbs, spices and a pinch of salt and pepper, and mix thoroughly.

Divide the mixture into 8 portions and shape into balls. Wrap each ball in a piece of caul fat, making sure it overlaps – it will seal as it cooks and hold the faggots together.

Place the faggots in a shallow ovenproof dish and bake in the oven for 10 minutes.

Turn the heat up under your onion gravy and reduce by about half (you should have about 500ml), then pour it over the faggots and return them to the oven to bake for a further 20 minutes.

Serve hot from the oven, with mashed potatoes or mushy peas.

4 pork chops, about 100g each

300g pigs' kidneys, skinned and cored

300g pork liver, trimmed

400g smoked bacon chops

4 pork sausages (Pepper Pigs for preference, *see* page 147)

4 shallots, halved

4 field mushrooms

4 plum tomatoes, halved

2 teaspoons olive oil

Maldon sea salt flakes and freshly ground black pepper

1 bunch of watercress, picked

140g Anchovy Butter (*see* page 340)

You will also need a charcoal barbecue

Mixed grill -- the preferred vittles of old-school private gentlemen's clubs, much abused, but treated with respect -- translates well to a meaty summer barbecue. The trick here is to undercook to medium and rest the meat long enough for the residual heat to finish the job.

MIXED GRILL WITH ANCHOVY BUTTER Serves 4

Cook all the meat on a charcoal barbecue to medium and allow to rest in a warm place at 60°C for at least 20 minutes.

Meanwhile, barbecue the shallots and the mushrooms.

Rub the cut side of the tomatoes, the shallots and mushrooms with the olive oil, sprinkle with salt and pepper, then bar-mark them on the grill and keep warm.

Return the rested meats to the barbecue for a few minutes to heat through, then serve neatly presented on a platter with the watercress and anchovy butter.

50g pork dripping

1 onion, baked in its skin, peeled and chopped

75g cooked pork, roughly chopped

75g cooked bacon, roughly chopped

100g pig's offal, heart, liver or kidneys, roughly chopped

250g cooked potato, diced

50g cabbage, chopped and blanched

Maldon sea salt flakes and freshly ground black pepper

1 pig's stomach, cleaned and washed

1 litre Master Pork Broth (see page 335)

1 faggot of fresh herbs, made with thyme, rosemary and bay

1 spice bag (made with black peppercorns, ½ cinnamon stick, 2 cloves and 1 star anise)

watercress salad, to serve

You will also need a trussing needle and trussing thread

When protein was so highly prized that every possible scrap of meat was utilized, the offal of an animal would often be stuffed into its stomach and cooked. The benefits are twofold -- seasoning and cooking helps preserve the offal for longer, while also making it more palatable. An example of this that is still common today is the mighty haggis. Here's another.

STUFFED PIG'S STOMACH Serves 4

Heat the pork dripping in a skillet, add the chopped onion and cook until golden. Add the roughly chopped meat, offal and potato and toss to mix thoroughly, then continue cooking over a low heat, tossing from time to time to caramelize the potatoes. Add the cabbage, mix and season aggressively with salt and pepper.

Preheat the oven to 180°C/gas mark 4.

Stuff the pig's stomach with this mixture and sew the opening firmly shut with trussing thread.

Place the stuffed stomach in a wide casserole and cover with the pork broth. Add the faggot of herbs and spice bag, cover and bake in the oven for 1 hour.

Remove the cooked stomach and keep warm. Strain the cooking liquid into another pan and reduce by half, then whisk in the butter and adjust the seasoning if necessary.

Remove the trussing threads and place the stomach on a serving dish. Pour over the sauce and serve with extra sauce and a watercress salad on the side.

2 whole pig's jowls

2 litres cold Master Pork Broth
(*see* page 335)

You will also need
a smoker or charcoal
barbecue

In times long past, when we ate every part of the pig except its squeal, Bath chaps were an example of a traditional delicacy that made the best of a lesser cut, the meat from the jaw. More recently we've come to believe that the pig is composed solely of ham, bacon and pork chops, so the Bath chap has lost its appeal and become difficult to obtain. Bath chaps can also be made from poached meat and finished with breadcrumbs in the manner of a ham.

BATH CHAPS OR SMOKED PIG'S JOWLS Serves 4

Remove the gelatinous skin from the jowls but keep as much fat as possible. Remove any gristle, veins or icky bits and you should have 2 roughly triangular pieces of meat. Place the cleaned jowls in the broth in a non-reactive container. Leave to brine for 2 days, then remove from the broth and dry completely.

Place in a preheated smoker at 110°C for 4 hours, or until an internal temperature of 89°C is reached.

To make the Bath chaps, spread out a double layer of clingfilm 60cm long. Carefully lay the warm triangles of meat in the middle, then enclose them in the clingfilm and wrap tightly. They should be conical in shape. Refrigerate overnight, to set firm.

The Bath chaps can now be reheated over a low charcoal grill for use in Smoked Pork Jowl Toast With Pickled Pear (*see* page 327), or sliced thickly and fried as part of a piggy breakfast, or sliced thinly and served cold with pickles and mustard.

1 pig's head, washed under cold running water

4 pig's trotters

2 onions

2 carrots

2 leeks

2 celery sticks

250ml cider vinegar

a faggot of fresh herbs, made with sage, rosemary, thyme and bay

a spice bag, made with 20 white peppercorns, 1cm cinnamon stick and 1 clove

Maldon sea salt flakes and freshly ground black pepper

To serve

crusty bread

mustard

pickles

You will also need a 1.5 litre terrine or loaf tin

Souse is the New World version of brawn, with the notable difference of being lightly pickled, a variation that I think is an improvement. The vinegar does break down the gelatine over time so it doesn't set so firm, but that's no bad thing.

SOUSE Serves 4

Remove the brain from the pig's head and discard the brain. Place the pig's head and trotters in a large saucepan and cover with cold water. Bring to the boil, then drain and refresh under cold running water.

Return the pan with the pig's head and trotters to the stove and pour over fresh cold water. Add the remaining ingredients and bring up to a gentle simmer, skimming the surface as you go.

After an hour remove the ears and dry carefully – reserve these for other dishes (*see* pages 290 and 292). After another hour, remove everything from the pot and discard the faggot, spice bag and vegetables. Boil the liquid until it has reduced by half.

While still warm, pick the head, tongue and trotters clean of all meat, particularly the cheeks, tongue and snout, taking care to peel the tongue and break any large pieces into small chunks.

Return the meat to the reduced cooking liquor and season heavily with salt and pepper, adding extra vinegar if needed – be bold, as when the brawn sets the seasoning will fade.

Line a terrine with clingfilm, leaving some overhanging, and fill with the meat mixture. Cover with a layer of the cooking liquid and chill until set or overnight.

Slice and serve with bread, mustard and pickles or a simple salad.

1 pig's head, split in half

2 large onions, halved

2 large carrots, halved

2 tablespoons cooking oil

250ml clear honey

Maldon sea salt flakes and freshly ground white pepper

2 sprigs of fresh thyme

1 bay leaf

1 teaspoon Chinese five-spice powder

2 litres Master Pork Broth (see page 335)

25g unsalted butter

To serve

800g triple-cooked chips (see method for the fries on page 234)

400g Cheddar cheese curds

Poutine could well be the national dish of Canada and it's surprisingly addictive. Unfortunately, cheese curds can be hard to find, but mozzarella makes a serviceable substitute -- unless you are Canadian, in which case nothing else will do.

PIG'S HEAD POUTINE Serves 4

Remove the tongue and brain from the pig's head and discard the brain. Put the split head and tongue into a saucepan, cover with cold water, bring to the boil, then drain and refresh in cold water.

Preheat the oven to 160°C/gas mark 3.

In a large flameproof casserole, brown the onions and carrots in the oil and add the honey to caramelize. Add the blanched pig's head and tongue and toss to coat in the honey mix. Season with salt and pepper, then add the herbs and five-spice followed by the pork broth.

Cover the pan and place in the oven for 3 hours, or until the jawbone is falling apart.

Remove the head from the pot and pick the meat from the cheeks, temples and snout. Peel the tongue and break any large pieces into small chunks. Reserve the meat.

Pass the stock through a fine sieve into a medium pan and reduce to a sauce, then whisk in the butter and add the picked meat.

Fry the chips until golden and drain on kitchen paper. Toss the hot chips with the cheese curds and place in a serving dish, then put into the oven to warm through before serving with the braised meat ladled over the top.

- 1 large pig's jowl
- 1 ham hock
- 1 litre Master Pork Broth (*see* page 335)
- 100g pork liver
- ¼ onion
- 4 garlic cloves
- 1 small faggot of herbs, made with rosemary, thyme and sage
- 250g cornmeal or oatmeal
- 10g fine sea salt
- a pinch of freshly ground white pepper
- a pinch of cayenne pepper
- a pinch of grated nutmeg
- 125g rendered pork fat, for sealing
- free-range eggs, to serve

> You will also need a 1.5 litre terrine or loaf tin

Scrapple is a mixture of the pork offcuts left after sausage-making, which are boiled, picked and chopped, then thickened with cornmeal or oatmeal. It's typically eaten at breakfast as a side in the States, and is very similar to the English breakfast slice or hog's pudding.

SCRAPPLE OR BREAKFAST SLICE Serves 6–8

Place the pig's jowl and hock in a heavy-based flameproof casserole and cover with cold water. Bring to the boil, then drain and refresh under cold water.

Pour off the cold water and add the flavoursome pork broth. Put the lid on the casserole and simmer gently for 1 hour, then add the liver, onion, garlic and faggot of herbs and cook for a further hour.

Strain the broth into a clean casserole or heavy-based saucepan and boil until reduced to 250ml. Pick the meat from the jowl and hock, discarding the bones, and chop or mince the meat.

Bring the reduced broth to a simmer, then combine the cornmeal and the seasonings and gradually add them to the simmering broth, stirring constantly. Reduce the heat to medium, add the chopped meat and stir until everything is well mixed.

Cook slowly for 30 minutes, stirring constantly to make sure it does not stick to the bottom of the casserole or pan – it will be quite thick.

After 30 minutes it will be ready to pour. Rub the terrine or loaf tin with rendered pork fat and pour in the scrapple to reach the top of the terrine. Cover with a layer of rendered pork fat and allow to cool, then refrigerate.

Turn the scrapple out on to a chopping board and cut into 2cm thick slices. Heat a skillet and fry the slices until golden brown. Serve with fried eggs and toast.

800g Braised Pig's Head meat, picked (*see* page 275)

80ml Barbecue Baste (*see* page 337)

80ml mustard of choice

100g fresh cheese curds or mozzarella

Maldon sea salt flakes and freshly ground black pepper

50g plain flour

4 free-range eggs

50ml milk

80g panko breadcrumbs

vegetable oil, for frying

Sriracha or other hot sauce, to serve

You will also need a deep-fat fryer

Chicken nuggets have been around since the '50s, when they were created by a food science professor at Cornell University in the US. These fellas owe more to a Spanish meat *croqueta* than to a chicken nugget, but I like the name and the down-and-dirty connotations.

PIG'S HEAD NUGGETS Makes 32

Mix the pig's head meat with the Barbecue Baste and mustard – the natural gelatine in the meat will help set the nuggets before frying. Add the cheese curds to the mixture and season with salt and pepper.

Put the mixture on a sheet of clingfilm and roll into a tight sausage about 5cm wide. Leave to set in the refrigerator overnight.

Cut the sausage into 2cm-thick discs. Line up 3 shallow bowls – sift the flour into one bowl, beat the eggs with the milk in another and put the panko breadcrumbs into the third. Coat the nuggets in the flour, then dip them into the egg mixture, then finally gently roll them in the panko breadcrumbs.

Heat the oil to 190°C in a deep-fat fryer. Fry the nuggets in small batches for 2 minutes, or until golden. Drain on kitchen paper and serve with hot sauce.

Maldon sea salt flakes and
freshly ground black pepper

2 pigs' tongues, about 400g
in total

600ml Court-bouillon
(*see* page 335)

200g Vinegar Slaw
(*see* page 341)

400g Baked Beans
(*see* page 282)

pork dripping, oil or
rendered fat, for brushing

fresh coriander leaves,
to garnish

You will also need
a barbecue

**Tongue is a lean and incredibly flavoursome meat that is often
overlooked by cooks, but with a little care and attention it can
be a star ingredient.**

GRILLED TONGUE
WITH BAKED BEANS & SLAW   Serves 4

Preheat the oven to 160°C/gas mark 3.

Season the pork tongues with salt and pepper and
place in a casserole with a lid. Cover with the Court-
bouillon and braise in the oven for 2 hours, or until
the tongues are easily pierced with a sharp knife.

Remove from the oven and allow the tongues to
cool a little in the cooking liquor. When cool enough
to handle, remove from the casserole, discarding
the liquid.

Peel the tongues gently by scraping them with a
sharp knife. Start at the bottom of the tongue and
work up a strip at a time – it's not easy, but persevere.
Then slice the tongues lengthways, about 2cm thick,
trying to make the widest slices possible.

Dress the vinegar slaw and set aside.

Warm your beans gently and light your barbecue –
charcoal for preference, but a gas barbecue will do
just fine. Brush the sliced tongue with a little fat, oil
or dripping and place on the barbecue. Leave until
nicely charred, a couple of minutes perhaps, depending
on the heat of your barbecue, then turn over and
repeat for a couple of minutes more.

Remove the tongue from the grill, brush with a little
more fat, oil or dripping, and serve with the hot beans
and a pile of Vinegar Slaw garnished with coriander.

500g white beans,
soaked in water overnight

3 whole onions

6 garlic cloves

1 pig's trotter

100g salt pork or bacon belly,
cut into 2cm chunks

100g Lardo (*see* page 247),
cut into 1cm dice

250ml tomato passata or
chopped canned tomatoes

100ml tomato ketchup
or Barbecue Sauce
(*see* page 337)

You will also need
preserving jars

We all love Heinz baked beans because they are delicious, but making your own is both easy and rewarding, and once you've tried these you might never open another tin. Might.

BAKED BEANS Serves 4

Drain the beans, discarding the soaking liquid, then place them in a large saucepan and cover with cold water. Bring to the boil and skim, then simmer for 20 minutes, or until the beans are cooked, but not so much so that they burst. Drain, reserving 500ml of the cooking liquid.

Preheat the oven to 160°C/gas mark 3. Place the onions, garlic and pig's trotter in a layer at the bottom of a casserole and cover with the drained beans. Add the reserved cooking liquid and the rest of the ingredients, and place in the oven for 2 hours, or until cooked. Either discard the trotter or, better still, pick it clean of skin and flesh to add to the beans.

Place your preserving jars in boiling water or steam at 160°C to sterilize them. Fill the jars with the hot beans and screw on the lids reasonably tightly. Put the jars back in the water or steamer for 30 minutes, then remove and allow to cool. Refrigerate until needed.

4 pigs' tongues

½ onion, plus 2 tablespoons very finely sliced onion

2 garlic cloves, smashed, with skin on

6 peppercorns

2 bay leaves

2 cloves

¾ small ripe avocado, roughly diced

3 finger-length medium-hot green chillies, finely chopped, seeds and all

30g coriander leaves and stalks, finely chopped

juice of 3 limes

1 tablespoon sunflower oil

2 tablespoons water

1 teaspoon Maldon sea salt flakes

1 teaspoon dried oregano

1 teaspoon ground cumin

400g grated mozzarella or mild Cheddar cheese

8 mini corn tortillas

I love all the 'lesser' parts of the pig, especially pigs' tongues, but these bits have not always delivered joy. Once, when giving a talk to a large gathering of respectable old ladies, I was asked what was the oddest thing I had ever eaten. I declined answering, saying it was maybe inappropriate for what had been such a nice morning. They were having none of it and asked again. 'Well,' I said, 'it must have been the braised pig's vagina tacos I ate in Mexico city.' Shocked silence fell on the room. I followed it up with more truth saying 'it was tender and giving so I ordered another one.' I was not invited to remain for a sherry after the talk.

CRISPY PIG'S TONGUE TACOS WITH FRIED CHEESE & GREEN SAUCE Makes 8 tacos (2 per person)

BY VALENTINE WARNER

Place the pigs' tongues in a saucepan and just cover them with water, then drop in the ½ onion, garlic, peppercorns, bay leaves and cloves. Bring the water up to a tremble and very gently simmer the tongues for 4–4½ hours, or until the tongues are tender to the prod of a knife. Add more water if needed.

Allow to cool, but score and then peel off the outer skin while the tongues are warm, as it's easier to do than when cold. Generally speaking, though, they can be hard to skin and sometimes it is just better to cut it off. Slice off any tatty underside to the tongue – although tasty it is unsightly. The broth from the poaching is delicious and should not be thrown away.

About 30 minutes before the tongues are ready, put the avocado flesh into a bowl with the chillies, coriander, lime juice and blitz with a stick blender

until as smooth and velvety as possible. Stir in the sunflower oil, water, salt and lastly the finely sliced onion. Leave to one side.

When the tongues are peeled, slice each one lengthways, about 5mm thick.

You will now need 2 frying pans – a large one for the tongue and cheese, and a large one for the tortillas. Season each slice of tongue with a little salt and a good sprinkle each of oregano and cumin. Fry the slices of tongue in a little splash of sunflower oil until well browned, then flip over each slice of tongue to brown on the other side. For each taco, pile about

50g of cheese into the frying pan, away from the tongue slices. Fry the piles of cheese until the undersides are brown and very crispy. While cooking the tongue and cheese, warm the tortillas over a medium heat in the other frying pan, flipping them once or twice. They should be hot and very floppy. Crispy – and they have been over-cooked.

Load a slice of tongue on to each tortilla, then flip on the cheese – crisped brown crust facing up. Spoon over a generous amount of the salsa and get the recipient to tuck in immediately while you make more. Fold the taco over and eat with the hands, accompanied with cold, cold, very cold beer.

1kg pigs' cheeks

1 onion, cut into 3cm chunks

1 carrot, cut into 3cm chunks

200ml red wine

Maldon sea salt flakes and
freshly ground black pepper

50g pork dripping

1 garlic clove

1 faggot of fresh herbs, made
from sage and rosemary with
celery and leek

1 litre Master Pork Broth
(see page 335)

1 large parsnip,
peeled and chopped

1 large turnip,
peeled and chopped

½ head of celeriac,
peeled and chopped

50g unsalted butter

Hard-working muscles benefit from long, slow cooking, and nowhere is this demonstrated better than in the cheek or buccinator muscle of an animal. Cheeks contain gelatinous layers among the fibres that disintegrate and dissolve during cooking, helping to moisten and lubricate the meat, especially when slow-cooked at a low temperature.

PIGS' CHEEKS IN RED WINE WITH MASHED ROOTS Serves 4

Trim any sinew off the pigs' cheeks and place in a non-reactive bowl with the onion and carrot. Pour the red wine over the pigs' cheeks and leave to marinate for a few hours.

Preheat the oven to 140°C/gas mark 1.

Remove the pigs' cheeks from the wine marinade and pat dry, then season them with salt and pepper and fry in the dripping until brown. Deglaze the pan with the wine marinade and reduce to a glaze.

Put the cheeks, reduced wine glaze, onions, carrots, garlic faggot of herbs and pork broth into a flameproof casserole cover, and place in the oven for 4 hours.

Remove from the oven and allow to cool, then remove the cheeks from the sauce and set aside. Reduce the cooking liquid by half, or until viscous

and a little sticky, then pass the reduced liquid through a fine sieve twice. Adjust the seasoning and put the cheeks back into the casserole.

Place the chopped parsnip, turnip and celeriac in a large lidded saucepan, add a splash of water and the butter, season with salt and pepper and set to cook over a low heat for 20 minutes, shaking the pan from time to time.

Mash the vegetables roughly, using a potato masher or ricer, then adjust the seasoning. Reheat the pigs' cheeks on the hob and serve with a large spoonful of the vegetable mash alongside.

2 pork cheeks

1 pig's trotter, well shaved

1 leek, roughly chopped

1 carrot, roughly chopped

1 celery stick, roughly chopped

1 onion, roughly chopped

1 sprig of fresh thyme

1 bay leaf

300ml Madeira

300ml chicken stock

Maldon sea salt flakes and freshly ground black pepper

2 garlic cloves, finely chopped

any neutral oil, for frying

500g clams, scrubbed

100ml Manzanilla sherry

100g peas (frozen is fine)

a handful of fresh coriander, chopped

BRAISED CHEEKS & TROTTER WITH CLAMS, PEAS & FINO Serves 4

BY MITCH TONKS

Pork and clams are a combination you will see all over Portugal. I think it works because of the saltiness of the clams and the similar texture of the meats. In many of the dishes I have had I found the pork to be a bit dry -- I like fat and softness, and paired here with soft cheeks and melting feet, clams are delicious.

First braise the cheeks and trotter. Preheat the oven to 150°C/gas mark 2. Trim the cheeks of fat and place them in a casserole with the trotter, the chopped vegetables and the thyme and bay leaf. Add the Madeira and the stock, cover with baking paper, then put a lid on the casserole and braise in the oven for 4 hours until all is meltingly soft.

Strain, then separate the meat from the vegetables. Pick all the fat and meat from the trotter and finely chop. Reduce the braising liquid by half, then season with salt and pepper.

In a frying pan, cook the garlic in a little oil, then add the clams. After a few minutes add the sherry, followed by 6–8 tablespoons of the reduced liquid, the pig's cheeks and the trotter meat. When the clams are open, add the peas and finish with the coriander. The juice should be salty and sticky on the lips! Discard any clams that remain shut before serving.

2kg pigs' ears

1.5 litres duck fat

15g Maldon sea salt flakes

For the apple sauce

200g Granny Smith apples, peeled and cut into 2cm pieces

25ml water

35g caster sugar

Slow-cooked confit pigs' ears, roasted, then seasoned and served with a chunky warm apple sauce. One of my head chefs, Richard Sandiford, came up with this little treat. It's interesting in that it is crispy-crunchy like crackling or scratchings, but retains little areas of soft, giving unctuousness that acts as a juxtaposition to the crunch.

CRISPY PIGS' EARS Serves 4

Preheat the oven to 150°C/gas mark 2.

Use a blowtorch to burn off any remaining hairs on the pigs' ears, then use a spoon to scrape off any remaining burnt pieces. Submerge the ears in warm duck fat, then bake in the low oven for 4–5 hours (the fat on the ears should be easy to pull apart).

Meanwhile, to make the apple sauce, put all the sauce ingredients into a saucepan and cook over a low heat for 10–15 minutes without browning, stirring regularly to break up the apples but not letting them get mushy. Set aside until needed.

Increase the oven temperature to 220°C/gas mark 7. Remove the ears from the fat and cool for 10 minutes, or until the ears are cool enough to handle, but cold enough to set. Gently pull away the skin and meat, keeping the pieces as big as possible. Place them on a baking tray lined with greaseproof paper, sprinkle liberally with the salt and roast in the oven for 10 minutes. The thinner pieces will be ready after this time, but the thick pieces will need a further 5 minutes at 180°C/gas mark 4.

Break the ears into pieces and serve with the warm apple sauce.

Use the following leftovers from the Master Pork Broth (*see* page 335):

2 ham hocks

2 pig's trotters

1 smoked gammon or bacon hock

2 onions

2 large carrots

2 celery sticks

2 large dried shiitake mushrooms

20g chopped fresh flat-leaf parsley

2 leaves of gelatine

500ml Master Pork Broth

Maldon sea salt flakes and freshly ground black pepper

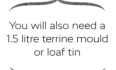

You will also need a 1.5 litre terrine mould or loaf tin

There is so much piggy goodness left over from the making of the master pork broth (*see* page 335) that it seems to me a crime not to write a couple of recipes utilizing it -- here's one.

PORK BROTH TERRINE Serves 10

Line the terrine mould with a double layer of clingfilm and set aside.

Pick all the skin off the cooked meat and all of the meat from the bones, then cut the meat into 1cm dice.

Cut all the cooked vegetables into 1cm dice and add to the meat along with the parsley.

Soak the leaves of gelatine in water for a few minutes, and meanwhile bring the pork broth up to a simmer. Remove the gelatine from the water, add to the hot pork broth and whisk. Correct the seasoning and allow to cool a little.

Strain the jelly over the meat and vegetables and put into the lined terrine to set.

Refrigerate overnight, then slice and serve with mustard, pickles and toast.

pig's ears, reserved from
Souse (*see* page 272)

vegetable oil, for deep-frying

salt and freshly ground
black pepper

100g dandelion leaves

100g sorrel leaves

5g fresh flat-leaf
parsley leaves

10g fine capers

30ml Honey & Mustard
Dressing (*see* page 342)

I have eaten many variations of this dish, both in England and
France, and it really is a splendid example of nose-to-tail cookery.
It's important the ears are sliced very thinly indeed or they can
be a little challenging against the delicate leaves of the salad.

CRISPY FRIED PIG'S EAR SALAD Serves 4

Slice the pig's ears as thinly as possible. Heat the
oil to 180°C in a deep-fat fryer or in a heavy-based
saucepan and fry the sliced ears in batches until
crisp, then drain on kitchen paper and season with
salt and pepper.

Wash and dry the salad and parsley leaves and place
in a bowl with the capers. Season, then toss with the
Honey & Mustard Dressing and serve topped with
the crispy fried pig's ears.

1 pig's trotter per person

chicken stock, to cover

1 glass of Madeira per trotter

black Périgord truffles (the amount depends on your funds, but I would suggest this is not the moment to hold back)

coarse sea salt

TRUFFLED PIG'S TROTTER Serves 1

BY FERGUS HENDERSON

Not a recipe for those of you who are deterred by a little grapple with your ingredients. It may seem that this is a long-winded recipe, but once you have boned out the trotter it is plain sailing!

Some say that boning out a trotter is like removing a lady's kid glove. It is not! Slit the trotter lengthways down the back, then gently follow the bone down to the trots and sever the skin and trots from the main bone.

Braise the skin in chicken stock and Madeira to the point when you can pinch through the skin with no resistance. Allow to cool and set in its own jelly. That was the hard part! Now to construction.

Thinly slice the truffles and lay them on a sheet of greaseproof paper. Remove the skin from its jelly, leaving some of it attached – the remaining jelly can be used for soup, or for future flavourings – then flatten out the skin on top of the truffles, covering them with the skin side to the air.

Sprinkle with coarse sea salt, pop on to a baking tray (the truffles will adhere to the sticky underside of the trotter) and finish under a preheated low grill. What you should end up with is crunch, lip-sticking give and, last but not least, the musk of truffle.

I must admit this has been a fantasy of mine for some time. This is one step nearer to reality!

500g assorted pigs' tails,
ears, snouts and feet

100g Pork Rub
(*see* page 334)

500ml Master Pork Broth
(*see* page 335)

100g plain flour

vegetable oil, for deep-frying

100ml Sriracha or other
hot sauce

125g unsalted butter

100ml cider vinegar

Blue Cheese Sauce
(*see* page 343), to serve

Not for the faint of heart, this snack makes use of all the icky
extremities of a hog, which are all about texture and the contrast
between a crispy exterior and a giving, unctuous interior.

BUFFALO-STYLE PIGS' BITS Serves 4

Singe the assorted pigs' tails, ears, snouts and feet to remove any hair. Wash and dry them thoroughly, then season all over with the half the pork rub. Place in a casserole and cover with the pork broth, then place the casserole uncovered in a smoker or oven at 120°C/gas mark ½ for 4 hours, or until tender.

When cooked, remove the bits from the broth and allow to cool. Cut large chunks of skin, fat and meat from the various porky bits, but keep the tails intact. Mix the remaining pork rub with the flour and dust the pork bits liberally in this mix.

Heat the oil to 180°C in a deep-fat fryer and fry the pigs' bits until crispy, then drain on kitchen paper.

Warm the hot sauce, butter and cider vinegar together until emulsified. Toss the crispy pigs' bits in the sauce and serve with pickled celery, apple and blue cheese sauce.

Use the following leftovers from the Master Pork Broth (*see* page 335):

2 ham hocks

2 pig's trotters

1 smoked gammon or bacon hock

Maldon sea salt flakes and freshly ground black pepper

2 onions, halved

2 large carrots, halved

2 celery sticks

2 large dried shiitake mushrooms

To serve

Honey & Mustard Dressing (*see* page 342)

Maldon sea salt flakes and freshly ground black pepper

romaine lettuce leaves

spring onions, chopped

Here's another recipe that uses any leftovers from the making of the master pork broth (*see* page 335).

PORK BROTH SALAD   Serves 4

Pick all the skin off the meat and all the meat off the bones. Shred the skin with a sharp knife and flake the meat with your fingers. Dress with the honey and mustard dressing and season with salt and pepper to taste.

Chop all the vegetables into small dice, dress with honey and mustard dressing and season to taste.

Place the romaine lettuce leaves on a plate and top with a strip of dressed meats and a strip of dressed vegetables. Sprinkle with chopped spring onions and eat with your fingers, using the leaves as spoons.

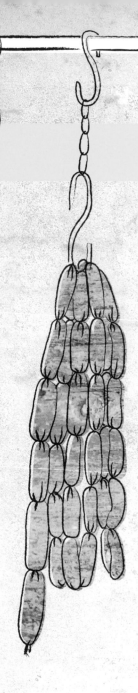

BUYING & BUTCHERY

Awesome meat starts well before it gets to the butcher or the chef -- it starts with the farmer, and conscientious cooks will want to know what it is they are buying and cooking. If you take this approach at home when sourcing your own meat, there is no doubt that over time you will have great satisfaction from eating and cooking meat you are proud to have purchased.

The first step is to find the best butcher you can – and if you are lucky, not only will they have pork of the highest quality but their meat will be sourced from dedicated farmers raising rare-breed pigs. Although it sounds contradictory, it is only through buying rare-breed meat that the rare-breed industry can grow and these passionate farmers can continue their great work.

BUYING

In my experience, the best meat will come from those farmers who value the importance of feed, husbandry, slaughter and breed. Look for meat from native breeds that have been grown slowly and naturally, have been fed without the aid of hormones and have not been pumped full of grain to fuel fast growth.

Not all rare-breed pigs are the same – each breed has its own characteristics, which become apparent when you eat the meat.

While many hybrids are fast-growing (and not very tasty), rare breeds are all slow-growing. The darker the flesh, the older the animal, and today's commercial pork is usually pale pink because it comes from young animals.

Driven by commercial considerations rather than the animal's natural maturity, the food industry slaughters animals far too early in their natural lifespan. If you grow a pig in an intensive system, it will be slaughtered at about 16 weeks. Given that a pig can live for up to 15 years, and will not begin to achieve proper maturity until it is at least a year old, you can see what a truncated life it leads. It is a crime against flavour – particularly when it comes to native-breed pork.

BUTCHERY

There is very little waste on a properly butchered pig, with almost every part of the animal being used. The phrase 'nose to tail' is derived from the versatility of pork and the fact that literally everything from a pig can be, and is, used. Rightly so: it is all delicious.

All carcasses are divided initially into five primal cuts – the shoulder, loin, belly, foreleg and rear leg – plus the head and offal. From here the primal cuts are usually broken down further into sub-primal cuts, which are defined by anatomical features (see overleaf). The names and exact specifications of cuts may vary a little depending on what part of the world you live in.

THE FAT FACTOR

The value of pork fat cannot be underestimated; its uses are endless and the need for it in the cooking of pork is clear. When buying pork, be sure that there is both a hard, thick layer of fat on the outside, firm meat that is greyish-pink in colour, visible marbling (the small flecks of white fat running throughout the meat) and white, not yellow, fat. Even if you do not intend to eat all the fat, it will aid the cooking, basting the meat as it begins to render and producing juicy, flavourful pork. This is only possible with proper fatty pork. Fat is one of the areas where a real difference between rare breeds and commercial pigs is visible. Rare-breed pigs mature and grow much more slowly than commercial breeds, whose natural ability to develop fat has been bred out of them. By the time the rare breeds reach maturity, they have usually developed a thick layer of back fat with prolific marbling throughout the eye of the loin and into the shoulder.

OTHER CONSIDERATIONS

Shoppers trying to buy ethical pork are met with a bewildering array of labelling, so here are some terms to look for.

Organic: The definition of organic varies from country to country, but usually means involving production without the use of chemical fertilizers, pesticides, or artificial chemicals and outdoor-reared for at least 80 per cent of their lives.

Free-range: While there is no firm definition of 'free-range pork', I believe this should mean pigs that are born and reared in outdoor systems throughout their lives, with permanent access to pasture. However, fewer than 2 per cent of pigs in Europe are free-range if this standard is used, and supermarkets regularly use the term for a much less free-range animal. In the U.S. the term is mainly used for marketing, meaning anything from, 'low stocking density,' 'pasture-raised,' or 'grass-fed,' and what constitutes free range is currently entirely decided by the farmer.

Outdoor bred: This means that the pigs are born in outdoor systems in straw-bedded arks with access to a large outdoor paddock. They are brought indoors for growing and finishing or shortly after, weaning, and should be clearly stated on the label.

Outdoor reared: In this system the pigs are born indoors, often in confined conditions, and then reared in outdoor systems for around half their lives. During this time they may not necessarily have access to pasture, but they will have access to an outside pen and a straw-bedded tent or ark.

Higher-welfare indoor systems: Pigs have no access to the outside world at any stage in their lives. If you do buy pork, bacon, sausages or ham from pigs reared indoors, look for 'straw bedded' or 'deep bedded' on the packaging.

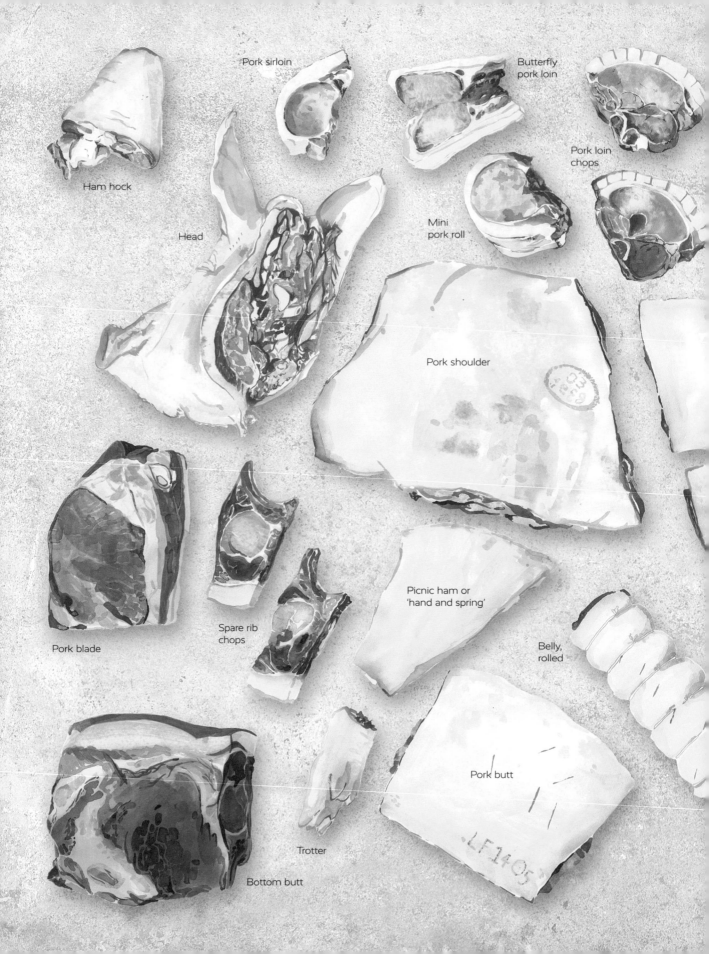

Ham hock

Pork sirloin

Butterfly pork loin

Pork loin chops

Head

Mini pork roll

Pork shoulder

Pork blade

Spare rib chops

Picnic ham or 'hand and spring'

Belly, rolled

Pork butt

Trotter

Bottom butt

LF1405

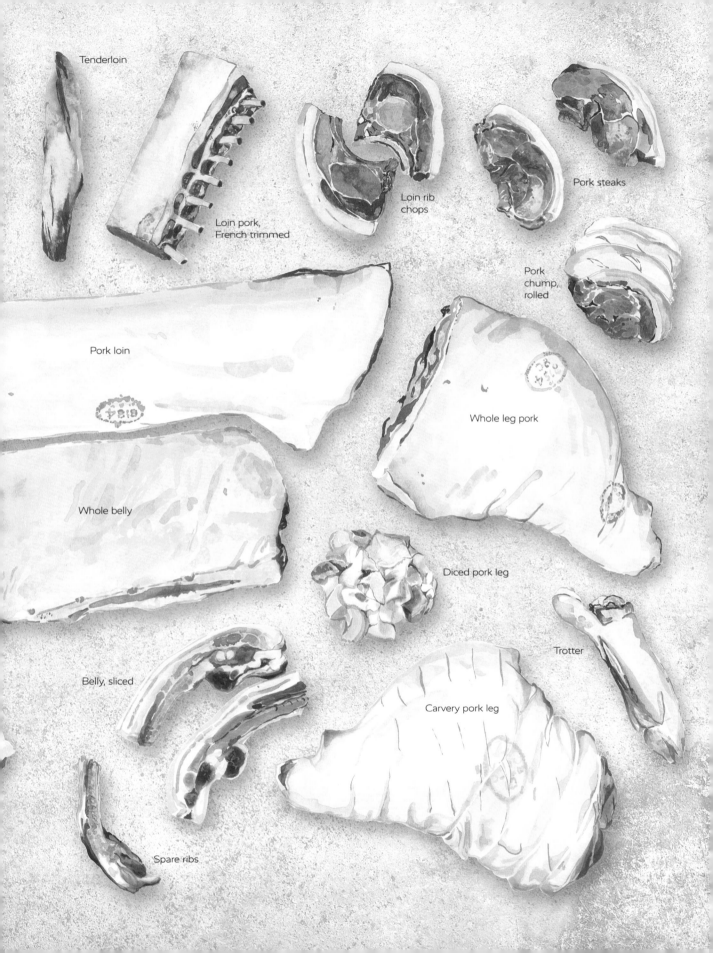

Tenderloin

Loin pork,
French trimmed

Loin rib
chops

Pork steaks

Pork
chump,
rolled

Pork loin

Whole leg pork

Whole belly

Diced pork leg

Trotter

Belly, sliced

Carvery pork leg

Spare ribs

Chapter 7
SMOKED

a 5-bone 'cote de porc' (rack of pork), untrimmed

35g fine salt

2 teaspoons sugar

1 teaspoon freshly ground black pepper

1 teaspoon smoked paprika

1 teaspoon mustard powder

Apple Ketchup (*see* page 339), to serve

You will also need a smoker or charcoal barbecue, oak chips soaked in water for 30 minutes and a meat thermometer

A simple smoked roast preparation. The trick as always is to smoke low, slow and long, with plenty of resting time -- this allows the pork to cook through without tensing up the meat fibres, making for a tender, moist roast. You could also brine the joint overnight (as in the brined dish on page 271).

SMOKED ROAST PORK CHOPS Serves 5

Remove the pork from the refrigerator and let it reach room temperature. Meanwhile mix the salt, sugar and spices.

Remove the skin for cooking as crackling, and sprinkle the pork with the salt rub, taking care to season evenly.

Prepare your smoker and set to 105°C. Seal the pork on a barbecue. Place your sealed joint in the smoker with your soaked oak chips and smoke for 2 hours, or until an internal temperature of 65°C is reached.

Allow to rest at 60°C for a further hour, either in the smoker or in a separate warm place.

Score the skin of the pork in a criss-cross fashion and poach for 20 minutes in simmering water, then season with salt and pepper and place on a wire rack. Either roast in a hot oven until crispy, or on the barbecue.

Carve 1 bone single portions and serve with Apple Ketchup and pork crackling.

50g Maldon sea salt flakes, pulsed in a blender

50g cracked black pepper

1 pork butt

6 spring onions, finely sliced

50g black sesame seeds

1 pear, sliced (optional)

For the barbecue sauce

200ml Sriracha or other hot sauce

200ml dark soy sauce

200ml sesame oil

10 garlic cloves

You will also need a smoker or charcoal barbecue, wood chips of your choice soaked for 30 minutes, some heat-resistant clingfilm and a meat thermometer

KOREAN-STYLE PULLED PORK Serves 20

BY NEIL RANKIN

There is nothing traditionally Korean about this recipe. Sriracha is not Korean, and you won't find pulled pork on any traditional Korean menus. This is just one of these recipes that shouldn't work, but does. It's salty and spicy, with a gentle sweetness that doesn't overwhelm the pork. It's a car crash of East meets West flavours that was meant to be.

Prepare your smoker and set to 140°C. Mix the sea salt and pepper and sprinkle evenly over the pork butt. Smoke in the smoker or on your barbecue for at least 3 hours at 140°C using your preferred wood (no peeking – as long as the smoke is clear and the temperature is right, trust it).

Remove from the smoker or barbecue and immediately wrap tightly in heat-resistant clingfilm. Cook in a low oven (110°C/Gas Mark ¼ or as low as possible) above an oven tray (still wrapped in clingfilm) for at least 8 hours. This can be done overnight. It may take 10 hours.

Remove the pork and unwrap when it starts to feel soft and the internal temperature is around 92°C.

It should pull relatively easily, but not fall apart. You should still have to tug it a bit in places. Keep it in large chunks and keep it moist using the liquid in the tray. There should be no need to season it.

Blitz the ingredients for the barbecue sauce in a blender until smooth and emulsified.

When you are ready to eat, get a pan roaring hot. Drop a portion of pork in, giving it a little colour, then pour in some of the barbecue sauce and toss it about.

Garnish with the spring onions and sesame seeds, and some sliced pear if you're feeling fruity.

200g smoked pork loin, chilled

60ml Green Chilli Dressing
(see page 341)

1 teaspoon fish sauce

fresh coriander and mint
leaves

30ml vegetable oil

40g easy-cook long-grain rice

4 smoked hotdogs or hot links

40ml Smoked Baconnaise
(see page 340)

4 brioche hotdog buns

200g Green Chilli Slaw
(see page 341)

Larb (also spelled laap, larp or lahb) is the national dish of Laos, but variations are found throughout northern Thailand. Larb is a spicy and sour meat salad, typically made from crispy minced meat, chilli, lime, toasted puffed rice and an assortment of fresh herbs. It is another Asian salad that can be happily married to smoky pork or, in this case, a smoked dog.

THE LARB DOG Serves 4

Chop the chilled pork loin across the grain into very fine pieces. In a hot pan, fry the slices for 5 minutes, until browned and cooked through.

Mix the cooked pork with the chilli dressing, fish sauce and a few coriander leaves.

To puff the rice, get a pan hot, add the vegetable oil and once smoking add the uncooked rice. Move the rice around the pan until all the rice has puffed up and the oil has been absorbed. Continue cooking the rice in the dry pan until it is an even light brown colour.

Cook your hotdogs on a barbecue or under a hot grill.

Spread Smoked Baconnaise on the inside of the buns and add your pork loin mixture. Sit the hotdogs on top, and top with the slaw, a few coriander and mint leaves and a small handful of puffed rice.

1 untrimmed boneless
pork shoulder half,
or a 3kg pork butt

Barbecue Sauce (see page 337)

For the dry rub

50g Maldon sea salt flakes

50g soft light brown sugar

50g fennel seeds, toasted

50g freshly ground black
pepper

For the vinegar mop

250ml cider vinegar

125ml water

20ml Worcestershire sauce

You will also need
a smoker, 3kg of
natural lump
charcoal, 500g of
hickory wood smoke
chips, soaked in cold
water and a meat
thermometer

Pulled pork seems to be everywhere at the moment, even some
fast food joints are serving it, but true pulled pork, or Carolina
Barbecue to give it it's correct name, takes skill and patience to
prepare. The stuff bought from fast food outlets or supermarkets
is a poor example of what can be a complex and delicious
preparation in the right hands.

CAROLINA BARBECUE OR PULLED PORK Serves 8

Mix the dry rub ingredients together in a bowl.

Place the pork, fat side up, on a clean work surface
and cut each piece in half lengthways, then place on
a large baking tray. Sprinkle 150g of the dry rub all
over the pork, pressing it into the meat. Cover with
clingfilm and refrigerate for at least 2 hours.

Prepare your smoker and allow to burn down as per the
manufacturer's instructions. Add half the hickory chips.

Mix together the ingredients for the vinegar mop
and stir in 40g of the leftover dry rub.

Place the pieces of rubbed pork shoulder on racks
in the smoker and cook at 105°C for at least 6 hours,
or until the internal temperature of the meat reaches
90°C. Every hour or so, brush the meat liberally with
the vinegar mop. You'll need to top up the smoker
fuel from time to time and add more hickory chips.

Remove the pork from the smoker and shred it into
bite-sized pieces. Collect the juices from the smoker
and pour over the top, then sprinkle with the
remaining dry rub to taste and mix thoroughly.
Serve warm, with Barbecue Sauce on the side.

4 soft buns, split

500g Carolina Barbecue or Pulled Pork (*see* opposite)

200g Vinegar Slaw (*see* page 341)

100ml Red Barbecue Sauce (*see* page 338)

100g Bread and Butter Pickles (*see* page 342)

Pulled pork buns vary from delicious to the downright actionable. True Carolina Barbecue is not too sweet, using vinegar to moisten the meat and red sauce, a tomato-based barbecue sauce, on the slaw instead of the usual mayonnaise. This version is my favourite, with plenty of freshness in the slaw.

PULLED PORK BUNS   Serves 4

Toast your buns until golden. Assuming it's not fresh from the smoker, gently warm the pulled pork through in a saucepan.

Toss your vinegar slaw in the red sauce and place on the base of your buns. Add plenty of pork and top with bread and butter pickles, then complete the sandwich with the lid.

You will need plenty of napkins to eat this, and it will be messy.

1.25kg pork shoulder

500g pork belly

250g pork fat

50g onions

2 garlic cloves

250g mixed (red, green and yellow) peppers

1 teaspoon freshly ground black pepper

1 teaspoon hot smoked paprika

50g smoked sea salt

a pinch of ground coriander

a pinch of wild fennel pollen or ground fennel seed

a pinch of crushed chilli flakes

200ml Barbecue Baste (see page 337)

You will also need a 1.5 litre loaf tin, a mincer and a smoker or charcoal barbecue

This impressive-looking hunk of sausage came about after a trip to an American BBQ festival. Slow-smoked, painted with sauce, sliced and served with soft white buns, coleslaw and salad, it would be a highlight of any 'cue!

BBQ SAUSAGE MEATLOAF Serves 4

Chill all your mincer attachments. Dice all the meats and finely dice the onions, garlic and mixed peppers, discarding the seeds. Mix with all the other ingredients except the Barbecue Baste.

Mince through the coarse plate on your mincer. Press the meat into the loaf tin and place in the refrigerator to chill and set for an hour.

Meanwhile, prepare your smoker or barbecue and set to 140°C. Place the tin in the smoker or barbecue for 30 minutes to allow it to set. After 30 minutes, remove from the smoker and discard the tin.

Lower the temperature of the smoker or barbecue to 120°C, then place the sausage 'loaf' directly on to the bars for a further hour, brushing it every 15 minutes with the Barbecue Baste.

Remove the loaf from the smoker and check the internal temperature – it should be at least 70°C. Allow to rest for 20 minutes, then slice and serve.

1 rack of pork full spare ribs, about 1.8kg

barbecue sauce (see below)

apple cider vinegar, in a spray bottle

For the dry rub

1 tablespoon coarse black pepper

1 tablespoon kosher salt

1 teaspoon paprika

You will also need a smoker or charcoal barbecue

SMOKED SPARE RIBS Serves 2

BY AARON FRANKLIN

Aaron is the finest exponent of American barbecue in the world today -- that's pretty much all any of us need to know.

Prepare your smoker and set to 135°C.

Mix all the dry rub ingredients together.

Trim the excess fat and breastbone from the spare ribs and peel the membrane from the inside of the rack.

Apply the dry rub to both sides of the ribs.

Place the ribs on the smoker or barbecue (meat side up), maintain the temperature at 135°C and spritz with cider vinegar from time to time whenever the ribs look dry.

When the ribs get to the desired colour (about 3 hours), spritz with cider vinegar and lightly brush with barbecue sauce. Let the sauce set up (dry out) for 5 minutes.

Place a sheet of foil on the table, shiny side down. Spritz it with cider vinegar and lightly sauce an area the same size as the ribs. Place the ribs meat side down on the foil and wrap tightly.

Continue cooking at 135°C until tender, about 2–3 hours, then let rest for 20 minutes. Cut between the bones and enjoy!

BARBECUE SAUCE

225g butter

½ onion, chopped

350g ketchup

125ml cider vinegar

50g light brown sugar

1 teaspoon salt

1 tablespoon freshly ground black pepper

¾ teaspoon chilli powder

¾ teaspoon garlic powder

juice of ½ lemon

Whisk and simmer, boil away, boil away, boil away...

½ unsmoked bacon belly, with ribs

For the marinade

100ml maple syrup

50ml French's mustard

50g Pork Rub (*see* page 334)

For the garnish

1 teaspoon crushed black peppercorns

Vinegar Slaw (*see* page 341)

You will also need a smoker or charcoal barbecue and a meat thermometer

These came about while creating the menu for Foxlow, one of my restaurants in London, and have proved extremely popular. Since they are already cured they are well seasoned, so don't be tempted to add further salt.

PEPPERED BACON RIBS WITH MAPLE MUSTARD GLAZE Serves 4

Prepare your smoker and set to 110°C.

Remove the skin and the inner membrane from the belly and massage with a small amount of maple syrup and mustard. Coat lightly in the rub mix and shake off any excess, then lay the ribs bone side down in the smoker.

Smoke for 5 hours until the bacon ribs reach an internal temperature of 89°C. Test the ribs by holding them with tongs to see if they bounce. If they have a bit of resistance, similar to the touch of a medium rare steak, remove the cooked ribs from the smoker.

Pull alternate ribs out of the cooked bacon belly with a twist-and-pull movement – this is also a good test of doneness. Cut into 300g portions, along the groove that has been left by the vacating rib so each portion contains 1 rib and coat with the marinade as you go.

Serve dusted with crushed black pepper and with a pile of Vinegar Slaw.

For the ribs

1 tablespoon Pork Rub
(*see* page 334)

1 tablespoon Chinese
five-spice powder

1 full rack of St. Louis cut ribs
(or baby back ribs if preferred)

For the sauce

100ml hoisin sauce

100ml tomato ketchup

100ml rice wine vinegar

30ml black bean sauce

1 garlic clove, crushed

To serve

3 spring onions, thinly sliced

1 teaspoon sesame seeds

You will also need a
meat thermometer

If using a smoker, an interesting flavour can be achieved by
using sandalwood and tea to smoke instead of the usual oak or
fruit-tree wood chips. Restraint is key though, as it would be
easy to overdo these flavours. This recipe could also be made
with baby back ribs, but cook for an hour less if you use these.

ASIAN-STYLE RIBS Serves 2

Mix the Pork Rub with the Chinese five-spice powder.
Sprinkle both sides of the meat with the mixture,
massaging it in, and refrigerate the ribs, uncovered,
for 2 hours so that the rub infuses the meat.

Preheat a smoker or oven to 110°C/gas mark ¼.

Place the ribs on a wire rack set over a roasting tin to
catch the drips, then smoke or bake for about 4 hours.
When the ribs are done they should have an internal
temperature of about 89°C. Remove them from the
smoker or oven and pour any cooking juices into a
bowl. Add the sauce ingredients and stir, then brush
both sides of the ribs generously with this sauce.

Heat a barbecue or griddle until you can't hold your
hand over the top and cook the ribs until the sauce
caramelizes slightly – 5 minutes or so. Brush the ribs
with more sauce, then remove from the heat and
sprinkle with the sesame seeds and spring onions.
Serve with the remaining sauce on the side.

1kg thick end boneless pork belly, skin removed and turned into crackling

1 tablespoon French's or Dijon mustard

100g Pork Rub (*see* page 334)

300g banana shallots, peeled and halved lengthways

500ml Master Pork Broth (*see* page 335)

300g Basic Pork Sausage mix, broken into chunks (*see* page 146)

500g cooked potatoes, roughly chopped

For the pickled apple

2 Granny Smith apples, peeled and cored

200ml good cider vinegar

100ml water

100ml lemon juice

50g caster sugar

10g Maldon sea salt flakes

2 cloves

You will also need a smoker or charcoal barbecue and a meat thermometer

Pickles are great accompaniments for pork, so it's worth keeping some in your store cupboard, but if you don't fancy making them there's a brand called Opies that is particularly good. This very combo graced the menu at Pitt Cue Co. in our early days, and damn tasty it was too.

SMOKED BELLY, PICKLED APPLE & SAUSAGE HASH Serves 4

First make the pickled apple. Peel the apples and shave on a mandolin to form ribbons or slice very finely and place in a plastic container.

Put the remaining pickle ingredients into a large saucepan and bring to the boil, allow to cool, then pour over the shaved apple and refrigerate. The pickled apple will be ready in a few hours and will keep for about a week. Remove the cloves before serving.

Remove the skin from the pork belly. Evenly score the fat on the belly in a cross-hatch, then rub the belly with the mustard and cover with the pork rub.

Prepare your smoker or barbecue and set to 110°C or preheat the oven. Place the shallots in a small baking tray and add the belly, fat side up. Add the pork broth

to the baking tray and cook in the smoker or in the oven for 6 hours, or until the internal temperature reaches 89°C.

Remove the belly and set aside. Separate the rendered fat from the cooking juices and reserve the juices.

Put the shallots and the rendered fat into a nonstick frying pan with the sausage chunks and cooked potatoes and fry slowly over a low heat, tossing regularly and allowing crispy golden bits to form.

In a separate pan, reduce the reserved cooking juices to a sauce. Slice or pull apart the pork belly and serve with the sausage hash, the sauce, crackling and some pickled apple.

1 bread roll

25ml Smoked Baconnaise
(*see* page 340)

10ml Sriracha or other
hot sauce

1 large light green romaine
lettuce leaf

30g Vinegar Slaw
(*see* page 341)

150g smoked pork rib meat

100g shredded smoked
bacon rib

25ml hot Barbecue Baste
(*see* page 337)

20g Bread & Butter Pickles
(*see* page 342)

Ah, the Ribwich. First seen at Krusty Burger in Springfield, home town of *The Simpsons*, the Ribwich consisted of only the meat, the bun and barbecue sauce. It was specifically not marketed as being nutritious or healthy. In the TV commercial for the Ribwich, the voice-over said, 'We start with authentic, letter-graded meat, and process the hell out of it.' The box the Ribwich was served in advertised it as 'Now without lettuce!' This version does contain lettuce, and pickles and slaw, and although I'll refrain from making any claims as to its health benefits, it certainly won't do you any harm, in moderation.

RIBWICH Serves 1

Slice the roll in half and lightly grill each exposed side.

Spread the Smoked Baconnaise on the base of the roll. Spread the hot sauce evenly across the lid. Top the bun base with the romaine leaf, followed by the Vinegar Slaw, the sliced pork, then the hot shredded bacon on top.

Lightly brush the bacon with the hot Barbecue Baste. Top this with the pickles, then close the lid and serve immediately.

2 Bath Chaps or Smoked
Pig's Jowls (or page 271)

200ml Barbecue Sauce
(or page 337)

a small sourdough loaf

100g Lardo (or page 247),
thinly sliced

extra pickles, to serve

For the pickled pears

2 firm comice pears, peeled,
cored and cut into wedges

200ml good cider vinegar

100ml water

100ml lemon juice

50g caster sugar

10g Maldon sea salt flakes

1 fresh red chilli, split in half

You will also need
a smoker or charcoal
barbecue

Pork jowl is an underrated cut. Cheeks are easy enough to
get hold of, but the gelatinous jowl area seems to be less highly
prized, which is a shame, as the proper treatment can lead to
many porky delights.

SMOKED PORK JOWL TOAST WITH PICKLED PEAR Serves 4

First make the pickled pear. Put the pear wedges in a
plastic container. Put the remaining pickle ingredients
into a large saucepan and bring to the boil, pour over
the pear wedges, then allow to cool and refrigerate.
The pickles will be ready in a few hours and will keep
for about a week.

Cook your Bath Chaps or Smoked Jowls slowly over
smouldering coals and brush with Barbecue Sauce
until sticky and shiny.

Slice the sourdough into 1cm slices and barbecue on
both sides until well toasted, then spread with Lardo.
Brush the jowls with more of the Barbecue Sauce,
then slice into 1cm slices. Top the toast with slices of
jowl, and serve with pickled pear and extra pickles.

LIVE-FIRE COOKING

Ah, live-fire cooks -- all men want to be us and all women want to be with us (or the other way round, depending on your fancy). There is strong evidence that learning to cook over live fire will make you attractive to the opposite sex and healthy, wealthy and wise. Well, maybe just the first two...

Live-fire cooking is all about managing time, heat and smoke – real results come through practice and an understanding of how this 'holy trinity' works. It is my medium of choice: the flavour of grilled meat is unique and addictive because of complex Maillard reactions occurring as meat hits a hot grill combined with the drippings from the meat hitting the charcoal. When the fats and juices from meat drip on to hot charcoal, they combust into smoke and flame and rise to coat the meat in a mixture of aromatic flavour compounds. Bear this in mind when deciding between charcoal and gas.

Maillard is the chemical reaction that occurs when meat is browned and is one of the main reasons that grilled or roasted meat tastes so delicious. Knowing that a grill needs to be hot for it to happen, recognizing when the time is right to season your meat and put it on the grill, and understanding how sugars and amino acids in meat combine at high heat to produce reactions and new flavour compounds will stand you in good stead on your journey into live fire.

Different cuts of meat have varying degrees of tenderness, which can largely be attributed to the collagen in each muscle. Collagen is made of proteins and is the main component of connective tissue in muscle. The strength of the collagen varies in different cuts of meat and is also dependent on the age, breed and sex of the animal. Those muscles that do very little work have weak collagen. Prime cuts of pork generally have less connective tissue and collagen and are consequently more tender. Lesser cuts usually have more connective tissue and

collagen and tend to be tougher. Understanding collagen is therefore an important part of understanding low and slow cooking. In order to turn a tough, collagen-rich cut such as brisket, shin or shoulder into something delicious, juicy and tender, the muscle must be cooked with a low and even heat for a long period of time so that the collagen molecules unravel, break down and dissolve into soft gelatin that bastes and moistens the meat. Luckily there are two types of live-fire cooking to deal with the two types of meat. One involves grilling the food close to hot charcoal to caramelize and give a smoky tinge, while the other is low and slow smoking.

Salt, sugar and vinegar added to food in conjunction with the 'holy trinity' of time, heat and smoke create a culinary alchemy. Good cooks do this naturally and often subconsciously, but for me it is in a conscious order. I often use umami-rich ingredients, then season to bring out the natural flavours, adding a touch of sugar and vinegar to balance, some spice to lift everything and some fat to bring it all together and help transmit the flavours to your taste buds.

DIRECT COOKING

In most of the world, direct grilling is what people think of when they hear the word barbecue. The heat from the charcoal or gas directly impacts the meat with high surface temperatures. The heat is not deflected or absorbed by anything during the cooking process, and convection currents are not utilized as they are with indirect cooking, when the barbecue is used like an oven.

Direct grilling

With a little bit of skill, direct live-fire cooking is one of the most exciting and important methods of cooking. Cooking over fire, whether it be direct or indirect, is down to the ability to control temperature, and while it is possible to guide someone as to how this happens, it is really only something that can be learned through practice. Just keep lighting your grill and cooking on it, and you will begin to understand the hot spots and cool spots; how long it takes for the coals to burn down for the optimum grilling temperature; which brand of charcoal cooks for longest and which brand cooks at a higher temperature; and how long a full load of charcoal will last you. The aim is to get a good char on the outside while keeping the meat juicy and tender inside, which is impossible with a thin piece of meat – ideally meat should be at least 4cm (1½in) thick.

It's easy to get started. Fire up the grill. Take your pork out of the refrigerator 20 minutes before cooking, to bring it up to room temperature. Get the grill fairly hot but not too hot – the charcoal should have burnt down and be coated in white ash. Quality free-range pork can be grilled at between 140°C (284°F) and 170°C (338°F), the point at which the Maillard reaction begins, to an internal temperature of 65°C (149°F) before resting for 15 minutes in a warm place —60°C (140°F) is ideal. At the last minute, season the meat well but do not use any oil on it; if the grill is hot enough, the meat will not stick. Put the meat on the grill and leave it for a couple of minutes before turning it, then carry on turning it every two minutes or so until you have achieved some enticing Maillard. If the meat is really thick, turn it more regularly to avoid burning. Move your meat if you see yellow flames from the barbecue, because this means that fat has caught fire, which can make the meat taste too smoky. Don't overcrowd the grill – make sure there is plenty of space between each piece of meat. It is impossible to give exact cooking times, as the time depends on the thickness of the meat, the animal it comes from and the temperature of the grill. However, as an example, a 400g (14oz) bone-in pork chop takes 8 minutes on each side over hot charcoal and a 15-minute rest, the key thing being the rest.

Direct dirty cooking

Also known as 'clinching', this method involves placing meat directly on the burning wood or charcoal or 'closing the gap' between meat and fire. There is then no room for flames as the heat is transferred directly and instantly into the meat and flames are smothered. This process in turn super-heats the fat and allows steam to penetrate the meat much more quickly than standard direct grilling. The flavour is incomparable and startlingly different – try it.

INDIRECT COOKING

Most people are inclined to use direct live-fire cooking, whereas for real connoisseurs it is all about trapping the smoke with a lid, cooking low and slow, and really getting the flavour out of the smoke with oak or fruitwoods. When the barbecue is used in this way as a smoke roaster, you can cook almost anything that you can in an oven. The hot coals are moved to one side, allowing you to smoke-roast big joints for hours.

If you have a look at the top of your barbecue, you will probably find a heat gauge, which is there precisely for when you want to use the barbecue as an oven. Fire up the barbecue in the usual way and make sure your coals and wood chips are really hot and white. Push the coals to the side, put the lid on, allowing air to pass out by keeping the vents open a little, then place your meat on the side without charcoal and cook as you would in an oven, turning the meat every so often to ensure the bits closest to the coals do not burn (*see* diagram, right).

With indirect live-fire cooking, the heat source and radiant heat should never be in direct reach of the meat. In the case of a ceramic barbecue, it is diffused through a thick ceramic plate. In an offset smoker, the fire pit is completely separate from where the meat is. In a kettle barbecue, a good set-up diffuses radiant heat through water trays, with the meat positioned as far away from the burning coals as possible so as to be affected only by the convection currents flowing through the barbecue, much as in a convection oven. The cooking is therefore a great deal more even than over direct heat. Whereas direct heat requires constant flipping, turning and attention in order to cook evenly, indirect heat requires a well thought-out set-up and patience.

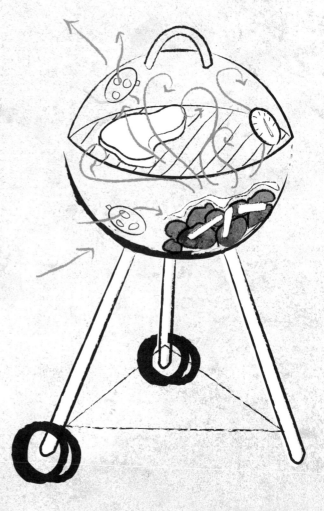

Indirect grilling or smoking

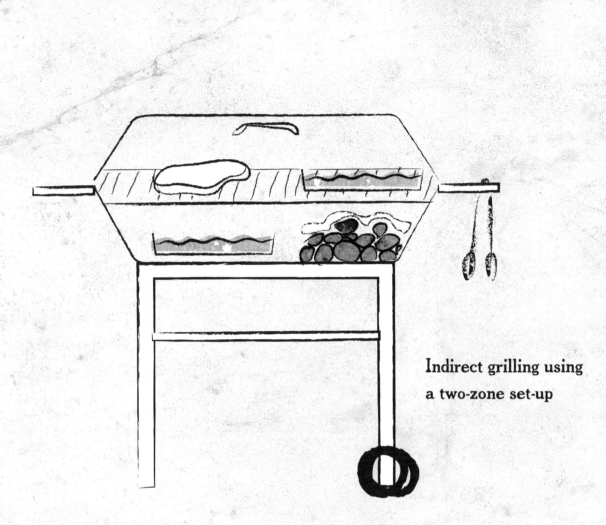

Indirect grilling using a two-zone set-up

BEST OF BOTH WORLDS

Getting the best out of your equipment, understanding what is happening at different temperatures and recognizing the benefits of cooking at those temperatures will come naturally the more you cook, but setting up a two-zone barbecue from the outset will stand you in good stead. The set-up is very simple and basically means that one side of your grill will be hot, producing direct heat that allows for fast grilling and the all-important Maillard reaction, while the other side of the grill will produce none of its own heat, relying on convection currents to create the temperatures ideal for smoking.

By controlling the temperature of your barbecue using the air vents, you will be able to implement techniques for taking prime cuts to medium-rare and smoking the lesser cuts low and slow. This set-up

also provides a safety net if you have a super-fatty piece of meat and do not want to suffer flare-ups that could ruin something so special. Being able to moderate the cooking using two different zones is particularly helpful in this respect – if the grill is getting a bit angry and things are at risk of burning, just sit them in the indirect area, where they can rest and take stock until the grill begins to behave again.

The aim with a two-zone set-up is to have two very different temperatures at either side of the grill. Ideally, the indirect zone will hover at around 105–130°C (221–266°F) and the direct zone will sit at around 170–190°C (338–374°F). Keeping the temperature at 105–115°C (221–239°F), the magical range for much great low and slow cooking, is not essential – but keeping the temperature as constant as possible within these parameters will help. It will allow you to get some idea of how long different cuts are going to take to cook when you try them again. I have tasted some unbelievable meat at barbecue competitions where smokers were set to 130°C (266°F) and up, but these people were militant in their checking and had honed their recipes over many years. Stick to 105–115°C (221–239°F) and you cannot go far wrong.

To achieve this set-up you need to fill up a chimney starter with charcoal. Light it and wait until it is ready to use (white, ash-covered coals are the best sign) before pushing all the lit coals to one side of the bottom ash grate in the barbecue. Place an aluminium tray filled with hot water next to the coals on the other side of the barbecue, then put the grill grate on and place another aluminium water-filled tray on the grill grate directly above the coals (*see* diagram on page 331). You can now cook indirectly on the other side of the grill grate, next to the top water tray. The two water trays will help moderate the heat from the coals and also provide an important source of moisture when cooking. The right humidity in the barbecue is important – cooking large volumes in one smoker creates a very humid cooking atmosphere, and often produces a moister and faster-cooked product, but cooking only one or two things for a long period of time at home is trickier, so the water trays are there to help. You are now ready to cook indirectly. Add a few wood chunks over the lit coals in order to begin smoking.

Smokin'

Barbecue at its most basic is the alchemy of wood, smoke and meat. An awesome barbecue can come from both wood and charcoal, but there is no doubt that the quality of the fuel can dramatically affect the flavour of your final offering.

The best hardwood will create the best barbecue. Hardwood cells contain large amounts of lignin, which is the main reason smoked food tastes so good. When hardwood is heated, this lignin breaks down, producing new volatile chemicals that are responsible for the aromatic smoke you find in great barbecue joints, and the sweet and aromatic flavours that this smoke imparts to the meat. Hardwoods such as mesquite, oak and hickory are all high in lignin and are unsurprisingly the most common woods used in indirect live-fire cookery, whereas softer woods such as pine contain low amounts of lignin and produce a bitter and acrid smoke.

At home, your best bet is to use lumpwood charcoal, made from good-quality hardwoods with none of the added chemicals that help lesser charcoals burn sufficiently well. This charcoal will become the backbone of your barbecue, the fuel that keeps the whole operation running. To this base different types and different quantities of hardwood chunks can be added, depending on the flavour profile you are looking for.

Keeping the temperature constant is the biggest challenge when smoking at home. The vents at the bottom of the barbecue are the key and should be used to control oxygen intake, which, in turn, dictates how fast and how hot the coals burn. Opening the bottom vents in the barbecue will increase the air flow, or draught, sucking more oxygen-rich air into the fire and causing it to burn faster and more fiercely. Closing the bottom vents will reduce the draught and the oxygen that reaches the fire, causing it to cool and burn more slowly.

In the search for complete temperature control, the top vents are less significant, as they do not provide the same control as the bottom vents. The top vents do affect the draught, however, and how easy it is for the smoke and air to leave the barbecue. They should remain half open to allow for draught in order to avoid the excessive build-up of smoke in the barbecue that could create acrid, sooty deposits and ruin your hard work.

Start with the bottom vents fully open, to allow the coals to get going. You will see the temperature begin to rise, and as you approach 100°C (212°F), close the vents by half. This should halt the rise in temperature, and from here it is a case of tweaking to get to your desired temperature for low and slow. The top vents need not be played with too much, but positioning the meat directly below these vents will force the smoke over the meat. It will also allow you to poke a thermometer through the vents to where the meat is cooking, so that you can work out exactly what temperature the most important part of the barbecue is at.

While cooking something for half a day at a low temperature provides the cook with greater margin for error, removing the meat at the right time is still crucial. There are so many variables in indirect cooking – the insulation of your barbecue, the fuel and the genetics of the animal all play a key role in how a piece of meat is going to cook. Timings are often approximate and need to be taken as a guide only. Indirect live-fire cooking is far from an exact science, but as long as you have a meat probe to hand, all will be well. A probe is an invaluable tool, but touch should not be forgotten, as will become apparent as you gain experience – and using touch and a probe alongside each other will allow you to train your touch without too many mistakes. There is no shame at all in using a meat probe, and it is the only way to produce consistent results early in your journey. If possible, buy a remote meat probe that allows you to read the internal temperature without lifting the lid of the barbecue. Lifting the lid releases all the moisture from the cooking chamber and lowers the temperature. The more moisture that is retained inside your barbecue, the better.

The ideal slow cooking temperature is around 110°C (230°F). The stall – when the meat reaches an internal temperature of around 70°C (158°F), stops and does not rise a degree in temperature for an hour or so – happens at 70°C (158°F). Finally, 87–90°C (189–194°F) is the internal temperature when your meat is ready to be removed from the smoker.

Don't panic when it stalls – this is normal and occurs when the collagen begins to break down into gelatin. The reaction absorbs energy and forces moisture to the surface of the meat, which cools it. So it's a good thing. Remember that opening the smoker or barbecue loses more moisture and temperature in the cooking chamber and contributes to a longer stall.

I find that the most flavour often comes from cooking low and slow first of all, as described here, and then finishing the meat over direct heat as in Direct Cooking (see page 328).

The lesser, collagen-rich cuts such as shoulder, belly, head, shins and hocks are all best suited to indirect cooking and smoking, where the low, even heat is able to break down the collagen into gelatin without the whole cut overcooking. For the larger cuts, like shoulder or even a suckling pig, you will have to light the chimney starter on numerous occasions to maintain the lit charcoal in the barbecue. The general rule of thumb is to add six chunks of lit coal every hour, which should help keep a constant temperature. This is where a ceramic barbecue like a Big Green Egg comes into its own, with one load of charcoal lasting longer than you will ever really need to cook a large joint.

All this complicated managing of temperature, time and heat really is worth the effort, and a little practice pays dividends for the stomach. Don't be surprised if by the end of the summer you are addicted to live-fire cooking and all the trappings (sex, health, wealth and wisdom) that ensue…

BASIC RECIPES

This is a basic rub suitable for pork. Do experiment with the spices, keeping the ratios of ingredients roughly the same.

PORK RUB

Makes 450g

200g Maldon sea salt flakes

200g light brown muscovado sugar

10g (1 tablespoon) wild fennel pollen

2 teaspoons Espelette pepper or paprika

2 teaspoons freshly ground black pepper

20g garlic cloves

Blitz all the ingredients in a food processor or blender and spread on a clean tray to dry. Blitz again, then store in an airtight container.

At its simplest a bacon cure can be pure salt, but every bacon curer wants their bacon to be unique. This is one of mine.

SMOKED BACON CURE

Makes 1kg

500g Maldon sea salt flakes

75g light muscovado sugar

10g cracked black pepper

10g fennel seeds, toasted and crushed

Mix all the ingredients in a bowl until they are thoroughly combined.

I was taught to use three basic stocks as the base for sauces – veal, chicken and fish – but in the back of my mind I've always had a nagging doubt: if making a sauce for pork or lamb, why would you use any other stock than one made from the bones of the meat you are cooking? This is my go-to stock for pork recipes, but a 50:50 mix of chicken and veal could be used to good effect.

MASTER PORK BROTH

Makes 4 litres

2 onions, halved

1kg pork bones, lightly roasted

2 pork hocks

2 pig's feet

1 smoked gammon or bacon hock

2 large carrots, halved

2 celery sticks

2 large dried shiitake mushrooms

1 head of garlic

1 faggot of fresh herbs, made with thyme, bay, rosemary and parsley

1 spice bag, made with 20 fennel seeds, 1 star anise, 2 cloves, ½ cinnamon stick, 1 small knob of fresh root ginger

250ml Madeira

250ml soy sauce

5 litres water

Blacken the cut side of the onions in a very hot dry pan. Place in a large pan with all the other ingredients and bring to a gentle simmer. Cook for 3 hours, skimming every 30 minutes or so. The trick here is to simmer at a bare roll and skim any impurities regularly, to achieve a clean, clear broth.

Without moving the pan, turn off the heat and gently ladle the broth out of the pot through a very fine sieve, taking care not to disturb the bottom too much. Cool and reserve the master pork broth until needed, and use the meats and vegetables to make Pork Broth Salad (see page 299) or Pork Broth Terrine (see page 291).

This is a basic court-bouillon for poaching piggy bits like heads, trotters, snouts, brains or tongues. Once made, it can be stored in the refrigerator for up to a week.

COURT-BOUILLON FOR PORK DISHES

Makes 2 litres

2 leeks

1 carrot

1 celery stick

3 onions

1 fennel bulb

1 head of garlic

1 knob of fresh ginger

1 star anise

2 cloves

½ cinnamon stick

10 mixed peppercorns

250ml white wine

2 litres cold water

1 lemon

1 sprig of fresh parsley

1 sprig of fresh thyme

Roughly chop all the ingredients except the lemon and herbs and place in a flameproof casserole.

Bring to a gentle simmer and cook for 20 minutes. Slice the lemon and add to the pot along with the herbs, then turn off the heat. Leave to cool and pass through a sieve, taking care not to disturb the solids.

Your court-bouillon should be clear and fragrant.

Adding much-needed gelatine, fat and unctuousness to pies, stews and casseroles, these extremities should be prized highly. A spoonful or two in most things could only improve the situation.

SNOOTS & FOOTS

Serves 4

4 pig's trotters, all hair removed

4 pigs' snouts, all hair removed

2 onions, halved

2 carrots, halved

2 celery sticks

2 leeks, split

1 head of garlic

1 faggot of fresh herbs, made with thyme, rosemary and bay

250ml Madeira

about 2 litres Master Pork Broth, to cover (see page 335)

Place the trotters and snouts in a large flameproof casserole. Cover with water and bring to the boil. Boil for 5 minutes, then drain.

Put the trotters and snouts back into the casserole with the vegetables, faggot of herbs and Madeira and cover with the pork broth – top up with water as required. Cook for at least 3 hours until the trotters are tender, then remove from the cooking liquid. Strain the liquid and reserve.

When the meat is cool enough to handle, pick off all the flesh, fat and skin, tearing the skin to shreds. Put into a pan with the cooking liquid and bring back to the boil, then place in jars, sterilized by placing them in boiling water or steaming them at 160°C. Fill the jars with the hot mixture and screw on the lids reasonably tightly.

Put the jars back into the water or steamer for 30 minutes, then remove and allow to cool. Refrigerate for up to a month, until needed.

A delicious Southern-style stuffing, often used for turkey at Thanksgiving but equally good with pork.

OYSTER & BACON STUFFING

Makes 1kg

6 streaky bacon rashers

60g unsalted butter

1 small loaf of Italian bread, pulled into 3cm chunks

1 small onion, chopped

2 celery sticks, thinly sliced

Maldon sea salt flakes and freshly ground black pepper

60ml dry white wine

250ml Master Pork Broth (see page 335)

1 free-range egg, beaten

6 oysters, shucked and cut in half

¼ bunch of fresh parsley, chopped

Sriracha or other hot sauce, to taste

Preheat the oven to 180°C/gas mark 4.

Cook the bacon in a skillet over a medium heat until crisp, stirring frequently – about 5–7 minutes. Transfer to a plate.

Butter a baking dish. Divide the bread between 2 rimmed baking sheets and bake until dry and crisp – about 10–12 minutes.

Meanwhile, wipe out the skillet and melt the butter over a medium heat. Add the onion and celery, and season with salt and pepper. Cook, stirring occasionally, until tender and golden, then add the wine and cook until evaporated. Transfer to a bowl and allow to cool.

Add the bread, broth, egg, bacon, oysters and parsley and toss to combine, adjusting the seasoning with salt, pepper and a splash of hot sauce if needed. The oyster and bacon stuffing is now ready to stuff into your chosen roast.

Used as a baste, this can be painted on throughout the smoking process, helping to create a bark on the outside of the meat.

BARBECUE BASTE

Barbecue Sauce
(*see* right)

Master Pork Broth
(*see* page 335)

pork dripping, collected
from the smoker or a roast

Mix equal quantities of the 3 ingredients and simmer until reduced by half.

This sauce has been in development for some years, and variations are in use in every restaurant I've opened. This is the current, but almost certainly not final, guise.

BARBECUE SAUCE

Makes 1.5 litres

2 white onions, grated

3 garlic cloves, grated

50ml vegetable oil

250ml apple juice

250ml cider vinegar

2 apples, peeled and grated

50g smoked sea salt flakes

125g canned chipotle peppers

250ml maple syrup

250ml French's mustard

250ml blackstrap molasses

250g apricot preserve

250g canned tomatoes

For the spice mix

2 teaspoons fennel seeds

2 teaspoons cumin seeds

2 teaspoons coriander seeds

2 teaspoons celery seeds

2 teaspoons black peppercorns

Put all the ingredients for the spice mix in a large dry saucepan and toast them lightly to release their flavours.

Add the onions, garlic and oil to the roasted spices and cook over a medium heat for 10 minutes, until the onions are cooked through. This is important, as undercooked onions will taint the final sauce with an unpleasant raw flavour. Add the apple juice and cider vinegar and simmer until reduced by a third.

Add the remaining ingredients and bring to a simmer for 10 minutes.

Blitz the sauce in a blender, then pass through a fine sieve and keep in sterilized jars until needed.

Red barbecue sauce, more often just called red sauce, is typical of Carolina barbecue. This recipe came from a South Carolina participant in the American Royal Barbecue contest in Kansas City.

RED BARBECUE SAUCE

Makes 1 litre

300ml tomato ketchup

250ml water

180ml cider vinegar

180g canned chopped tomatoes

100g dark brown sugar

125ml maple syrup

30ml molasses

20g Maldon sea salt flakes

20ml Worcestershire sauce

100g grated apple

200g onion, quartered

2g mustard powder

2g cayenne pepper

2g freshly ground black pepper

2g toasted celery seed

2g toasted coriander seed

5g toasted fennel seed

5g crushed chilli flakes

1 fresh red chilli

1 garlic clove, crushed

Combine all the ingredients in a large saucepan and bring to the boil, then simmer over a low heat for about 20 minutes.

Pass through a sieve and bottle in sterilized jars.

Long before the mighty Heinz created its iconic tomato ketchup, cooks in medieval England were making ketchups to serve with meat. Mushroom may well have been the original ketchup, but certainly fruit ketchups were also made, and with the incredible variety of fruit available today the possibilities are endless.

FRUIT KETCHUPS All make 500ml

Place all the ingredients in a stainless steel pan and bring to the boil, then reduce to a simmer and cook for 20 minutes.

Remove the spice bag and blend the sauce to a smooth purée. Pass through a fine sieve, place in sterilized bottles or jars, and refrigerate until needed.

RHUBARB KETCHUP FOR ROAST & GRILLED PORK

500g forced rhubarb, pink stems only

150g fruit sugar

100ml cider vinegar

1 spice bag, made with ½ cinnamon stick, 2cm piece of fresh root ginger, 2 cloves and 8 black peppercorns

50ml orange juice

a pinch of Maldon sea salt flakes

PINEAPPLE KETCHUP
FOR BACON & HAM

500g peeled and cored
pineapple

100g fruit sugar

100ml cider vinegar

1 spice bag, made with
1 split hot red chilli, 1 vanilla
pod and 20 black
peppercorns

50ml lime juice

a pinch of Maldon sea
salt flakes

APPLE KETCHUP
FOR ROAST & GRILLED PORK

500g peeled and cored
Granny Smith apples

150g fruit sugar

150ml cider vinegar

1 spice bag, made with
½ cinnamon stick, 2 cloves
and 8 black peppercorns

50ml lemon juice

a pinch of Maldon sea
salt flakes

CRANBERRY KETCHUP
FOR CHRISTMAS HAM

500g fresh cranberries

150g caster sugar

150ml red wine vinegar

50ml orange juice

1 spice bag, made with
fresh root ginger, nutmeg,
black peppercorns, allspice
berries

a pinch of Maldon sea
salt flakes

If fat is flavour, then this is the daddy of flavour. It is particularly good on burgers and sandwiches.

SMOKED BACONNAISE

Makes 300ml

2 free-range egg yolks

20ml cider vinegar

20ml water

10g English or Dijon mustard

Smoked Bacon Cure (*see* page 334)

250ml warm rendered smoked bacon fat

Mix the egg yolks, vinegar, water and mustard in a blender and season with the smoked bacon rub.

Slowly trickle the warm liquid smoked bacon fat into the emulsion until entirely incorporated, then taste and adjust the seasoning. Use while still warm.

Gentleman's Relish is a Victorian spiced anchovy butter that's eaten by the well-to-do as a post-dinner savoury. It's also good to have on hand for serving with a mixed grill, or in fact any grilled meat. Be sure to use good-quality anchovies – it really does make a difference, and don't worry, they won't make the meat taste fishy.

GENTLEMAN'S RELISH (ANCHOVY BUTTER)

Makes 450g

125g canned anchovy fillets

250g unsalted butter, diced

a small pinch of cayenne pepper

a small pinch of ground nutmeg

a small pinch of freshly ground black pepper

a small pinch of ground cinnamon

25ml lemon juice

25ml Worcestershire sauce

25ml water

Put all the ingredients into a food processor or blender and whizz until smooth.

Roll into a log, then wrap in clingfilm and refrigerate until needed. When required, cut a thick slice and serve alongside your mixed grill.

This lighter slaw cuts through the richness of pork in a pleasingly fresh manner. Use it in sandwiches, in burgers or on tacos.

VINEGAR SLAW

Serves 4–6

1 teaspoon fennel seeds

200g white cabbage

100g red cabbage

100g fennel

1 red onion

mixed handful of fresh herbs (parsley, coriander and mint)

1 teaspoon Maldon sea salt flakes

1 teaspoon freshly ground black pepper

For the dressing

50ml cider vinegar

50ml white wine vinegar

35ml extra virgin olive oil

35g caster sugar

juice and zest of 1 unwaxed lemon

Whisk all the dressing ingredients together until the sugar has dissolved, and store in a sealed container.

Toast the fennel seeds in a dry pan until golden, then set aside.

Slice the cabbage, fennel and onion 1mm thick, using a mandolin – the thinner the better. Finely chop the herbs using a very sharp knife.

Toss together with all the remaining ingredients so that they are well combined and the herbs are evenly spread throughout the slaw.

Whisk the dressing again 20 minutes before serving and add to the slaw. Toss thoroughly and check and adjust the seasoning.

This spicy little fellow has oriental flavours that marry well with pork.

GREEN CHILLI SLAW

Serves 6–8

½ white cabbage, finely sliced

¼ red cabbage, finely sliced

1 small fennel bulb, finely sliced

125g mayonnaise

¼ bunch of fresh coriander leaves

Maldon sea salt flakes

For the green chilli dressing

25g fresh green chillies

25g fresh root ginger, peeled and roughly chopped

25g light brown muscovado sugar

25ml soy sauce

zest and juice of 1 lime

To make the dressing, grill the chillies over direct heat on a barbecue or in a griddle pan until charred and blistered. Discard the stalks. Put the blackened chillies in a blender with all the remaining dressing ingredients except the soy sauce and blitz, gradually, until emulsified and smooth.

Lightly salt the cabbage and let it sit for 1 hour in a colander to allow the excess moisture to drain off. Transfer to a serving bowl and mix in the fennel. Add the mayo, coriander leaves and 50ml of the green chilli dressing and toss, then season with salt to taste. Add more dressing if you like, then serve.

This version of a classic dressing was developed during the early days of Hawksmoor. It has stood the test of time and has remained unchanged for years now.

HONEY & MUSTARD DRESSING

Makes 180ml

2 teaspoons wholegrain mustard

2 teaspoons clear honey

20ml lemon juice

20ml cider vinegar

120ml light olive oil

salt and freshly ground black pepper

Whisk together the mustard, honey, lemon juice and cider vinegar. Slowly add the olive oil in a thin stream.

Adjust the seasoning and store in sterilized bottles in the refrigerator until needed.

A sweet and sour Southern pickle that's perfect with barbecued pork. This is really easy to make and much better than store-bought.

BREAD & BUTTER PICKLES

Makes 1 litre (serves 20)

5 large cucumbers

2 onions

80g salt

600ml cider vinegar

400g soft brown sugar

2g ground turmeric

10 cloves

1 teaspoon black mustard seeds

1 teaspoon fennel seeds

1 teaspoon coriander seeds

Wash the cucumbers and onions and slice into 4mm-thick pieces. Layer them in a non-reactive container, with the salt distributed in between the layers. Cover with clingfilm and put a heavy weight on top to help extract the water from the vegetables. Leave for at least 4 hours, until limp but crunchy.

When ready, pour away the liquid and rinse the cucumbers and onions under cold running water, tossing constantly for 5 minutes, until no longer salty. Leave to dry.

Put the vinegar, sugar and spices into a saucepan and stir over a medium heat until the sugar has dissolved. Bring to the boil, then add the cucumber and onions to the pan. Cook for 2 minutes, until the cucumber has browned through but not cooked. This is important, as overcooked cucumbers will soften. Remove from the heat and leave to cool.

Transfer the pickles to sterilized jars and store in the refrigerator for 2–3 weeks to mature.

Almost not a recipe, this is my preferred blue cheese sauce. It can also be made using a fork for a more rustic appearance.

BLUE CHEESE SAUCE

Serves 4

50g blue cheese
100ml soured cream

Add the cheese and soured cream to a blender, then blend to combine and serve.

A spoon or two of this stuff can liven up any pork dish and it can also be served on the side as a fresh and zingy condiment.

GREEN SAUCE

Serves 4

2 tablespoons chopped fresh flat-leaf parsley

1 tablespoon finely chopped fresh mint

extra-virgin olive oil

1 medium clove garlic

1 tablespoon finely diced shallots

1 tablespoon salted capers

1 tablespoon Dijon mustard

1 tablespoon red wine vinegar

Maldon sea salt flakes and freshly ground black pepper

Place the chopped parsley and mint in a bowl and add just enough oil to cover. Add the chopped garlic, shallots and capers to the parsley-mint mixture and stir to combine. Add the mustard and vinegar, along with more oil to your desired consistency. Season with salt and pepper to taste. Serve at room temperature.

A slightly sweet carbohydrate side for when pork alone isn't quite enough.

PARSNIP, POTATO & APPLE CAKE

Serves 4

2 large waxy potatoes, peeled

1 large parsnip, peeled

1 large cooking apple, peeled

Maldon sea salt flakes and freshly ground black pepper

1 tablespoon butter

1 tablespoon pork lard or dripping

Parboil the potatoes and parsnip in salted water until just tender, but not soft. Allow to cool, then chill for a couple of hours.

Coarsely grate the potatoes, parsnip and apple over a clean tea towel, then squeeze dry. Place in a bowl and season with salt and pepper.

Heat half the butter and half the lard in a small, heavy-based frying pan over a medium heat, then add the grated mixture and allow to cook for a couple of minutes. Shape into a flat cake, pressing down as lightly as possible. Allow to cook for a few more minutes, then gently shake the pan to loosen. Flip the cake over, add the remaining fats and continue to cook for about 8 minutes until golden and crisp, then turn out on to your plate to serve.

INDEX

ABOUT THE CONTRIBUTORS

Meredith Erickson is a writer for the *New York Times*, *Elle*, *The National Post* and *Lucky Peach*. Based in London and Montreal, she is co-author of *Le Pigeon: Cooking at The Dirty Bird* (2013) and *The Art of Living According to Joe Beef: A Cookbook of Sorts* (2011).

Aaron Franklin is an American chef and owner of the legendary Franklin Barbecue in Austin, Texas. Renowned as being among America's BBQ elite, *Bon Appetit* magazine hailed Franklin Barbecue as the best in America.
franklinbarbecue.com

Fergus Henderson is the founding partner and chef at St John restaurant in London which champions his philosophy of nose-to-tail eating. Henderson has been awarded an MBE for services to gastronomy, and was awarded the Lifetime Achievement Award at the World's 50 Best Restaurant Awards. He is author of the award-winning *Nose to Tail Eating: A Kind of British Cooking* (1999) and *Beyond Nose to Tail Eating* (2007).
stjohngroup.uk.com

Diana Henry is one of Britain's best-loved food writers. She has a weekly column in *The Sunday Telegraph* and was named Cookery Writer of the Year at the 2013 Fortnum & Mason Food and Drink Awards. Diana has twice been named Cookery Journalist of the Year by the Guild of Food Writers. Her books include *Crazy Water Pickled Lemons*, (2012) *Food From Plenty* (2010), *Salt Sugar Smoke* (20132) and *A Change of Appetite* (2014).
dianahenry.co.uk

Judy Joo is a Korean-American chef with a love of Korean food. She is one of four UK Iron Chefs and the Executive Chef for The Playboy Club in London. Joo regularly appears on Food Network TV and UK Food Channel's Market Kitchen and hosted *Korean Food Made Simple* on US TV's Cooking Channel.
judyjoo.com

Josh Ozersky is an American food writer and the founder of Meatopia – the so-called 'Woodstock of Edible Animals' festival in New York City and London. Ozersky is Restaurant Editor of *Esquire*, writes the 'Taste of America' column for *TIME* magazine and is author of several books including *Meat Me in Manhattan: A Carnivore's Guide to New York City* (2003) and *The Hamburger: A History* (2008).
ozersky.tv | meatopia.co.uk | meatopia.org

Neil Rankin, pioneer of high-end barbecue cooking, is a British chef and owner of Smokehouse in London, the UK's only real-wood barbecue restaurant, which opened to critical acclaim in 2013. He was formerly head chef at the revered Pitt Cue Co. and John Salt in London.
smokehouseislington.co.uk

Mitch Tonks is an award-wining seafood chef and restaurateur – his acclaimed Seahorse restaurant in Dartmouth was awarded Best UK Restaurant by the Observer Food Magazine Awards in 2012. He has also opened three RockFish seafood restaurants in southwest Britain, and is author of five cookbooks including *Fish Easy* (2012).
mitchtonks.co.uk

Turner & George supplied all the pork for this book, and they like to think it's the kind of meat you'll always want at your table. They visit every farm they source from, and select the finest, naturally-reared native, traditional and rare breeds. In celebration of the whole animal, Turner & George try to stock and sell as much of the animal as their customers will buy, and are avid supporters of the nose-to-tail revolution.
turnerandgeorge.co.uk

Valentine Warner is a London-based food-writer and cook with a passion for nature, the seasons and being outdoors. He has made a variety of television series for BBC2, UKTV Good Food, ITV and Fox International. He has written four cookbooks including *What to Eat Next* (2014).
valentinewarner.com

AUTHOR'S ACKNOWLEDGEMENTS

As with any creative project there are loads of people I must thank for helping to get this book off the ground. First and foremost, Stephanie Jackson at Octopus who, for some obscure reason, felt I had another book in me after *Pitt Cue Co. – The Cookbook*. Her support, patience and humour were, I'm sure, tested at times. Also at Octopus Sybella Stephens and Juliette Norsworthy who kept me company, styled, directed and cajoled on the photo shoots, all the while maintaining saint-like tolerance. A big thanks to Kat Mead for early-morning shopping trips, kitchen assistance and translating chef speak into human speak. An equally huge thank you to the inimitable Paul Winch-Furness and his shirts, without which my days would be considerably duller.

Thanks also to Diana Henry for allowing me to devastate her kitchen during photo shoots and for writing a delightfully gushing tribute. Also Josh Ozersky, my partner in Meatopia, who wrote a typically idiosyncratic foreword and who regularly reminds me that some Americans have a better grasp of our language than I do (as well as a deluded version of the history of the hamburger, but that's another story...).

I should also thank Hawksmoor and Foxlow, and in particular Will Beckett, Huw Gott and Tim Gould, for allowing me time to pursue outside interests, such as pig worrying and writing, with good humour.

Thanks to David Ezrine of The Big Green Egg, a piece of kit I literally couldn't have done without on some of the recipes.

A huge thank you to the chaps at Turner & George, for putting up with my frantic demands for ever-increasing quantities of pork for the photo shoots – you guys rock!

Last, but not least, a humongous thank you to James George, my butcher, business partner and buddy for more years than I care to consider.